UNMASKING THE MASCULINE

'Men' and 'Identity' in a Sceptical Age

Alan Petersen

SAGE Publications
London • Thousand Oaks • New Delhi

SAGE Publications Ltd
6 Bonhill Street
London EC2A 4PU

SAGE Publications Inc
2455 Teller Road
Thousand Oaks, California 91320

SAGE Publications India Pvt Ltd
32, M-Block Market
Greater Kailash – I
New Delhi 110 048

British Library Cataloguing in Publication data

A catalogue record for this book is
available from the British Library

ISBN 0 7619 5012 5
ISBN 0 7619 5013 3 (pbk)

Library of Congress catalog record available

Typeset by M Rules
Printed in Great Britain by The Cromwell Press Ltd,
Trowbridge, Wiltshire

Contents

Acknowledgements

I wish to thank all those who have assisted me in the writing of this book, particularly Chris Rojek, from Sage Publications, who has been sympathetic and helpful from the outset, and has offered useful comments on early draft chapters. Special thanks are also due to Ros Porter, Robin Bunton, Lesley Jones, Dorothy Wardale and Don Abbey for their ideas, encouragement and companionship. I am grateful to the anonymous reader of an earlier version of the manuscript who offered useful critical feedback. Finally, I wish to acknowledge the support of Murdoch University which allowed me a period of study leave in which I was able to write much of the book.

1

Introduction: the epistemology of 'masculinity'

This book focuses on contemporary constructions of masculinity and masculine identity. It examines the frameworks of knowledge that have shaped conceptions of manhood in the modern West, and it outlines a number of challenges posed to these conceptions by a recent shift in our theoretical understanding of the world. The 1990s saw a rapidly growing interest in men and their lives, as witnessed by a proliferating number of enquiries into men's emotions, men's relationships with partners, parents and siblings, men's health and sexuality, and the 'masculine crisis of identity'. While much research has been generated by academic feminists and gay male scholars, an increasing amount of work has also been undertaken by self-identified heterosexual men involved in what is a highly diverse 'men's movement' and in teaching and research in universities. A developing area of 'men's studies' has found a niche in many universities in the United Kingdom, North America, and Australia, and 'masculinity' and its discontents has become a popular topic of research among postgraduates and established scholars. This work has given rise to some interesting and provocative analyses, helping to highlight many issues long in need of exposition and analysis. However, questions concerning the construction of knowledge about men and 'masculinity' have remained marginal. Relatively few scholars have asked how modern Western societies have arrived at a conception of what constitutes normal masculine identity and behaviour, why certain research questions get raised while others remain unarticulated, and what assumptions about male bodies and selves are embedded in theories. In short, important questions of epistemology have been largely overlooked. This book directs attention to the epistemology of 'masculinity', and discusses the challenges posed to this epistemology by recent trends in social thought. I begin, in this chapter, by outlining my aims, assumptions, and arguments, and providing an overview of the individual chapters.

The recent turn towards deconstruction, postmodernism and poststructuralism in the social sciences and humanities has led scholars to reappraise basic categories of social analysis. Many people have begun to rethink assumptions upon which identities have been constructed, especially the assumption that there exist natural bodies and essential selves. The conventional modernist concepts of identity and identity politics have been critiqued across diverse fields of social thought and this has led to discussions about alternative ways of conceiving the personal and the political, and the relationship between the two. Recent work has highlighted, in particular, the role of the natural and social sciences in the construction of knowledge of human subjects and in the shaping of people's awareness of themselves *as* subjects – i.e. their subjectivities. Although, in the broader culture, natural knowledge and social knowledge have appeared as mutually exclusive, it has become increasingly clear that *all* knowledge, including biological knowledge, is socially produced and reflects prevailing assumptions about normal embodiment and subjectivity. Feminists, for instance, have recently pointed out that knowledge about 'sex' and 'sex differences' is shaped by cultural constructions of gender. A nature/culture dualism has underpinned a range of expertise over the last 200 years – including biology, biomedicine, sociobiology, phrenology, craniology, anthropology, sociology, psychology, psychiatry, and psychoanalysis – serving to construct knowledge of human subjects and to delineate boundaries between normal and pathological bodies and selves. However, more and more, Western systems of thought have come under scrutiny, raising profound challenges for research and practice in relation to questions of identity.

Given its subject matter, one would expect that 'men's studies' would be a vibrant field of new ideas on questions of identity. However, theoretically, the area has been rather insular and dominated by a few perspectives – notably sex-role theory, gender theory, learning theory, Jungian theory and object-relations theory – that were originally developed in psychology, psychoanalysis, sociology, philosophy, and sociobiology, and then often subsequently reworked by the so-called 'second-wave' feminists. Many texts do not acknowledge feminist studies at all, which is perceived as a discourse parallel to the study of 'men' (McMahon, 1993: 675). Male scholars seem unwilling, in the main, to engage in the kinds of interdisciplinary and critical enquiry undertaken by feminists. Those male writers who claim to be pro-feminist have engaged with only a fragment of the vast number of *feminisms* that have emerged over the last two decades. The field of contemporary feminist thought has become so diverse it defies easy categorisation, but can be seen to encompass various egalitarian and sexual difference strands of thought, spanning virtually all disciplinary areas. Feminist history and philosophy of science, postmodern feminism, poststructuralist feminism, ecofeminism, and lesbian feminism have generated numerous and useful insights into gender, gender relations, and sexuality that have been largely neglected by 'men's studies' scholars. Male scholars often completely fail to address the power relations of sexuality, and their writings are seen to often reflect a strong heterosexual bias (Edwards, 1990: 111). There has been little analysis of how heterosexual masculine identity became institutionalised as the ideal, and the implications of this for non-normative sexual identities (Kinsman, 1993). Most research takes as given, rather than problematises, the dominant epistemology of sexuality and what Sedgwick (1994) refers to as the 'consensus of knowingness' implied by the hetero/homosexual division.

The separatism of 'men's studies' has been interpreted by some feminist writers as a strategic response to feminism, as a means of preserving masculine privilege (see, for example, Young, 1993: 318). Feminist suspicion of 'men's studies' is understandable. 'Men's studies' has emerged in a context very different to that giving rise to 'women's studies' and, arguably, addresses a different set of concerns. The effort to make 'women' the object of theory has been integral to the effort to unmask the seeming 'naturalness' of women's invisibility. For women, 'becoming an object in theory was the inevitable result of becoming a subject in history' (Guillaumin, 1995: 166). As Mary Evans has recently pointed out, the retention of the label 'women's studies', rather than the adoption of 'gender studies', a commonly suggested alternative, 'is a constant, and constantly politicizing, reminder that women have been, until relatively recently, largely excluded from the academic curriculum both as subjects and as agents' (1997: 13). Although it has been argued that universities have also taught little that was explicitly about men, the human subject has been simply assumed to be male. This is reflected in language where the words 'he' and 'mankind' have often been used to denote a generic human being. Many feminist academics are rightly sceptical towards any attempt to develop a new field of study which focuses specifically on men and 'masculinity', especially when feminists have had to struggle to gain institutional recognition of 'women's studies'. In a context of limited resources, feminists have reason to be anxious about the potential for resources to be 'siphoned off' by men who are keen to 'get in on the act', especially in light of historical experience which shows that white, heterosexual men have been more successful in monopolising the means of academic production (Johnson, 1997: 16). One of my goals in this book is to draw attention to what I see as some major limitations of contemporary approaches to the study of men and 'masculine identity', as manifest in particular in the academic speciality of 'men's studies', and to help shift the focus of thinking and research. In my view, those undertaking research on men and masculine identity have not given enough attention to questions of epistemology, to the analysis of power relations, and to interdisciplinary enquiry. Scholars and activists, I believe, need to be more critical in their use of concepts and categories, and much more attentive to the implications of their adherence to particular perspectives.

The essentialism of 'masculinity'

One of my starting premises is that 'masculinity' has been essentialised and that this has provided a major impediment to theoretical and political work. In order to properly explain what I mean by this, I should first clarify my own use of the term 'essentialism' since it figures prominently throughout this book. Essentialism has a long and illustrious career within Western thought, although its meaning is often left undefined in academic discussions. As Stanley and Wise note, there is no 'essence' to essentialism; it is an invention of social scientists and philosophers (1993: 209). However, it is increasingly used in a rhetorical sense, to dismiss positions with which one does not agree, which has often lead to polarisation in debate (Fuss, 1989: xi). In his recent overview of the uses of essentialism in the social sciences, Andrew Sayer observes that reference to 'essentialism' in the social scientific literature is nearly always derogatory; indeed it is widely seen as a term of abuse which often silences argument, being tainted by association with racism and sexism (1997: 453). He notes that there are many essentialisms and many critiques of essentialism, arising in different contexts and relating to different issues. However,

> [i]f there is anything common to all the critiques of essentialism in social science, it is a concern to counter characterisations of people, practices, institutions and other social phenomena as having fixed identities which deterministically produce fixed, uniform outcomes. Whether they are talking about cultural identity, economic behaviour or gender and sexuality, anti-essentialists have argued that people are not creatures of determinism, whether natural or cultural, but are socially constructed and constructing. (Sayer, 1997: 454)

According to Sayer, the take-up of anti-essentialism as an emancipatory strategy represents a 'remarkable shift in radical academia' from the 1970s when radicals used to attack pluralists for not recognising structures or essence behind superficial appearances. There are now relatively few theorists who actively defend any kind of essentialism in its own right, although some critics recognise the necessity of occasionally employing essentialist descriptions for strategic purposes (Sayer, 1997: 454–5).

The concept of essentialism has been of central concern to feminists, principally in connection with discussions about the binary categories of sex/gender, women/men, male/female and feminine/masculine, and it is they who have offered some of the most detailed exposés of the term. In Fuss's poststructuralist feminist account, 'essentialism is classically defined as a belief in true essence – that which is most irreducible, unchanging, and therefore constitutive of a given person or thing' (Fuss, 1989: 2). As she explains, the idea that men and women are identified as such on the basis of 'transhistorical, eternal, immutable essences' has been rejected by poststructuralist feminists on the basis that it 'naturalises' human nature. Poststructuralists dismiss the attempt to find an absolute grounding for knowledge and instead embrace the notion of 'fractured identities', insisting upon the need to recognise differences *among* women and men (Bacchi, 1990). Although poststructuralist theory is widely seen to have inaugurated an anti-essentialist movement within feminism, the foundations for the deconstruction of essentialist categories can be seen to have been laid by 'second-wave' feminists.

'Second-wave' feminists can be seen to have critiqued essentialism in so far as they questioned the assumption that social differences between men and women are rooted in biological or natural differences (i.e. biology-as-destiny), although they may not have used the term 'essentialism' in their own writings. In their efforts to contest the naturalisation of sexual difference, they appropriated the concept of gender from the social sciences. However, in the process, they carried over essentialist assumptions into their own work through the sex/gender distinction; that is, 'sex' was seen to correspond with 'nature', and 'gender' with 'culture' (see Chapter 2). Poststructuralist and postmodern feminists have subsequently problematised that which was left implicitly unproblematised by the 'second-wave' feminists, namely the natural or the biological. However, their critique is not limited to explanations of natural or biological 'essences'. They also focus on psychological characteristics such as nurturance, empathy, support, non-competitiveness, and the like, and 'activities and procedures (which may or may not be dictated by biology) observable in social practices – intuitiveness, emotional responses, concern and commitment to helping others, etc.' (Grosz, 1995: 47). As Grosz explains, essentialism is seen to entail the belief that those characteristics defined as women's 'essences' are shared in common by all women at all times and underlie all apparent variations differentiating women from each other. It is seen to imply a limit on the variations and possibilities for change and thus of social reorganisation, and for this reason has been of central concern to most contemporary feminisms (1995: 47–8).

Following Grosz (1995), essentialism may be distinguished from biologism, naturalism, and universalism – all of which are centred on the question of the nature of women and men, and also figure at various points in my discussion. Biologism is a form of essentialism perhaps the most widely recognised form, in which women's and men's 'essences' are defined in terms of biological capacities. As Grosz explains, biologism tends to involve reductionism in that social and cultural factors are seen to be the effects of biological factors. In feminist analysis, it is commonly seen as tying women to the functions of reproduction and nurturance, although women's possibilities are also seen as limited through the use of evidence from neurology, endocrinology, and neurophysiology. Biologism is clearly evident in recent accounts of sex differences in the brain. However, it is also apparent in explanations of sexual behaviour, such as male heterosexual behaviour and 'homosexual orientation' (see Chapter 3). Naturalism is a form of essentialism in which a fixed nature is postulated for women and men; for example, women are seen as being 'naturally' caring, and men as 'naturally' aggressive (see Chapters 3 and 4). While this 'nature' is usually given by biology, it may be asserted on theological or ontological grounds. Thus, women's and men's natures may be seen to be God-given attributes that are not explicable in biological terms. Or, following Sartrean existentialism or Freudian psychoanalysis, it might be asserted that there exist some ontological invariants that distinguish the two sexes; for example, 'the claim that the human subject is somehow free or that the subject's social position is a function of his or her genital morphology' (Grosz, 1995: 48).

Universalism, although usually justified in terms of biology, may be conceived in purely social terms; for example, the sexual division of labour or the prohibition of incest. As Grosz argues,

> unlike essentialism, biologism, or naturalism, in which not only the similarities but also the differences between women [and between men] may be accounted for (race and class characteristics can also be explained in naturalistic, biologist, or essentialist terms), universalism tends to suggest only the commonness of all women [and men] at all times and in all social contexts. (1995: 48–9)

Universalist explanations posit a unity among women and among men based on ahistorical and cross-cultural qualities. Charges of universalism have been increasingly made against Western academic feminism by women from non-European cultures and of different 'racial' and socio-economic backgrounds whose experiences are at odds with feminist theories. I examine these critiques in more detail in Chapter 2. A similar kind of critique has yet to emerge in respect to 'men's studies', but it is clear that the same tendency to generalise also exists here.

Essentialism is rife in writings on men and 'masculinity'. That is, it is assumed that there exists a relatively stable masculine 'essence' that defines men and distinguishes them from a feminine 'essence' that defines women. Although the essentialism of 'masculinity' often entails biologism, it is also frequently based on psychology or other disposition or practice. This essentialism may be found in both scholarly and 'popular' writings on men, and recent efforts by theorists to avoid charges of essentialism by positing the existence of multiple 'masculinities' (i.e. simply pluralising 'masculinity'), I believe, does not overcome this basic problem. Bob Connell (1993) is right in pointing out that 'masculinity' has been reified, and treated in isolation of particular historical and cultural contexts. As he notes, the area of 'men's studies' has thus far been dominated by psychological accounts, and there has been a failure to take account of global history, comparative and historical perspectives, and power relations. However, in adopting 'masculinities' as a major analytic category in his own work (see particularly Connell, 1995) Connell, too, can be accused of reifying that which is in need of critical deconstruction. Given that most pro-feminist 'men's studies' scholars avowedly reject the idea of a universal masculine 'essence' and argue that there is nothing inevitable about male perspectives and behaviours, it seems ironic that they so frequently reify and essentialise 'masculinity' in their own work. The reification and essentialism of 'masculinity', I believe, is an artifact of the way in which scholars have conceived the object of their enquiries. The tendency has been to use 'masculinity', or 'masculinities', as the basic analytic category in research and writing, rather than to view this category as a specific social and historical construction; as a product of power and knowledge.

The constant and uncritical use of the category 'men' in research and writing also reflects a tendency towards universalism. The unstated assumption is that there exists a universal category of human subject defined by biology and/or common experience. However, none of the concepts of 'men', 'women', 'gender', 'sexuality', and so on, has cross-cultural and trans-historical significance: all are relational terms whose identities derive from their inherence in a system of differences. (On this point, see Parker et al., 1992: 5.) Researchers have failed to deconstruct the category 'men', and to examine how different constructions of 'men' have emerged historically and become inflected with racialised, sexualised, and classist meanings. One of the key arguments of this book is that essentialism and universalism are instrinsic to Western thought and that their elimination will require a radical change in epistemology. Our ways of knowing in the modern West have been limited by the assumption that the only true knowledge is objective, universal knowledge – i.e. knowledge that is independent of time and place, and of the power relations between the knower and the known. In Chapter 2, I outline some of the key assumptions of Western rationality and some recent criticisms that have been made by postmodern and poststructuralist theorists, and others. Feminist philosophers have been at pains to point out that the drive to develop an impartial, total, view of the world is not only unrealisable but has exclusionary and marginalising effects. Western knowledge is seen as based on a foundation of first principles that involves the ordering of reality into dualisms. The dualistic ordering of knowledge always involves the privileging of one side of the dualism over the other: identity over difference, reason over unreason, being over negation, culture over nature, self over other, mind over body, male over female, and so on. Critics have not found it easy to avoid dualistic thinking in their own work, however, as is evident in recent scholarly work on the links between 'masculinity' and reason (see Chapter 4).

Essentialism and universalism are perhaps most apparent in 'popular' genres of writing on men. These works have been overlooked by more critical scholars as a source of insight into the operations of the epistemology of 'masculinity'. Such works both reflect and generate cultural knowledge of the masculine. They offer simple messages to mass audiences. Their wide appeal would seem to lie, at least in part, in the fact that they are unencumbered by what is seen to be 'high theory' and the detailed (and often complex) qualifications characteristic of more scholarly contributions. They are products of a relatively new and rapidly expanding publishing industry surrounding the 'crisis in masculinity'. Writings are dominated by two main styles of narrative, both of which have their origins in Christian tradition, namely the confession and the sermon. (On the use of the confessional style in recent writings on men and 'masculinity', see my discussion, 'Uncovering the male emotions', in Chapter 4: 88–94.) Each is characterised by strong appeals to 'common sense' (i.e. 'what "we" all know') and tends to offer gross generalisations about men and women, and their relationships. They make liberal use of essentialist and universalist categories. In deploying these categories, many, if not most, are implicitly heterosexist, and often racist. It is not always easy to distinguish these works from more scholarly contributions, however, in that both frequently share similar assumptions and theories, although these theories are usually more implicit in 'popular' works.

Perhaps the most well-known strand of the 'popular' writings is of the so-called mythopoetic variety, of whom the most notorious contributor is Robert Bly, of *Iron John* fame (see Bly, 1990). The authors of the mythopoetic works look to a mythical past to find the models for contemporary 'manhood' – for example, the warrior figure. Drawing heavily on Jungian psychology, they argue that men must reclaim their cultural heritage which has been destroyed by modern society. Men are seen to suffer profound grief at the loss of 'masculinity', which needs to be restored to its rightful and ritualistic place (Young, 1993: 324). In Blazina's (1997) view, during a period of 'masculine crisis', 'myths can become tools for cultural and personal transformation by

giving men alternative ways of conceptualizing "what is masculine"'. He suggests that men emulate generative myths such as Odysseus, the Greek hero
who symbolises the emotion of reunion between father and son, and the
Green Man, a prehistorical figure who symbolises peaceful coexistence and
respect for nature, in order to 'guide them toward a deeper understanding of
self and object relations' (1997: 292). The mythopoetic 'men's movement', and
Robert Bly's work in particular, has been criticised extensively by feminists
and a number of male scholars. Criticisms have included the charges of separatism, 'masculinist nationalism', contempt for the 'other', authoritarianism,
and the reinforcement of invidious distinctions between women and men
(see, for example, Caputi and MacKenzie, 1992; Young; 1993).

    There are other kinds of 'popular' writings which also enjoy widespread
commercial success and are equally essentialist. Writings roughly divide
between those of the 'men's rights movement' and those of the 'pro-feminist
men's movement'. The former seek to expose 'the myth of male power'
(Farrell, 1994), and to reclaim and protect masculine power and privilege, and
can be seen to represent a reactionary response to feminisms. Writers tend to
employ essentialist and naturalist arguments to justify normative hierarchies
of gender, while actively ignoring the specificity of the history of relations
between women and men, often pitting all women against all men at all times
and depicting feminism as strategies 'to get men' (Frank, 1993: 337–8). 'Pro-
feminist' writings, on the other hand, generally seek to identify the absences
and needs in men's lives and posit 'action plans' (for example, Biddulph,
1995; Stoltenberg, 1989). As mentioned earlier, the term 'pro-feminist' is
deceptive in that it often conceals ignorance of the complexities of feminist
positions and a reluctance to engage critically with feminist theories.
Proponents rarely fully articulate the privileged position of white, heterosexual, middle-class men, or their implicit support for those positions (Frank,
1993: 339). Like the mythopoetic and 'men's rights' advocates, 'pro-feminist'
advocates tend to cast men as 'victims of society', effectively side-stepping
awkward questions about the power relations of gender and sexuality.

Towards a critique of the epistemology of 'masculinity'

Problems such as these, which are common to some extent to both scholarly
and 'popular' writings on men, underline the need for a thorough critique of
the epistemology of 'masculinity'. Such a critique should aim to show how
the frameworks of knowledge about the masculine have historically evolved
and how they structure what is known, and what can be known, about men
and their experiences. Such an analysis has been sadly lacking in 'men's studies', even in the more critical works which have been attentive to historical
and socio-cultural contexts. As Frank (1993) has commented, in so far as
'men's studies' fails to critically examine 'man-made explanations' of the
world, it offers no profound oppositional discourse. Although gender has
become an object of enquiry, this is conceived as yet another variable to be

added to 'the already long list of variables to be measured', while business continues as usual (Frank, 1993: 336).

> Even with the awareness of the social construction of gender within patriarchal relations, there is still either the lack of recognition – or the purposeful avoidance – of any analysis of the historicity and the social construction of the actual theories and the methods themselves that produce knowledge. The power of these historical and social products (the theoretical stance and methodological procedures) produced within the patriarchal gaze used to gain an understanding of people's lives and the resulting consequences, are taken for granted, and thus temporalized and depoliticized. In-so-far as these disciplinary practices produce women, and some men, as subordinate, their methods of observation and inquiry and the resulting production of theory do little to reorganize the objectified 'ways of knowing'. (Frank, 1993: 336–7)

To be sure, there is an emerging body of scholarship examining changing definitions of masculinity, showing how conceptions of masculinity are enmeshed in the history of institutions and of economic structures. These histories are highly provocative and provide one source for my arguments: for example, work showing how particular constructions of masculine behaviour and masculine embodiment have been effected through disciplines of the military (see Chapter 3). However, few histories focus *explicitly* and *systematically* on the frameworks of knowledge within which 'masculinity' and male subjects have been constructed. That is, there has been little effort to examine the 'assumptions about the nature of the subject (and hence about *human* nature) and about the relationship between the subject and the "thing" known' (Flax, 1981: 1007; emphasis in original).

Male bodies as objects and sites of power

A critical analysis of the epistemology of 'masculinity', I believe, should include an account of how male bodies have been objects and sites of power, and how this affects the subjectivities of different men. It needs to be asked why some male bodies are invested with more visibility and more power than others, and how natural knowledge is deployed in the construction of difference. Under the influence of Michel Foucault, many writers have challenged the naturalistic view of the body which has a fixed structure and immutable desires and behaviours. For example, the idea of a normal masculine heterosexual desire is questioned by recent Foucauldian-inspired social constructionism (see Katz, 1995). (See Chapter 2.) Rather than seeing bodies as biologically given, or pre-discursive, bodies have come to be seen as fabricated through discourse, as an effect of power/knowledge (see, for example, Butler, 1993). As yet, there has been relatively little detailed analysis of how different male bodies have been constructed in discourse, and how differences between men and women, and *within* men, have come to be seen as *natural* differences. Appeals to natural differences have long been used to rationalise the 'inferiorisation' of homosexuals, as well as other sexual minorities, women, and people of colour.

Racism, sexism, and heterosexism operate through the imputation of negative characteristics to the bodies and corporeal existence of different peoples. This is perhaps most evident in the construction of 'race' which has been dependent on the efforts of dominant nations and peoples to classify humans on the basis of corporeal characteristics such as skin colour (Shilling, 1993: 59). However, sexism and heterosexism, too, have relied on the classification of physical bodies into types; for example, there have been numerous attempts to classify and differentiate male and female bodies, and sexual types (see Kaplan and Rogers, 1990). There has recently been a resurgence of interest in biological, particularly genetic, explanations of human differences, for example between men and women, between different racial groups, and between 'homosexuals' and 'heterosexuals' (see Garber, 1995: 268–83; Nelkin and Lindee, 1995). Such theories have appeared with renewed vigour during a period in which there has been a conservative reaction against virtually all minority groups and against the gains made by feminists, gay and lesbian people, and peoples of non-European descent. They have been strategically employed to draw boundaries between Self and Other, to justify rights, and to deny rights. The findings of genetic research can be used by those who believe that education will make no difference to the social status of indigenous peoples; by those who would seek to change homosexual behaviour through medical intervention; and by those who are opposed to equality in general (Nelkin and Lindee, 1995: 399). It needs to be asked why there has been a renewed interest in genetic explanations of human differences in popular culture and science, and how such work is used to argue for discriminatory policies and practices.

Work such as that of Simon LeVay (1994) and Dean Hamer (Hamer and Copeland, 1994) in the United States, which focuses on the biological bases of male homosexuality, and of Moir and Jessel (1991) in the United Kingdom, which focuses on biological differences between men and women, has struck a resonant chord among a broad section of the population. There has also been some interest in the findings of racial science, particularly research pointing to genetic differences in the mental abilities between 'blacks' and 'whites' (see Kohn, 1995).

Research on sex differences and homosexuality has been welcomed by some women and some gay people who believe that it affirms and validates their difference. However, it is important to recognise that it can be used to delineate boundaries between that which is considered normal, and hence superior, and that which is viewed as pathological, and hence inferior, with deleterious consequences for those so labelled. There have been numerous efforts in the past to intervene into the bodies and lives of women on the assumption that their bodies are 'naturally' inferior, and various forms of 'treatment' have been meted out to lesbians and gay men on the assumption that their 'condition' is a result of a failure of some biological function (see, for example, Birke, 1982; Ehrenreich and English, 1979). It is likely that studies of biological difference will continue to be used in these ways so long as science, and biological science in particular, remains a privileged arbiter of the 'truth' on questions of difference. A critique of the idea of the natural body and of supporting discourses is necessary, I believe, if one is to counter essentialism and naturalism and the tendency to control or annihilate that which is deemed to be different.

The research contributions of Thomas Laqueur (1990), Londa Schiebinger (1989, 1993) and Nellie Oudshoorn (1994) illustrate well the value of historical deconstruction in undermining the essentialism and 'naturalisation' of the body – especially in relation to its sexed and gendered dimensions. This corpus of work has been one of the sources of inspiration for this study, and is referred to at various points in the discussion (see particularly Chapters 2 and 3). Such work unsettles a number of deeply held cultural assumptions of people in the modern West about the 'naturalness' of the body, emphasising the particular role played by biological and bio-medical knowledges in the fabrication of the 'normal', 'healthy', sexed and gendered body. Sex, the supposed biological bedrock for the social constructions of gender, is shown to be a social product. It has been constructed in line with cultural assumptions about normal gender and sexuality. Work such as this offers a profound challenge to the epistemology of 'masculinity', based as it is upon the premise that there exist relatively stable bodily 'essences', desires and behaviours. It brings into question taken-for-granted understandings of the normal and the pathological, and the stability of the boundaries that have been erected between normal selves and the abnormal others. Far from having stable, immutable properties and potentialities, bodies are shown to be highly variable – both historically and culturally.

In so far as the body has been discussed at all in 'men's studies', most analyses have been ahistorical and inattentive to the specifics of culture and to the operations of power relations. The body is rarely seen as a product of power/knowledge. Although social constructionism has increasingly influenced analyses of the body, theoretical development has been limited by a discourse about whether the body is a natural or biological given *or* a socially-constructed entity. I believe that it is important for scholars to move beyond the terms of this debate if they are to avoid essentialism and dichotomous thinking in their work. Recently, many scholars have claimed that the body is 'socially constructed', without specifying exactly what they mean by this. Social constructionism is an umbrella term encompassing a range of perspectives which suggest that the body is somehow shaped, constrained and even invented by society. Those who take this approach tend to share the view that the 'meanings attributed to the body, and the boundaries which exist between the bodies of different groups of people, are social products' (Shilling, 1993: 70). However, beyond this basic level of agreement, there exists a great diversity of social constructionist perspectives on the body.

The naturalism/constructionism dichotomy is useful in underlining the distinctiveness of recent problematisations of the body in the social sciences and humanities. However, as an abstraction, it cannot do justice to the full range and complexity of contemporary theoretical and political positions in respect to the body. Many writers are guilty of essentialising social constructionism, overlooking the fact that this is a generic term encompassing a diverse range of shifting perspectives and projects, including but not limited to discourse analysis, deconstruction, and poststructuralism, which have been developed in different ways by scholars at different times according to their own particular theoretical and political purposes. Although all social constructionists may be seen to share a broadly similar epistemology, in that they all claim to eschew essentialism and realism, and view knowledge as historically and culturally specific, they are not of one voice (see Burr, 1995). Some researchers give explicit theoretical attention to the body as an object or site of power, and seek to undertake detailed genealogies of supportive discourses. For example, those feminists and gay and lesbian scholars who have been influenced by Foucault's ideas have examined the ways in which women's bodies and the bodies of 'homosexuals' have been subject to the disciplinary powers of bio-medicine (for example, Plummer, 1981; Sawicki, 1991; Weeks 1985). However, not all social constructionists can be considered poststructuralists, and not all articulate a clear theoretical perspective on power relations. Commentators often gloss over considerable differences in perspective, using 'social constructionism' as a 'catch-all' descriptive phrase, sometimes dismissing 'it' on the basis that 'it' denies biology. For instance, in his discussion of men's bodies in his book *Masculinities*, Bob Connell criticises 'social constructionist approaches to gender and sexuality' (which he simplistically, and misleadingly, equates with the 'semiotic approach') for 'disembodying sex' and for their inattention to 'an irreducible bodily dimension in experience and practice' (see Connell, 1995: 51), effectively dismissing the substantial social constructionist contributions of feminist and gay and lesbian scholars focusing precisely on these dimensions. Postmodernism and poststructuralism have ushered in sophisticated, historically informed approaches to the study of the body, which recognise both the materiality of the body and the fact that that materiality is itself a product of power/knowledge.

Rethinking the concept of identity

The anti-essentialist trend within contemporary social theory has had a profound impact on thinking about 'identity'. This is reflected in the proliferation of academic writings in the 1980s and 1990s on 'the question of identity'. Much of this writing has originated in the areas of feminist theory, anti-racist and post-colonial theory, and gay/lesbian/queer theory where academics have debated the possibilities of developing a new or reconceptualised identity politics. This work challenges some basic premises underlying the dominant epistemology of 'masculinity'. Scholars have tended to leave 'identity' unproblematised, uncritically adopting conceptions originally developed in the social sciences in the 1950s (Gleason, 1983, cited by Epstein, 1993/94: 28). As Epstein (1993/94) notes, social science conceptions of identity lean towards either one of two oppositional views, one a psychological reductionism, the other a sociological reductionism. The first view treats identity as a relatively fixed and stable characteristic of the person. It reflects the notion that we can know who someone *really is*. The second conception treats identity as 'acquired', involving 'the internalisation or conscious adoption of socially imposed or socially constructed labels or roles' (Epstein, 1993/4: 28–9). According to the 'acquired' definition, identity is not so deeply inscribed in the psyche of the individual, and so there is scope for changing one's identity. It reflects the belief that the individual can voluntarily 'choose' to 'identify as' a such-and-such (Epstein, 1993/94: 28–9).

Of course, these are ideal-type conceptions, and 'men's studies', like the social sciences in general, has been characterised by attempts to mediate between these positions. For example, psychoanalytic explanations of identity posit a complex interaction between 'intra-psychic' processes and social expectations. However, the above two basic conceptions have dominated thinking about 'identity' up to the present, and have influenced the development of so-called 'identity politics', whereby one bases one's politics on a sense of personal identity – as gay, as Jewish, as black, as a male, a female, and so on (Fuss, 1989: 97). As Fuss argues, the tendency has been to assume that there is a causal relationship between 'identity' and 'politics', with the former determining the latter. Thus, there is the expectation that the individual will 'claim' or 'discover' their 'true' identity before they elaborate a 'personal politics'. This is especially evident in both the gay and lesbian literature, where there is a familiar tension between a view that identity is something which is always present (but has been repressed) and that which has never been socially permitted (but remains to be created, or achieved). This has often led to the reduction of the political to the personal, and the limitation of political activity to 'self-discovery' and personal transformation (Fuss, 1989: 99–101). (See Chapter 5.) In feminist psychology, in particular, the dictum 'the personal is political' has usually meant that the 'political' is personalised, as can be seen in the use of the notions of 'empowerment', 'revolution from within', and the focus on 'validating' women's reality (Kitzinger, 1996).

The essentialism of identity mirrors the essentialism of the self, seen within the Enlightenment tradition as 'a stable, reliable, integrative entity that has access to our inner states and outer reality, at least to a limited (but knowable) degree' (Flax, 1990: 8). The 'search for identity' and concerns about 'identity crises' can be seen as contemporary manifestations of the preoccupation with the 'essential' self. These themes are widespread in both scholarly and 'popular' writings on men and 'masculinity', and are a preoccupation of the mythopoetic and a number of other strands of the 'men's movement'. The concern with the link between identity and selfhood is reflected in recent sociological writings, such as in the work of Anthony Giddens who has explored the dilemmas posed to the question of 'self-identity' in a context in which tradition increasingly loses its hold. Giddens' view is that in the post-traditional order of modernity, 'self-identity' becomes a reflexively organised endeavour in which there is a multiplicity of available options for shaping one's own identity (Giddens, 1991). According to Giddens, this extends to the most personal aspects of one's existence. Thus, even one's 'sexual identity' involves an element of choice and, with the severing of the link between sexuality and reproduction, a growing number of possibilities for intimate relationships has emerged (Giddens, 1992). (See also Chapter 6.)

Some of the harshest critiques of identity as a category of knowledge and politics have been offered by non-heterosexual people, people of colour, and peoples from the 'Third World' – those who have been most excluded and marginalised by modern categorising and naming practices. Academic feminism has not been immune to criticism in this regard. Lesbians, women of colour, and women in the 'Third World' have been among those who have questioned feminist categories, which are seen often to be underpinned by an implicit heterosexism (see, for example, Phelan, 1994; Richardson, 1996a), racism and Eurocentrism (see, for example, James and Busia, 1993; Mohanty et al., 1991). (See also Chapter 2.) Black feminists and black male writers have also pointed to the tendency for writers to essentialise black and ethnic male identities. This essentialism is seen to affirm white European notions of manhood and masculinity, while denying the historical and social contexts of domination within which identities have been forged (hooks, 1992; Julien, 1992; Mercer, 1994; Mercer and Julien, 1988). The trend to 'de-essentialise' 'identity' is an important one in the social sciences and humanities and, as I will point out at various points in the chapters that follow, has significant implications for how one views the masculine self.

Increasingly, 'identity' is seen as a discursive construction – one that is arbitrary and exclusionary, and acts as a normative ideal for regulating subjects. This is not to deny human agency and the possibility for the self to fashion itself (on this point, see Chapters 5 and 6). However, to view 'identity' as fabricated disturbs the widely held assumption that 'identity' is relatively stable and is 'made up' of various fixed components, particularly gender, sexuality, race, and ethnicity, conceived as relatively independent aspects of one's being. As Edwards (1990) points out, there has been a tendency to treat 'sex' and 'gender', and 'sexuality' and 'gendered identity' as separate entities, or aspects of 'identity'. Moreover, 'race' has been either totally neglected or viewed, like 'sex', as a natural category. The separation of these categories in 'men's studies' reflects the aforementioned dualism between nature and culture that has been part of Western thinking since the nineteenth century (Edwards, 1990: 111). One of the legacies of this dualistic thinking is that 'male identity' is seen to be simply a composite of various natural and socially constructed attributes. Thus, one is a 'homosexual man', a 'black man', a 'white heterosexual man', an 'able-bodied young man', and so on. The problem with this so-called additive model of identity is that no matter how exhaustive the description, there will always be exclusions, and disjunctions between imposed identity labels and personal experiences. There is literally an infinite number of ways in which the 'components of identity' can intersect or combine to 'make up' masculine identity. There is an arbitrariness about any identity construction, which will inevitably entail the silencing or exclusion of some experiences.

The utility of 'identity' and of 'identity politics' continues to be debated. I examine these debates at various points in the book, but particularly in Chapter 5 where I examine the challenge posed by queer theory to 'identity', and to 'sexual identity' in particular. At this point, it should be emphasised that contemporary theorists do not necessarily disavow identity, as some writers have suggested. Rather, their aim has been to draw attention to the fictitious character of identity, to the dangers of imposing an identity, and to the necessity to resist attempts to replace identity with something else, especially with a 'new identity'. They question the imperative to have coherent identities, and the notion that political identities must be secure in order that one can do political work (Fuss, 1989: 105). In introducing these often complex arguments, I do not aim to propose a clear resolution, but rather to highlight what I believe are some important challenges to prevailing conceptions of men, masculinity and masculine identity, and to emphasise the need to rethink basic categories of analysis and critique. I see this book, then, as offering a synthesis and assessment of recent trends in social thought as they impact on contemporary understandings of the masculine and masculine identity and, hopefully, as serving to stimulate further thinking and research.

Outline of the book

In Chapter 2, I examine the context shaping contemporary concerns about 'masculinity' and 'masculine identity'. The so-called 'crisis of masculinity' can be understood as an aspect of a broader 'crisis of modernity', involving the critique of the mode and categories of Western thought. Belief in objective knowledge has been undermined, and scholars across the social sciences and humanities have begun to interrogate all categories and concepts, including 'the body', 'the self', 'society', 'reason', 'community', and 'history'. The ideas of writers such as Derrida, Deleuze and Guattari, and Foucault emerge and find a receptive audience in this context, influencing established disciplines and inspiring new critical enquiries. As I argue, within the humanities and social sciences, identity is increasingly seen as a normative ideal that is assured through the use of categories such as 'gender', 'sexuality', 'sex' and 'race', rather than as a descriptive aspect of experience. In the chapter, I focus on challenges posed by a growing 'gender scepticism' within feminism and the recent impact of social constructionism on our understandings of heterosexuality and of 'race'. Work generated by poststructuralist and postmodern feminists, gay and queer scholars, and anti-racist/post-colonial theorists offers new critical and historical insights into the bases of masculine privilege and unsettles some of the key assumptions upon which constructions of the masculine have relied. I conclude this chapter by noting that the wide range of responses to the 'crisis of masculinity' is indicative of the extent to which political positions have polarised in the current sceptical climate. In so far as writers retreat into various forms of essentialism, none of the recent responses proves satisfactory. I contend that if one is to open up possibilities for conceiving new ways of being, it is strategically important to critique and expose the operations of essentialism. In respect to the study of men and 'masculinity', I believe it is important that one appreciates how these categories have been sustained, historically, through various exclusions.

It is in light of these observations and beliefs that I develop my perspective on male bodies in Chapter 3. As I have mentioned, in so far as the body has figured at all in 'men's studies', it is rarely viewed as a product of power/ knowledge. An examination of the ways in which male bodies have been constructed and of the implications of these constructions for different subjects, I would argue, is integral to the ongoing effort to expose the operations and implications of essentialism. Starting from the premise that the very materiality of bodies is an effect of power, I examine the processes through which particular male bodies, or bodily qualities, come to matter more than others. Clearly, some male bodies are more visible, powerful and valued than others and, since the nineteenth century, the bodies of white, European, middle-class, heterosexual men have been constructed as the standard for measuring and evaluating *all* bodies. I explore the role of science, particularly biological science, in constructing knowledge of male sexuality and male identity. The categories of 'sex', 'race' and 'sexuality' have been extensively employed in the construction of human differences. These categories have interacted in various and complex ways in different contexts and at different times, each helping to constitute the others. Historically, 'race' has been a major division of body classification and evaluation and, in the mid to late eighteenth century, when racial theories were beginning to be developed, both women and non-Europeans were defined as being inferior species within the great chain of being. Theories of 'race' and sex have been used to construct, marginalise and stigmatise particular male bodies. Various physical markers of sex and race (for example, skin colour, skull capacity, circumcision) have been employed as the basis for identifying and stigmatising male Jews, 'black' men, and other groups. In this chapter, I explore the impact of Darwinism on the disciplining and shaping of male bodies from the late nineteenth century. Darwinism is seen to provide the master metaphor for thinking about categories of difference, and in particular for thinking about male bodies and their capacities, and its influence has extended to the training of male bodies and male minds, and to theories of natural male aggressivity and a natural male sex drive. One of the themes explored in this chapter is the stigmatisation of the homosexual body, which came to be seen in the late nineteenth century and early twentieth century as an 'inversion' – a pathology – and as the binary opposite of the supposed normal, heterosexual male body. Biological theories of difference continue to hold sway in scientific and popular discourses, as evidenced by the recent search for the 'gay gene' and in a number of studies of sex differences. I examine some of this work and its attendant dangers. The chapter finishes with a plea for greater recognition of the ways in which the corporeal body is 'made' and 'remade' in various contexts, and of the implications of this for subjectivity and for social action.

Chapter 4 examines some critiques of the cultural link between 'masculinity' and rationality, as articulated in the work of various feminist scholars and 'pro-feminist' male writers. The privileging of the 'mind' over the 'body' is widely seen to be characteristic of 'masculinist' rationality, and to be implicated in the domination of men over women, of culture over nature and of Europeans over non-Europeans. In the chapter, I examine the areas of feminist psychoanalysis, feminist theories of moral development, ecofeminism, and 'pro-feminist' men's writings on male emotionality, focusing on the contributions of a number of key authors. As I explain, the works that are examined should be seen as more than simply critiques of 'masculinist' rationality. In different ways, and to varying degrees, they reflect and contribute to the maintenance of the very discourse which their authors claim to challenge. One of the key aims of this chapter is to emphasise the difficulty of escaping the dichotomous, hierarchical, and essentialist thinking that is characteristic of Western rationality. Given the dominance of scientific rationality in modern culture, it is hardly surprising that scientific institutions, methods and practices have been subjected to sustained criticism by feminists and other critical scholars. The insights of the feminist critics of science have informed my arguments at many points in this book. In this particular chapter, however, I draw attention to some difficulties encountered by feminist critics in their analyses of 'masculinist' rationality. Continuing commitment to rational science, an implicit heterosexist bias in some influential versions of some theories (such as psychoanalysis), and dualistic and essentialist thinking are among the problems identified. A number of these problems, and others, are also evident in the work of 'pro-feminist' male writers who have critiqued men's emotionality. I conclude the chapter by emphasising the need for scholars to remain reflexive in their use of *all* categories and dualisms and alert to the challenges involved in developing 'situated knowledges' in a context profoundly shaped by the drive to achieve 'logocentric knowledge', or the generic human viewpoint.

In Chapter 5, I examine some important challenges posed to understandings of identity and identity politics by the recent development of queer theory. The emergence of queer theory, I argue, is indicative of growing disenchantment with the modern proclivity to name and categorise, and of recognition of the dilemmas of basing one's politics upon the assumption of a fixed identity. The chapter examines the context giving rise to queer theory and the particular problems it addresses. It asks such questions as: what does it mean to mobilise around men and 'masculinity' when the ground upon which these categories are constructed has been de-stabilised? Is it possible to base an identity on something other than an 'essence'? Should one abandon the concepts of identity and identity politics? As I point out, queer theory does not constitute an homogeneous body of thought. Although there is broad agreement among scholars regarding problems with the essentialism of identity, there are divergent views on the strategic value of an appeal to essentialist categories. While some scholars emphasise the strategy of deconstruction, others advocate the deployment of 'strategic essentialism' in order to protect basic rights. In the chapter, I outline these debates, and indicate some problems with translating queer theory into practice, evident, for instance, with the practice of 'outing'. Despite its problems and unresolved dilemmas, queer theory raises some important questions about the sexual and its relationship to the social. Importantly, it focuses attention on the production and effects of the putative norm, and on processes of marginality and power relations that tend to be neglected in conventional analyses of sexuality. Queer's critique of gay identity politics raises questions about the meanings of non-sexist and gay affirmative work as promoted by many 'men's studies' scholars and by sections of the contemporary 'men's movement'. Queer theorists have exposed the heterosexist biases of those disciplines that have produced knowledge about the masculine, such as psychoanalysis and sociology, and the implicit heterosexism in theories of gender. In brief, queer theory's particular approach to the sexual unsettles some deeply held assumptions about men and identity, and poses significant challenges for future theoretical and political work.

In Chapter 6, the concluding chapter, I draw together the main themes of the book and discuss some implications and questions arising from the analysis as a whole. In a postparadigmatic context, characterised by scepticism towards all categories and concepts and a focus on the politics of representation, the meanings of the concepts 'men', 'masculinity' and 'identity' should no longer be simply assumed. As I argue, an opportunity has been presented for rethinking the question of identity, and for developing ways of being that are less constrained by the sex/gender system. Many people, it is clear, are receptive to rethinking traditional assumptions about manhood and about relationships between men of different backgrounds and between men and women. In this chapter, I outline some likely directions of change that are suggested by developments in those societies where there has been a substantial redefinition of gender roles. Although it is unlikely that established ideals of manhood will suddenly vanish, and that changes will be abrupt, uniform and without resistance, the conditions of late modern society would seem to be ripe for the emergence of reconceptualised models of identity.

2

From essentialism to scepticism

As a number of writers have recently pointed out, over the last two decades, 'masculinity' is seen to be in 'crisis' (see, for example, Badinter, 1995; Horrocks, 1994; Rutherford, 1992). Although there is by no means agreement about the exact nature of this 'crisis', or indeed about whether this is the most apt description for the changes afoot (on this point, see Connell, 1995: 84), there is a widely felt sense that the contemporary period marks a decisive point in terms of thinking about established cultural understandings of the masculine and about the possibilities for reshaping male identities on the basis of radically new conceptions of the person. In recent years there has been a proliferation of discourses on men and 'masculinity', as evidenced by the rise of new academic specialities of 'men's studies' and enquiries into men's lives. And at least some men have shown a preparedness to explore their own lives and relationships. There has been an increasing number of conferences and seminars organised around such themes as men's health, men's violence, and the sexual abuse of men; men's festivals (including gay men's festivals); residential workshops for men; psychotherapy groups and counselling services for men; and Internet discussion groups on men. Many men, and women, it would seem are confused about 'what makes a man', and while some men have begun the search for a 'lost identity', others see new opportunities for recasting the masculine script.

According to both Badinter and Kimmel, there have been at least two earlier such 'crises in masculinity' in modern history, such as in France and England in the seventeenth and eighteenth centuries, and in Europe and the United States at the turn of the nineteenth and twentieth centuries (Badinter, 1995: 9–20; Kimmel, 1987: 126–53). As Badinter and Kimmel argue, such crises, involving a radical questioning or redefinition of the meaning of 'masculinity', have occurred in countries where there have been great ideological, economic, or social upheavals precipitating changes in social values, including the creation of greater freedoms for women. According to Badinter, the first crisis involved a questioning by the French *précieuses* ('ladies "refined" in sentiment and language') and English feminists of the institution of marriage and the demand for dignity, education, the possibility of social ascension and, in the case of England, the demand for total sexual equality and the right not to be abandoned when they became pregnant. In both countries, women demanded not only the equality of desires and rights, but also that men 'be gentler, more feminine'. This led to an inversion of roles involving the emergence of the new 'feminised' man who adopted behaviour similar to that of women. In the event, in France at least the development was put an end to by the French Revolution of 1789 when political action against women's demands for rights as citizens reaffirmed forcefully the separation of the sexes (Badinter, 1995: 10–13).

The second major crisis occurred in Europe and the United States in response to feminist demands following economic and social upheavals generated by industrialisation and democracy. A new type of woman appeared 'who threatened imposed sexual frontiers', and who demanded education, greater participation in public life, and 'equal pay for equal work'. Although the 'masculine anxiety' created by these changes took different forms in different countries, there was a hostile reaction from a certain class of men 'who felt their identities threatened by this new creature who wanted to do what they did, be like them' (Badinter, 1995: 14). The men who were most threatened by these changes made a concerted effort to resist the 'feminisation of culture' that was seen to undermine both the traditional family unit and established identities. One of the responses of this period involved an emphasis on the 'natural' differences between men and women as the basis for social differentiation. The assault against women's gains originated with religious and medical authorities, but was supported by new biological and social science theories which rooted social differences in the 'natural order of things' (Kimmel, 1987: 143–5). At the end of the nineteenth century, there was an outpouring of new natural science and social science work seeking to demonstrate women's ontological inferiority and close relationship to the animals and 'lower races'. According to Badinter, this particular 'crisis of masculinity' was temporarily resolved by the two world wars which 'served as an outlet and a "test of manliness"' for many men (1995: 20).

These two previous 'crises', Badinter claims, can be distinguished from the present one by their socially limited nature. The first involved only the dominant classes, the aristocracy and the bourgeoisie, while the second involved mainly industrial working-class and middle-class men whose work, which was redefined by the process of industrialisation, no longer provided opportunities for the demonstration of qualities that were seen to underpin male identity, such as strength, agility, and initiative (Badinter, 1995: 10–15). In both cases, the respective social orders would seem to have produced a relatively coherent set of norms for 'manliness', even though the fragility of those norms was made apparent by the reaction of those groups most directly threatened by change. In the present 'crisis', however, there has been widespread questioning in many contemporary societies of not only the norms of 'manliness', but also of supportive frameworks of knowledge. A number of converging developments have served to undermine modernist constructions of the natural and social worlds, and the apparent mutual exclusivity of these two worlds, and in the process have called into question the utility of categories that have been foundational to modern thought on men and 'masculinity' and women and 'femininity'. The notion of a fixed human essence that defines and differentiates people, particularly according to biophysical criteria, has come under scrutiny within the social sciences and humanities, and many scholars have drawn attention to the limits of an identity politics based upon stable categories of gender and sexuality.

These developments can be seen to be inextricably connected with a broader 'crisis of modernity', involving a questioning of the grand synthesising theories of the nineteenth century and the progressionist impulse of science. The rationalist search for objectivity and truth has come to be seen by writers of diverse backgrounds and perspectives as no longer tenable, and notions of 'the self', 'the body', 'society', 'community', 'reason', and 'history' are all being vigorously interrogated. As Jeffrey Weeks (1995) has pointed out, the late twentieth century is characterised by great uncertainty about values, particularly values around sexual identity, and a critical interrogation of what have been taken to be the essential truths about human sexual nature. The binarisms that have come to dominate thinking about gender and sexuality since the nineteenth century, such as the repression/liberation model, the homo/hetero sexual distinction and the sex/gender distinction, have been subjected to intense scrutiny. And some writers have begun to explore the possibilities of fashioning new models and practices of the self that are not wedded to an essentialist notion of identity. In this chapter I outline some important dimensions of these developments, and begin the task of exploring the implications for 'masculine identity' and the power relations of gender, sexuality, and 'race'.

Critique of Western thought

A fundamental challenge has been offered to the social sciences and humanities by the critique of 'logocentrism', the idea that it is possible to gain unmediated access to reality. The idea that the truth about the human subject can be arrived at through rational knowledge is questioned by various overlapping and complementary theoretical and practical projects going by the names of postmodernism, poststructuralism, social constructionism, and deconstruction. Jacques Derrida, whose work has been especially influential among scholars in the humanities, maintains that modern philosophy (and his argument can be extended to almost any modern knowledge system, anatomy, biology, psychology, sociology, and so on) has been dominated by the so-called 'metaphysics of presence' the desire to bring things into a unity or under a universal essence (Sarup, 1993: 35; Young, I.M., 1995: 234–5). According to Derrida and his followers, any effort to define an identity always involves excluding some elements, separating the pure, authentic, and good from the impure, inauthentic, and bad. Any definition or category involves the drawing of inside/outside distinctions, and the logic of identity seeks to keep those borders firmly drawn (Young, I.M., 1995: 235). Western philosophy is seen to be built upon a foundation of first principles which involves the ordering of reality into 'dualisms': identity and difference, reason and unreason, being and negation, nature and culture, self and other, mind and body, and male and female. This dualistic ordering of knowledge always involves the privileging of one side of the dualism over the other: identity is privileged over difference, reason over unreason, being over negation, nature over culture, self over other, mind over body, male over female, and so on. Whatever is other – difference, absence, unreason – is marginalised and devalued (Hollinger, 1994: 108). One of the important implications of this work is that the assumption of an immediately available area of certainty is no longer seen as tenable. There is no 'single definable moment which is now', but rather an endless play of signifiers (Sarup, 1993: 35). The method of deconstruction advocated by Derrida and others involves the close reading of texts in order to show the ultimate failure of the conceptual distinctions on which arguments rely because of their inconsistent and paradoxical use.

For Deleuze and Guattari, the problem with Western thought is its adherence to the metaphor of the tree (the 'arborescent schema'), whereby the mind organises knowledge of reality according to systematic and hierarchical principles (branches of knowledge) which are grounded in firm foundations (the roots). This involves a politics of identity which is premised upon either/or distinctions, and leads to the repression or denial of difference and the marginalisation of those who do not conform to narrowly prescribed norms. For example, the construction of the unitary subject 'man' as white, European, adult, heterosexual, and 'rational' provides the standard against which women, non-Europeans, children, homosexuals, and those seen as 'irrational' are negatively evaluated, excluded, and marginalised (Deleuze and Guattari, 1987: 291–3). It is because of these exclusions that postmodern feminists, such as Hélène Cixous, Luce Irigaray, and Rosi Braidotti, have described Western thought as 'phallogocentric'. The critique of phallogocentrism offered by feminists has been important in drawing attention to the social and historical construction of categories of distinction, such as male and female, nature and culture, and rational and irrational, and in opening up space for a thorough appraisal of current strategies around those categories.

In her book, *The Man of Reason: 'Male' and 'Female' in Western Philosophy*, Genevieve Lloyd contends that Western philosophy has been deeply implicated in the organisation of sexual difference through its ideals of reason. From the beginnings of philosophical thought, argues Lloyd, femaleness has been symbolically associated with what reason supposedly excluded – the dark powers of the earth goddess, sensuality, emotion, desire, embodied experience, and nature. All the early Western philosophers, such as Philo, Augustine and Aquinas, presented femininity as somehow derivative of the male paradigm of rational excellence. However, beginning with the Enlightenment, philosophers began to see the minds of men and women as quite different in ways that make them 'complementary'. Both Kant and Rousseau, for example, insisted that although the 'fair sex' possessed just as much understanding as the male, it was a different kind of understanding that had its integrity, merit, and indeed beauty. As Lloyd explains, this complementation was supposed to be to the advantage of both sexes, since the attributes together were seen as making up a single moral being: 'he becomes more perfect as a man; whereas the woman becomes more perfect as a wife'

(1984: 76). In practice, it served to reinforce male dominance and women's exclusion from the public realm. In the work of Rousseau, for example, women's closeness to nature is seen to make them moral exemplars – she is both what reason leaves behind and that to which it aspires in the reconstruction of man in his natural state – while at the same time providing a rationale for their exclusion from the public sphere. Women's strengths were seen to reside in the domestic domain where they were contained in order to control the destructive effects of passion on civil society (1984: 58–64, 76–8).

Londa Schiebinger (1989) has argued that the theory of sexual complementarity advocated by Kant, Rousseau and others was compatible not only with ancient views on natural sex differences but also with the dominant strands of liberal democratic thought that were emerging from the late eighteenth century onwards. This theory proposed that women's unique role within the new democracies was as mothers and nurturers. Increasing fears that 'learned ladies' were eschewing traditional forms of marriage and motherhood – which were indeed justified since women were increasingly demanding productive lives free of the cares of parenting – led to a concerted campaign to reassert the virtues of mothering and women's natural disposition to nurture. Differences between the sexes were seen to be grounded in nature and not in social convention, and hence were believed to have universal applicability. Rational science was increasingly used as a bulwark against the demands of women to enter the public sphere. Doctors allied themselves with the complementarians and began to enquire into the anatomical and physiological basis for social differences. From the late eighteenth century, there was a flood of drawings of female skeletons which sought to describe and represent the 'perfect', universal female body. Male and female bodies were depicted as perfect in their difference, with the females seen as inferior to the males, but ideally and naturally adapted to their role as mothers (Schiebinger, 1989: 189–213). Such an understanding of history leads one to question whether it is possible to affirm the strengths of distinctly 'feminine' traits, particularly those seen to be based on biological distinctions (see, for example, Badinter, 1995; Christen, 1991), without at the same time covertly reinstating assumed 'masculinist' norms; that is, to revert to Rousseau's idea that the female mind is equal, but different. As Lloyd argues, 'women cannot easily be accommodated into a cultural ideal which has defined itself in opposition to the feminine' (1984: 104–5). Writers who have valorised the distinctly feminine (for example, women's greater capacity for nurturing relationships or for caring) (see Chapter 4) run the risk of reinforcing those very structures within which the masculine and the feminine have been historically constructed as essentially different but complementary.

As explained in Chapter 1, much feminist work has been concerned with the question of essentialism, or the attribution of an invariable essence to women usually, but not necessarily, identified with women's biology (Grosz, 1990a: 333–5; see also Gatens, 1996: 77–9; Grosz, 1995: 47–9). Essentialism is seen to emerge from the dualistic ordering of Western social science and Western philosophy which gives rise to identities and categories of difference which appear as natural, exclusive, complementary, fixed, and inevitable. An increasing amount of scholarship has focused on the dualistic distinction between natural science and social science which has been shown to have created an illusion of value freedom in scientific understandings of the human subject while operating in support of phallogocentrism. Writers such as Donna Haraway and Evelyn Fox Keller have pointed out that natural knowledge inevitably makes its appearance in social science theories of the female subject and is used to justify social inequalities which are seen as being 'natural' outgrowths of the 'facts of biology'. Such work has provided the opportunity for a more critical and thoroughgoing analysis of how presently constructed divisions in knowledge sustain hegemonic understandings of the masculine and the feminine, and for reflecting upon the possibilities for developing new systems of thought which break with the totalising gaze of modern Western philosophy and social science. As part of their efforts to de-stabilise (phal)logocentrism, a number of feminists and other scholars have proposed new modes of thought and an attendant language.

In Deleuze and Guattari's scheme, the metaphor of the rhizome is used to designate the deterritorialised movement of patterns of thought and language which subvert binary logic. The rhizome is suggestive of dynamism, multiple roots, multiple connections, and heterogeneity, which they see as being more in line with philosophical systems of the East and Oceania than of the West. Rhizomatic thought is spontaneous, not constrained by orthodoxy, the canon, or the search for origins. It implies eclecticism in style, recognition, and indeed celebration of difference, and the abandonment of the search for ultimate 'truths'. Rhizomatic thought is 'nomadic thought' that is opposed to state-centred thought that tries to discipline rhizomatic movement through totalising forms of theory and normalising practices of the state. The nomad provides a new model of existence and struggle: it attempts to free itself from roots, bonds, and identities, and thereby resist the state and normalising powers (Best and Kellner, 1991: 102–3). Rosi Braidotti (1994), for instance, advocates nomadic thinking as a feminist strategy in a context characterised by new conservative rationalities and patterns of domination based upon linear systems of thought. Feminists have been among those at the forefront of efforts to explore the limits and political implications of existing categories and to develop new modes of thinking employing such fictions as the 'nomadic subject' (Braidotti, 1994) and the 'cyborg' (the hybrid machine/organism) (Haraway, 1991). As recent work in feminism and in some other fields of critical enquiry has emphasised, the idea of fixed identities, including those based upon stable genders and stable sexualities, is itself a fiction – a regulatory one at that – that is sustained by adherence to logocentrism and arborescent schemes of thought.

The regulations of identity

There is a growing trend within the humanities and the social sciences to see 'identity' as a normative ideal that is assured through the use of categories such as 'sex', 'sexuality', 'gender', and 'race' rather than as being a descriptive feature of experience. Much recent critical scholarship has been concerned with revealing and analysing the role of these categories in the regulation of identity, and in this section I wish to draw attention to what I believe are some important implications of this work for conceptions of the masculine and for identity politics. I begin by drawing attention to recent feminist and other scholarship critiquing established 'second-wave' feminist categories, before moving on to discuss the regulations of sexuality and 'race', and then spelling out some implications of this work for reconceptualising the masculine.

Gender scepticism

The libertarian project of 'second-wave' feminism was increasingly questioned in the 1980s and 1990s. This has direct implications for how the category of the masculine is understood and for the possibilities of an identity politics based upon the category of gender. Judith Butler is an important figure among those who have asked whether the identity categories presumed to be foundational to feminist politics work to limit and constrain in advance the very cultural possibilities that feminism is supposed to create. As Butler (1990a) argues, feminism has assumed that 'women' denotes a fixed, coherent category that exists cross-culturally, and can be used as the basis for mobilising those who are seen to share that identity. Furthermore, discussions about the 'oppression' of 'women' assume a universal or hegemonic structure of 'patriarchy' or 'masculine domination'. However, the notion of a coherent category of 'women' has been criticised for ignoring 'differences' *among* women, and 'patriarchy' is seen as unable to capture the complexity of the operations of power in concrete cultural contexts. These criticisms have tended to originate with women themselves – especially black women, women from non-Western cultures and lesbians – whose experiences do not accord with the descriptions offered by white Western feminists (see, for example, Butler, 1990a; Collins, 1990; hooks, 1991; Mohanty et al., 1991; Phelan, 1994; Spivak, 1993). In a globalising and postmodernising context, appeals to old certainties about sisterhood and unity have ceased to have any meaning (Evans, 1997: 12). As poststructuralist feminists have pointed out, the concept 'woman' is a social construction, and hence a fiction in that it is an idealised version of what women should be (Bacchi, 1990: 232).

In tracing the history of the construction of feminist categories, Judith Grant (1993) argues that in order to draw attention to the fact that 'women are oppressed as women', 'second-wave' feminists needed to invoke the idea of a universal 'women's experience' of male domination, or 'patriarchy'. In the absence of a developed body of theory, it was simply assumed that 'women' were united by common feelings about oppression by 'men'. And since male domination was presumed to be present across time and cultures, and to affect all institutions, virtually anything could be defined as political and subject to contestation. However, in assuming the universality of 'women's experience' and a universal 'patriarchy', feminists have made themselves vulnerable to engaging in the very same kind of grand theory building and essentialism that they set out to challenge. Feminist theory had, in a sense, been 'captured by the patriarchal ideas it sought to oppose'. It had 'created a stereotypical Woman, a monolithic, abstract being defined only by her source of oppression' (Grant, 1993: 31).

> The problem of using an experiential standard was reflected in the Redstockings 'prowoman line', an explicit, political position that basically held that, in the name of sisterhood, women should not criticize each other. The idea of experience was necessary because of the need for some kind of evidence that women were oppressed. That is, it was necessary to prove that the category Woman existed because if women did not have something in common, the full analytic value of the major foundational category of feminist theory would disappear. The idea behind experience was that it would unite women through what it was assumed would be their common feelings about oppression. (Grant, 1993: 31)

As Grant explains, the problem with 'experience' has been that white, middle-class women have generalised from their own experiences to arrive at the experiences of women in general. It led to the view that if women did not feel oppressed then they were suffering 'false consciousness' or were 'male iden-tified'. However, this suggested that there existed an objective 'truth' by which one could gauge that which is 'false' – a notion which feminists have spent a good deal of time debunking. The 'false consciousness' idea also implies that 'women' are hapless victims of an 'oppressive patriarchy', thereby effectively denying subjects agency and the fact that they creatively engage with, and routinely resist and subvert, the norms of gender. In some writings, there has been a strong hint of a male conspiracy, whereby 'men' knowingly and delib-erately seek to keep 'women' blinded to their own 'true' interests, and that all 'men' benefit equally from this situation. With subjective experience placed firmly in feminist theory, however, no space was left for a notion of 'truth' apart from 'experience'. If women were allowed to define their own ideas of oppression there remained no theoretical grounds by which radical feminists could claim that women's perceptions of those experiences were 'false'. If feminists were to base their analyses upon 'women's experiences', the false consciousness argument was no longer tenable. Loss of faith in the very idea of objectivity (as gender-neutral knowledge) meant that 'female knowledge', subjectively determined, was the only knowledge women could trust. All this became attached to a new notion of politics: 'the personal is political' (Grant, 1993: 31–3).

The notion of 'experience' continues to hold a central place in many strands of feminist theory. Its importance is often emphasised in feminist critiques of science, where it is posited as a kind of antidote to the objectify-ing gaze that is seen as characteristic of 'masculinist' rationality (see Chapter 4). For example, in their critique of 'the social sciences claim to provide us with objective knowledge independent of the personal situation of the social scientist', Liz Stanley and Sue Wise argue that 'women's perspective, women's knowledge, and women's experience, provide an irrefutable critique of such claims' (1993: 163). The tendency for feminists to turn their back on theory and take refuge in 'experience' has been criticised by a growing number of academics, however, on the grounds that it rests on the liberal-humanist assumption that subjectivity is the authentic source of 'true' knowledge, unmediated by power/knowledge. Under the influence of postmodernism and poststructuralism, feminists have come to recognise that theory *per se* is not a problem, but rather the *type* of knowledge that is produced. Chris Weedon, for instance, argues that a central task for feminism is to transform the social relations of knowledge production and to 'tackle the fundamental questions of how and where knowledge is produced and by whom, and of what counts as knowledge' (1987: 7). As Weedon notes, this is not to deny the personal and political importance of 'experience', but rather to argue for the development of a theory of the relationship between 'experience', knowledge and power, and to carefully consider what sort of theory should be developed (1987: 8). Many contemporary feminists have now abandoned previous feminist understandings of the unified female subject, and rejected unproblematised notions of 'women's experience' and of patriarchy as a monolithic power structure, in favour of an analysis of the 'discursive construction' of the gendered subject and of the reiterative practices of gender (for example, Butler's performative theory of gender), without necessarily referring to an overarching patriarchy. Attention has shifted from viewing 'gender identity' as a fixed essence, defined by biology, psychology, theology, or ontology, and that holds across situations, to seeing 'identity' as a specific social and historical production. Both male and female subjects are viewed as 'discursively constructed', although are differently positioned within different discourses according to the cultural context and time period. 'Gender identity' has come to be seen as playing a crucial role, historically, in the discursive fabrication of two complementary 'sexes', and hence in reinforcing the institution of heterosexuality. (For a more detailed discussion of this point, see Chapter 5: 114–17.)

This growing unease with the use of 'gender' as a category of identity and experience is by no means universally applauded by feminists. Susan Bordo (1993) has cautioned against what she refers to as growing 'gender skepticism' within certain sections of contemporary feminism. She finds it troubling that feminists are questioning the integrity of the notion of 'female reality' at that very point in time when they are beginning to get a foothold in those disciplines that can be most radically transformed through feminist practice, and asks whether feminist gender scepticism is serving white, male 'power/knowledge', especially the demands of professionalism which 'require us to abandon our "female" ways of knowing and doing' (1993: 240). (On this point, see also Hoff, 1996.) The work of such writers as Dinnerstein, Chodorow, and Gilligan, argues Bordo, grew out of concrete experiences of exclusion and 'were neither grounded in a conception of adequate theory nor demanded a theoretical response' (1993: 220). As Bordo explains, feminism has not been inattentive to racism and ethnocentrism, but rather has needed to make visible a dimension of shared experience that has for thousands of years remained largely invisible. There are key differences between

the universalisations of gender theory and the metanarratives arising out of
the propertied, white, male, Western intellectual tradition. In Bordo's view,
although feminism can benefit from more local, historically specific enquiry
and from paying greater attention to the relations of the diverse axes of identity (sexuality, 'race', ethnicity, age, and so on), postmodern feminists deceive
themselves in their pursuit of the adequate representation of 'difference'.
Theory can never be adequate in the sense of doing justice to heterogeneity,
locality, and complexity. Although Bordo agrees with the postmodern feminists that there is no Archimedean viewpoint from which to 'read' history and
culture, she believes postmodernism continues to adhere to the 'fantasy of
transcendence' in its emphasis on the adequate representation of textual 'difference'. Thus, despite the appeal for feminists of new archetypes (for
example, Haraway's hybrid of machine and organism, the 'cyborg'), theoretical positions are always located, limited and partial, and reveal the *'always*
personally invested nature of human "story telling"' (1993: 228; her emphasis). Bordo proposes that *for practical purposes* feminism needs to reserve
spaces for both generalist critique ('suitable when gross points need to be
made') and for attention to complexity and nuance (1993: 242). In the context
of this debate, some feminists have proposed the adoption of the notion of
'strategic essentialism', that is, the idea that feminism can make effective use
of the universalising categories of patriarchy to advance feminist goals.
Writers who put forward this view argue that feminists should not be bound
by an adherence to theoretical purity, but rather should develop strategies
that suit a situation even if this involves reference to an essence as a mobiliz-
ing slogan (see Grosz, 1990a: 343; Spivak, 1993: 3–5).

   While many feminists are wary about entirely abandoning an identity politics founded on the category of gender, others have embraced scepticism as
a theoretical and political stance, and have begun to cast a critical gaze on the
discursive construction of the category of gender and to consider the implications of such a critique for gendered subjects. Some feminists have
suggested a more explicit focus on the origins, deployment and political uses
of the category 'women', such as Denise Riley (1988) who argues for an
exploration of the implications for feminist theory and practice of the discursive historical formation of 'women'. In obvious sympathy with this
argument, Carol Bacchi has recently examined how 'women' is used in relation to affirmative action policies and how those uses which undermine
feminist goals might be challenged (1996: 163). Others have been concerned
about the theoretical and practical implications of feminists' appropriation of
the concept of gender as it has been developed through research in biology,
linguistics, and psychology. As a number of writers have pointed out,
although 'second-wave' feminists appropriated the concept of gender as a useful strategy for contesting the naturalisation of sexual difference (i.e.
biology-as-destiny) in different arenas of struggle, they also inherited some of
its problems (see, for example, Braidotti, 1994: 261; Delphy, 1993; Haraway,
1991: 133–4). Haraway notes that the concept of gender was formulated
within the so-called gender identity paradigm in the decades after the Second

World War as part of a broad liberal reformulation of the life and social sciences. (See also Chapter 5: 115.) However, this reformulation 'failed to interrogate the political-social history of binary categories like nature/culture, and so sex/gender, in colonialist Western discourse' (Haraway, 1991: 134). While early 'second-wave' feminists criticised the nature/culture dualism, argues Haraway, they hesitated to extend their criticism fully to the derivative sex/gender distinction. Biological determinism and dualistic thinking was carried over into feminist theorising in the correspondence of 'sex' with 'nature' and 'gender' with 'culture'. The development of a 'second-wave' feminist politics based on 'biological determinism' versus 'social constructionism' and the sex/gender distinction, was pre-structured by a discourse that was functionalist and essentialist in its orientation and took the field of biology as a given rather than as a discourse open to intervention. Within this discourse, the world is posited as an object of knowledge in which the resources of nature are to be appropriated by culture. In their arguments against 'biological determinism' and in favour of 'social constructionism', Haraway maintains, feminists have failed to enquire into how bodies, including sexualised and racialised bodies, appear as objects of knowledge and sites of intervention in 'biology' (1991: 134). Towards the end of the 1990s, however, it could no longer be said that feminists had ignored these questions. A growing number of feminists had begun to rethink the status of the body in feminism, and there was an explosion of feminist writings concerned with exploring the specific constructions of, and significations attached to, women's bodies.

The body and sex/gender

Christine Delphy (1993) has been among those who have criticised the assumption common in both the social sciences and feminism that biological sex precedes, and implicitly causes or explains, gender, even if it is not seen to determine the exact forms that gender divisions take. As Delphy has noted, the basis for this assumption has remained largely unexamined, reflecting the view that 'sex' is a 'purely natural' category. Like other recent theorists (for example, Laqueur, 1990, and Butler, 1990a), she has argued that *gender* precedes sex, and that sex itself simply marks a social division that identifies those who are dominant and those who are dominated (1993: 3–5). Moira Gatens (1996) has suggested that the feminist tactic of 'degendering' or 're-socialising' society is built upon an implicitly rationalist view in that it posits the body as neutral and passive with regard to the formation of consciousness, and is ahistorical in that it denies the effects of history and culture on one's 'lived experience', particularly one's experience as an *embodied* subject. In its focus on the determination of personal identity at the level of ideas, Gatens contends, the orthodox account of the sex/gender distinction neglects the social and historical specificity of the network of relations obtaining between the female body and femininity and the male body and masculinity. Feminists have long been wary of attempts to link women's subjectivities and social positions to the specificities of their bodies, as Elizabeth Grosz (1994: x) observes. However, in her view, it is crucial that feminism attempts to rescue the body from this status and to contest the view that 'it' is an ahistorical, pre-cultural, or natural object. Grosz is interested in the ways in which women's bodies 'are not only inscribed, marked, engraved, by social pressures external to them but are the products, the direct effects, of the very social constitution of nature itself' (1994: x). She is particularly concerned with uncovering the implicit conceptions of the body and of the role that it plays in social, cultural, and psychical life, within the writings of male social theorists. These theorists, she argues, have constructed a 'corporeal universal' which has

> functioned as a veiled representation and projection of a masculine which takes itself as the unquestioned norm, the ideal representative without any idea of the violence that this representational positioning does to its others – women, the 'disabled', cultural and racial minorities, different classes, homosexuals – who are reduced to the role of modifications or variations of the (implicitly white, male, youthful, heterosexual, middle-class) human body. (1994: 188)

Grosz's effort to rethink the body is seen as integral to the effort to challenge the phallogocentrism of Western rationality, referred to above, which disavows the role of the body. The so-called 'crisis of Reason', Grosz argues, is in fact a consequence of the historical privileging of the purely conceptual or mental over the corporeal, and of the neglect of the ways in which the production of knowledge relies on and yet denies the role of the body (see Grosz, 1993).

Judith Butler has been a significant contributor to the recent critique of the identity politics of feminism, premised as it has been upon a distinction between a physical 'sex' and a culturally constructed 'gender'. In her book *Gender Trouble*, Butler (1990a) argues that this distinction presumes the existence of a prediscursive, natural realm constituting a 'politically neutral surface on which culture acts'. Taken up within feminism to dispute the biology-as-destiny argument, the distinction implies that 'sex' is neither congruent with, nor causes, 'gender'. However, as Butler notes, if 'gender' is the cultural meaning that the sexed body assumes, then a 'gender' cannot be considered to follow from 'sex' in any one way. The logic of the sex/gender distinction suggests a radical discontinuity between sexed bodies and culturally constructed genders. Even if one assumes the stability of binary sex, it does not follow that the construction of 'men' will accrue exclusively to the bodies of males or that of 'women' to only female bodies. And, even if the 'sexes' appear as binary in their morphology and constitution, there is no reason to assume that genders ought to be restricted to two (1990a: 6–7). For Butler, the performative character of 'gender' and its contingent relationship to 'sex' is clearly revealed through the cultural practice of drag which plays upon the distinction between the anatomy of the performer and the gender that is being performed (1990a: 137–8). As she explains, 'when the constructed status of gender is theorized as radically independent of sex, gender itself becomes a free-floating artifice, with the consequence that man and masculine might just as easily signify a female body as a male one, and woman and feminine a male body as easily as a female one' (1990a: 6). In her more recent book, *Bodies That Matter* (1993), Butler theorises 'sex' not as a static condition of the body, but rather as a cultural norm that governs the 'materialisation' of bodies, so that those bodies appear bounded, fixed, stable, and 'pre-discursive'. Against those feminists who would argue that the body's irreducible materiality is a necessary pre-condition for feminist practice, but congruent with Grosz's views, outlined above, Butler suggests that its very materiality may well be constituted through an exclusion and degradation of the feminine that is profoundly problematic for feminism. As Butler argues, feminists ought to be interested, not in taking materiality as an irreducible, but rather in conducting a 'critical genealogy of its formulation' (1993: 30–31). Viewing the materiality of 'the body' as a historically and culturally specific construction leads to important questions about why some bodies (i.e. European, heterosexual, male bodies) come to matter more than others, and what kinds of constructions are foreclosed through the figuring of the material body as outside discourse (see Chapter 3).

Increasing recognition among feminists and other scholars that the sexed body is 'discursively constructed' has led to a more systematic historical analysis of the processes of body regulation through sexology, biology, and biomedicine. Foucault's (1980) work on the history of sexuality from the late eighteenth century has been a highly influential source in this research, as has the Foucauldian-inspired research of Thomas Laqueur. In his book *Making Sex* (1990), Laqueur argues that 'sex, as much as gender, is made', and is very much a product of post-Enlightenment science which has focussed on sex differences. I have already referred to the development in the eighteenth century of the theory of complementarity and the search for differences between the sexes. The construction of the 'two-sex' model, which sees fundamental differences between the male and female sexes, and thus between man and woman, in discoverable biological distinctions, is seen by Laqueur to represent a fundamental paradigm shift from the pre-Enlightenment 'one-sex' model in which women were seen to have the same sex organs as men, but on the inside of their bodies rather than on the outside. In support of his argument, Laqueur presents anatomical diagrams of male and female sexual organs from the pre-Enlightenment period which supposedly demonstrate that the vagina is an inverted penis and the uterus an inverted scrotum. Although the one-sex model has reappeared at various points in different guises, the model of the two opposed sexes has remained predominant throughout most of the nineteenth and twentieth centuries. Laqueur's fundamental point is that claims about sex always involve claims about gender and power (Laqueur, 1990: 11). While in both the one-sex model and the two-sex model there is a hierarchy obtaining between men and women, in the one-sex model the differences between the sexes are of degree rather than of nature. Man is the yardstick of perfection against which the female sex is measured. Before the emergence of the two-sex model, to be a man or a woman was above all a rank or cultural role, and not one form of being biologically different from the other (Badinter, 1995: 6). The development of the two-sex model, which involved a shift in theories of sexual differentiation from difference of degree to difference of nature, can be directly linked to the aforementioned rise of the theory of sexual complementarity from the late eighteenth century. As Badinter explains, during this period the body began to appear as real and cultural significations as epiphenomena; that is, 'biology became the epistemological foundation for social prescriptions' (1995: 7). Clearly, Foucault and Laqueur have been key figures in the development of a new historical and critical approach to the study of 'gender' and 'sex' and of their relationship that has served to destabilise contemporary understandings of 'sex/gender' (see, for example, Oudshoorn, 1994; Hausman, 1995).

Ethnographic and cross-cultural research

Finally, it is important to acknowledge the challenge to the dominant formulations of sex/gender offered by a growing body of evidence deriving from ethnographic and cross-cultural research focusing on cross-dressing, sex-changing and gender ascription. The emergence of a *transgendered* community in the 1990s has been an important stimulus to research on the study of non-normative genders. Transgenderists seek to expose and undermine binary and essentialist thinking through, among other strategies, autobiographical writing, lobbying for legislative change, and undertaking ethnographic studies (see, for example, Ekins and King, 1996; Nataf, 1996). This work underscores the enactment and contingent character of gender identity, and its reliance upon historically and culturally specific definitions of 'sex' and body deportment. Work on 'gender blending' – that is, the mixing of various aspects of male and female gender – disturbs cultural notions about the 'correct' blend of such things as dress and demeanour, object choice, occupation, leisure pursuits, and so on (Ekins and King, 1996: 2). Research in the United States on 'gender blending females' – that is, biological females who successfully project themselves as sufficiently masculine to enjoy the status and privileges usually limited to men and/or to avoid sexual and physical violence by men – has demonstrated both the arbitrariness of the link between physical sex and social gender and the significance of cultural assumptions about male and female physical characteristics, appearances and behaviours in ascriptions of gender (for example, Devor, 1987; Young, 1996). Such examples of gender 'passing' challenge the cultural logic that the physical body is the site of an authentic intelligibility, and expose the essentialism that is often the foundation of identity politics (Ginsburg, 1996: 4).

Cross-cultural research shows that not all societies make a strict distinction between sexed bodies, and not all see gender as being linked to discrete and fixed binary categorisations of sex. Among the Hua people of the Eastern Highlands of Papua New Guinea, the binary categories 'female' and 'male' are neither discrete ones nor premised on discrete binary categories of biological sex differences evidenced by external genitalia. Individuals are classified according to both external anatomical features *and* the amount of certain male and female substances they have in their bodies which are thought to be transferable between individuals through eating, heterosexual sex and everyday casual contact. The Hua insist that the gender of a person changes over their lifetime as their body takes on more of the substances and fluids transferred by the other sex (see Moore, 1994a: 23–4). Among the Yorùbá people of southwestern Nigeria, there was, traditionally, no concept of gender as a dichotomous biological category. The use of body-type to delineate social categories in Yorùbá society was imposed by the colonialists, who brought their 'biologic' interpretation of the social world, imposing gender-based (and associated public/private) distinctions as part of their effort to extract wealth from local labour. In the precolonial context, the categories 'men' and 'women' were absent; the primary principle of social organisation was seniority, defined by age. Although bodily distinctions were linked to reproduction, and were based on recognition of the distinct roles played by the two categories in the reproductive process, these distinctions did not carry over to other areas of life (Oyěwùmí, 1997: 31–79; 149–56).

Evidence of the existence in some societies of institutionalised intermediate or 'third genders' – for example, biological males who behave, dress, work and are treated in most respects as social women further undermines the notion that gender is necessarily attached to a biological substratum (Lorber, 1994: 17). These cross-over genders have been observed in a wide variety of contexts, including Polynesia (for example, the Tongan *fakatangata* and Samoan fa'atama), India (the hijras) and North America (the berdaches) (Besnier, 1994; Nanda, 1994; Roscoe, 1994). There are African and American Indian societies that have a gender status called *manly hearted women*, who are biological females who work, marry and parent as men. But they do not have to dress or behave as men in order to have the social responsibilities and prerogatives of husbands and fathers; rather, their status as men is defined by having enough wealth to buy a wife (Lorber, 1994: 17). As Lorber explains, the categories of 'transsexuals' and 'transvestites', although being the nearest equivalent of these cross-over genders in modern Western societies, are not institutionalised as third genders. Transsexuals are seen as biological males and females who have sex-change operations to alter their genitalia in order to bring their physical anatomy in line with their own sense of gender identity; transvestites are males and females who change genders, either temporarily or for most of their lives, but do not have sex change surgery. The problematic status of these categories underlines the normative power of the sex/gender system in modern Western societies (Lorber, 1994: 17–18). Viewed as a whole, the above evidence underlines the dangers of assuming the stability of the dualistic and 'bio-logic' conception of gender in theoretical and political work, and the need for caution when generalising across contexts.

The social construction of 'sexuality'

The idea that there exist stable categories of sexual subject has also been undermined by a growing corpus of social constructionist research on 'sexuality'. As pointed out in Chapter 1, the term social constructionism is used by writers in different ways, and so it is important that one clearly specifies one's intended meaning. When employed in relation to the analysis of sexuality, social constructionism usually refers to the project of exposing the *historical* processes whereby sexual categories are created, thereby challenging the belief that categories of human behaviour are 'natural', pre-determined by biology, genetics, or physiological mechanisms (see Vance, 1989: 14; Stein, 1992: 5). According to Vance, social constructionism is oriented to the theoretical and political task of showing that sexuality is 'a product of human action and history rather than the invariant result of the body, biology, or an innate sex drive' (1989: 13). The term social constructionism is sometimes taken by its critics to imply that the socially constructed identity is less real, or less significant for individuals, than biologically determined phenomena and can therefore be willingly jettisoned. However, this confuses the individual level with the cultural level: there is no necessary congruence between sexuality as historically and culturally constructed and the individual's personal sexual identification and experience. The question of why lesbians and gays, rather than heterosexuals, should be concerned that their sexual identities have been 'constructed' is a vexed one. Vance suggests that gay and lesbian scholars initially undertook history in order to reclaim the past and to insist on the visibility of lesbian and gay identities in different periods and places, but that discoveries proved the great variability and hence the constructed nature of experience (1989: 27). The growing popularity of social constructionism during the 1970s and 1980s was undoubtedly due in part to the efforts of many gays and lesbians to counter the dominant repression hypothesis and medicalisation of homosexuality by revealing its historical construction (Carrigan et al., 1987: 84; Jeffreys, 1993: 2).

Clearly, the emergence of social constructionism as applied to sexuality has been bound up with gay and lesbian struggles to make visible and legitimate their sexual identities in a heterosexual-dominant society. Although there have now been many enquiries into the historical construction of homosexuality (for example, Halperin, 1990; Plummer, 1981; Weeks, 1977, 1985), there have been relatively few systematic historical analyses of heterosexuality. Heterosexuality is seen as 'innate'; determined by reproductive demands, evolutionary strategies, or the natural differences in the physiology of men and women (Wilkinson and Kitzinger, 1994a: 309). However, within lesbian feminist and queer scholarship, heterosexuality has come to be seen as occupying a key position in the social construction of gender and the re-inscription of gender-based and sexually based patterns of dominance and subordination (see, for example, Butler, 1990a; Katz, 1990, 1995; Richardson, 1996a; Wilkinson and Kitzinger, 1993, 1994a, 1994b). Queer scholars have recently begun to expose the heterosexist biases in theories of gender as articulated, for instance, in feminist sociology (see Chapter 5). Heterosexuality has been described by some feminist writers as a 'compulsory' or 'obligatory' institution into which men and (especially) women are 'coerced'. They are coerced, it is claimed, through a variety of forces such as rape, child-marriage, sexual harassment, oppression of homosexuals, pornography and economic sanctions (Rich, 1980; Rubin, 1975). From the gay perspective, heterosexual masculinity is seen as a privileged masculinity that is in part created and maintained through homophobia at the expense of homosexual men and women. Many gay people share with radical feminists the premise that the dominant heterosexual order is maintained through sexual violence and the threat of violence (Clatterbaugh, 1990: 132). Although it would seem to be generally recognised that experiences of heterosexuality are diverse and its 'compulsory' nature varies according to such factors as class, 'race', ethnicity, and generation, it is nevertheless seen to have a coercive quality, a fact which is most evident to those who are *not* heterosexual (Wilkinson and Kitzinger, 1994a: 309).

Jonathan Katz, who is a pioneer in critical historical research into heterosexuality, argues that heterosexuality is a relatively recent 'invention' that has been 'normalised' through processes of medicalisation and commodification. According to Katz, during most of the nineteenth century, the terms heterosexuality and homosexuality were absent from discourses on gender and eroticism, and opposite-sex attraction and same-sex attraction were not identified by two mutually exclusive categories of desire, identity and love. The concept of 'true love', used by the middle classes in the first half of the nineteenth century, reflected the view that the body was a means of love's expression and the penis and vagina were for procreation, not pleasure parts. Indeed, it is Katz's contention that up until the end of the nineteenth century and even early in the twentieth century, libidinous pleasure was seen as wasted energy, which was to be used in work, in rearing children and sustaining the family. Erotic pleasure with a different sex was seen as a problematic distraction from a heavenly God, as ultimately threatening the reproductive viability of society and, when pursued for its own sake, as a perversion. In the American colonies at least, sex between men was not thought to 'demasculise' either party, but rather was thought to be a waste of procreative seed (Katz, 1995: 128). However, in the course of the nineteenth century there was a gradual transformation from the emphasis on the body as an instrument of work and procreation towards an emphasis on the body as a source of consumption and pleasure. This corresponded with a broad shift in economic emphasis away from production and towards consumption and its 'commoditized culture of pleasure' (Katz, 1990: 13). Beginning in the 1860s, heterosexuality and homosexuality gradually emerged as two opposite forms of eroticism in Germany, England, France, Italy, and America (Katz, 1995: 51). New medical discourses began to focus on women's sexual pleasure and to define 'a new ideal of male–female relationships that included, in women as well as men, an essential, necessary, normal eroticism' (Katz, 1990: 13).

Writers such as Havelock Ellis and Sigmund Freud, although offering different arguments about the origins of heterosex, can be seen as major proponents of the different-sex erotic among a 'progressive' public in the early twentieth century (Katz, 1990: 18; 1995: 87–8). In Katz's view, the focus on normative heterosexuality in the late nineteenth century reflected the deep anxieties of men about changing social roles, and the power of men over women – the so-called 'crisis of masculinity', referred to earlier. The focus on physiological and gender dimorphism as the basis for a universal, normal erotic attraction, arose at that very point in history when male dominance was coming under challenge (1995: 89–90). Those forms of sexuality which did not conform with this ideal, particularly same-sex intimacy, were seen as based upon deviant desire and came to be increasingly marginalised. As Katz has discovered, the discourse of heterosexuality had a protracted 'coming out', and the association of heterolust with perversion continued well into the twentieth century, only gradually becoming established as 'the stable sign of normal sex'. However, once entrenched, this norm worked to affirm the superiority of men over women and heterosexuals over homosexuals, and to construct in time 'a sexual solid citizen and a perverted unstable alien' (Katz, 1995: 112).

The work of Katz, Wilkinson and Kitzinger, Butler, and others, builds on and extends the 'second-wave' feminist critique of the heterosexual order, undertaken in the 1960s and 1970s by writers such as Betty Friedan, Kate Millett, and Gayle Rubin. In recent research and writings, there has been an attempt to make more central and explicit the historical links between the dominant heterosexual order and the dominant gender order. The political importance of this work lies in the challenge it poses to the dominant 'masculinist' idea of a stable, exclusive heterosexuality and heterosexual desire linked to an invariable male gender identity. It exposes the historical basis of the deep-seated homophobia evident among many heterosexual men, while bringing into question the 'naturalness' of their own sexual identity. There is the danger, however, of assuming the existence of a monolithic normative heterosexuality that applies equally to all men and all women. As mentioned, different groups have different experiences of heterosexuality, and even among radical feminists there is a great deal of disagreement about the 'coercive' power of heterosexuality, and about the relationship between pleasure and power within heterosexual relationships. (On this point, see particularly the debate following the special issue on heterosexuality appearing in *Feminism and Psychology*, 2 (3), 1992, and subsequently published in Wilkinson and Kitzinger, 1993, and elsewhere: Hollway, 1993, 1995; Kitzinger and Wilkinson, 1994.) Furthermore, as Karin Martin (1993) has shown in her historical study of medical opinion on homosexuality in men and women in the United States, the relationship between sexuality and gender varies in historically and socially specific ways and reflects broader, ongoing, social struggles. Thus, while the effort to medicalise lesbianism in the first two decades of the twentieth century can be seen as a response and a resistance (at least in part) to the suffrage and early women's movement, later attempts (in the 1930s and 1940s) to pathologise male (and only occasionally female) homosexuals by pointing to their gender deviancy are best understood as a means of resisting and regulating the new sexual communities that were forming in urban areas (1993: 246–60). Work such as this serves to emphasise the complex and historically specific ways in which the regulations of identity operate and the fact that one should be wary in generalising about the links between sexuality and gender.

The regulations of 'race'

Like the categories of 'sex' and 'sexuality', the category of 'race' has come under critical scrutiny, particularly by those most subject to its regulations, in this case mainly black women and black men. The writings of black men have exposed the role of racism in the production of 'white masculinity' (Clatterbaugh, 1990: 144). With the relatively recent change in the situation of minorities, 'who are still exploited, oppressed and racialised, but no longer subject to appropriation' through colonialism, there is greater opportunity for questioning and deconstructing the dominant discourse on 'race' (Juteau-Lee, 1995: 14). As Juteau-Lee puts it, 'it is now easier to put a wedge in the crack, and to show that "race" is a construct' (1995: 14). It has become evident that 'race', like the other regulatory categories described above, has been, and continues to be, produced in the context of social relations of domination. There is a growing number of historical and contemporary studies into the processes sustaining the category of 'race', many of which analyse it as a product of racism. As with 'sex' and 'sexuality', theories of natural, bio-physical difference are seen to play a crucial role in the mapping out of social destinies. Within the dominant racial discourse, the categorisation of humans into separate 'races' is considered to be self-evident, not requiring an explanation, thus effectively obscuring the historical and social construction of racial categories. However, recent research has shown that skin colour became a key signifier of difference, and the basis for the establishment of taxonomies of human and cultural value, *after* racial taxonomies were historically constituted. According to this taxonomic system, white European males and European culture are located at the top of the hierarchy and provide the standard against which other human subjects and cultures are judged. Although the explicit theorisation of 'race' began in the late eighteenth century, theories became increasingly scientific during the period of British and European colonial expansion in the nineteenth century. Clear connections have been established between racial theories of white superiority and the justification for that expansion (see, for example, Goldberg, 1993: 148–205; Wieviorka, 1995: 27–8; Young, R.J.C., 1995: 91–2). Colette Guillaumin has shown how the term 'race', previously used among a small class, the nobility, to designate a legal line of descent, began to acquire its biophysical connotations during the period in which the bourgeoisie were achieving economic, political and global dominance (1995: 29–107). New scientific theories of 'race' began to infect the entire academic establishment in the nineteenth century, and most areas of culture were defined explicitly or implicitly in terms of racial categories. The sciences of eugenics and physiognomy provided a means by which the upper and middle classes marked out their differences from the working classes, and disciplines such as social anthropology and criminology began to develop an obsessive concern with delineating British and European people into 'types' (Young, R.J.C., 1995: 95). It should be kept in mind that the new category of 'race' was applied *globally* and that people from diverse ethnic backgrounds and geographical locales were classified on the basis of universal categorisations of skin colour and other physical features: Caucasians, black-skinned people, yellow-skinned people, and so on. (For a recent historical account of the idea of race and of its diverse applications, see Hannaford, 1996.)

Recent social constructionist research on 'race' has been important also in exposing the historical links between the regulation of sexual relations and the regulation of 'race' relations, and in showing how this has ultimately served the supremacy of white, middle-class males. As Robert Young (1995) has argued, in the nineteenth century the question of racial difference was very much focused on the degree of fertility of the union between different 'races'. The major dispute was between, on the one hand, the monogenetic position, which argued that different human 'races' descended from a single human source, as is suggested in the biblical account, and that racial differentiation could be explained by degeneration; and, on the other, the polygenetic view that held that different races were in fact different species, and had been different all along, which supported the argument that they would and should continue to be so. In the context of this debate, the question of hybridity – of whether or not the sexual unions between different 'races' were, or were not, fertile – was of central concern. Victorian racial theory was preoccupied with determining the fertility of human hybrids, those of mixed race, since if it could be shown that hybrids were fertile through several generations this would undermine the polygenetic argument that the different 'races' were fixed for all time (Young, R.J.C., 1995: 101–2). Supporters of the polygenetic view expended much effort in demonstrating the fundamental differences between the sexual mores of the European middle class and those of foreign Others, especially 'blacks' who were seen to be 'the lowest exemplum of mankind in the great chain of being'. For example, black females were seen to have an animal-like sexual appetite and 'primitive' genitalia that defined their natural difference from European peoples (Gilman, 1985: 83). The development of the discourse on hybridity reflected increasing anxiety about racial and cultural degeneration accompanying the intermixing of the 'races' during the period of colonialist expansion. Since the slave order depended upon the reproduction of slaves, and that reproduction could only be assured by maintaining the continuity of the slave 'race' (i.e. children born of enslaved black women were themselves slaves), efforts were made to prohibit sexual relations between the white and black 'races' (Collins, 1990: 50). According to the prevailing ideology, racial intermixing had potentially deleterious implications for the continuity of the social order as a whole. In the work of the notorious racial theorist Count Gobineau (*Essay on the Inequality of Races*, 1853–5), for example, the key concern was the effects of racial intermixing on the rise and fall of civilisations. It was Gobineau's view that racial differences and the relative values of the 'races' could be measured by the presence or absence of (Aryan) 'civilisation' and that, since it was clear that not all 'races' were equal, degeneration was bound to accompany the intermixing of races (Young, R.J.C. 1995: 99–117). The links between efforts to maintain racial purity and efforts to regulate sexuality have perhaps been most clearly articulated by the eugenicists who mounted campaigns to prevent the 'lower elements' – the poor, blacks, immigrants, and so on – from producing so many children (Bullough, 1994: 51).

As black, ethnic, and 'Third World' feminists have pointed out, the history of racism has been largely overlooked by the mainstream academic disciplines, including feminism, and racism is perpetuated through both the refusal to acknowledge this history and the continuing uncritical use of theoretical categories. The failure of Western academics to thoroughly scrutinise their work for underlying racist assumptions is hardly surprising given the racialised relations of power shaping academic work. Anthropology, sociology, psychology, economics, and more recently feminism, have all been criticised for their Eurocentrism and racism. bell hooks, Chandra Mohanty, and Gayatri Spivak, among others, have criticised Western feminist thought for its assumption that all women (and by implication, all men) can be defined by either an invariant 'essence' (for example, biological or psychological attributes) or by a common social situation. Western feminist work on the 'Third World' has, for example, often posited a singular 'third world woman' without adequate consideration of the effect of hegemonic Western scholarship on the construction of third world differences. The assumption of the already constituted group with identical interests, desires, and class, ethnic and racial location, Mohanty (1991) has argued, serves implicitly to denigrate non-Western women (who are seen as poor, ignorant, uneducated, domestic, family-oriented, victimised, etc.) while reinforcing the self-representation of Western women as educated, as modern, as having control over their own bodies, sexualities and decisions. Western feminists who make such a distinction constitute themselves as the normative referent, and can be accused of undertaking the same kind of colonising, ethnocentric endeavour characteristic of humanism in general (Mohanty, 1991: 73). The academic area of 'men's studies' has also tended to marginalise issues of 'race' and racism, and this area has as yet produced few systematic analyses of how racism interacts with other forms of oppression in different settings. (Some recent notable exceptions are the studies of Duneier, 1992, and Majors and Billson, 1992.) The work of recent black feminists points to the essentialism involved in using the category of gender without reference to other factors, particularly 'race' which has been shaped by the history of white domination and colonialist exploitation. Recent African-American academic debate has begun to explore different constructions of 'black masculinity' and how this expresses a relative lack of black male power within societies that are racist, sexist, and homophobic (see, for example, hooks, 1991: especially 57–77; hooks, 1992: 87–113; Collins, 1990; Harper, 1993; Skelton, 1995; Wallace, 1990). This writing points to the need for a more subtle and complex analysis of the power relations of gender which recognises the profound influence of racist thinking on constructions of the masculine in different settings.

The limits of 'identity' and constructions of the masculine

The developments described above, which signal a growing *post*modern or postparadigmatic wariness in relation to the use of generalised, or essentialist, categories of identity, serve to unsettle the foundations of the dominant constructions of the masculine. As such, they have profound implications for individuals' sense of self, and for how one conceptualises the power relations of gender and the prospects for social change. The wide range of responses manifest in the 'crisis of masculinity', from militant reactionism and separatism, at one extreme, through to the uncritical adoption of totalising, 'pro-feminist' positions, at the other, indicate the extent to which political stances have polarised in the current context of uncertainty. In so far as they retreat into forms of biological or social essentialism, none of the responses articulated so far is satisfactory. Those who have responded to uncertainty by recourse to narratives of essential difference, such as those which emphasise biological sex differences, seem not to recognise the extent to which the categories of identity to which they appeal have been historically and socially constructed through processes of exclusion and marginalisation. One of the important insights of recent work, such as that described in this chapter, is in pointing to the links between power and knowledge, and particularly to the ways in which power operates by defining social difference as a 'fact of nature' and therefore, by implication, immutable.

One of the central assumptions of this book is that it is strategically important to critique and expose essentialist thinking, for, in doing so, one makes it easier to imagine alternative ways of being. So far, there has been little systematic analysis of how categories of the masculine have been discursively constructed in specific historical and social contexts. The representational practices by which, and through which, white, European, heterosexual masculine identity has been constructed as the cultural 'ideal' and standard for evaluating other identities need to be systematically and critically appraised. This will require a more adequate understanding of the ways in which power operates by 'normalising' certain categories and practices through making them appear as inevitable outgrowths of 'nature'. With these points in mind, I turn, in the next chapter, to an exploration of the ways in which male bodies have been socially and historically constructed as 'naturally' different from female bodies and how *particular* male bodies have been constructed as the standard for measuring and evaluating other bodies.

3
Male bodies that matter

One of the important implications of recent theoretical work has been to recast people's thinking about the status of the body in the analysis of gender and sexuality. Foucault's insight that bodies are discursively constructed within modern systems of power has been especially influential in feminist and gay and lesbian writings (for example, Butler, 1990a, 1993; Diamond and Quinby, 1988; McNay, 1992; Ramazanoğlu, 1993; Weeks, 1985), and has helped stimulate research into the ways in which female bodies have been 'naturalised' and homosexual bodies 'pathologised' through scientific knowledge (for example, Jordanova, 1989; Laqueur, 1990; Oudshoorn, 1994; Russett, 1989; Schiebinger, 1989; Weeks, 1985). This research has emphasised the crucial role of science in making knowledge of bodies – their forms, experiences, and relationships – seem independent of particular social contexts (i.e. universal), as reflecting the 'natural order of things'. In line with their concern to reveal the regulations of identity, scholars have sought to expose the ways in which scientific knowledges and practices have constructed the 'truth' about gender and sexuality in such areas as sexual science and biomedicine. This is important and exciting work, and opens the path to a more explicit focus on the discursive construction of male bodies in different contexts. There is a need for a more systematic analysis of how male bodies have been constructed through scientific and cultural practices as 'naturally' different from female bodies and how particular male bodies, namely the bodies of white, European, middle-class, heterosexual men, have been constructed as the standard for measuring and evaluating other bodies.

As many feminists have pointed out, theories of power have been blind to the specificities of male and female bodies – to the fact that they are subject to different technologies of power – and that this blindness also often applies to postmodern theories (see, for example, Grosz, 1990b; Harstock, 1990). Feminists' rejection of the supposed universality of the knowing subject, and their critique of the complicity of 'masculinity' and rationality, has led them to advocate a sex-specific analysis of the subject and of *embodied* subjectivity. So far, this strategy has not been without its own problems, as I point out later. However, feminists have at least endeavoured to redress the shortcomings of 'male-stream' theories of power. They, and a growing number of other scholars, have also called attention to the need to recognise how 'race' operates in the regulation of bodies and identities. Methods of deconstruction can be employed to expose the ways in which power 'works' by constructing *particular* male bodies as normal or natural and others as pathological or unnatural.

Clearly, some male bodies do matter more than others. It goes without say-ing that bodies have a different materiality in that they come in a large variety of shapes, colours, and sizes, and exhibit different capacities, and that this materiality has significant consequences for embodied subjects. What is not widely recognised or acknowledged, however, is that this materiality is itself an effect of power (Butler, 1993: 2). This chapter examines the processes through which particular male bodies come to matter more than others. I emphasise the historical role of science, particularly biological science, from the nineteenth century onwards in constructing what has come to be widely accepted as 'truth' about male sexuality and male identity. I begin by exam-ining the ways in which the male sexed body has been historically and socially constructed through biological knowledges, and the categories of difference – specifically 'race' and 'sexuality' – that have been employed in those con-structions, before exploring the particular techniques deployed for the disciplining and shaping of male bodies in more recent times. As I endeavour to show, biological essentialism and determinism underlies a diverse range of modern discourses of sex and sexuality, and continues to influence thinking – for example, in so-called difference feminism and in 'popular' accounts of sex difference.

The fabrication of the 'ideal' male body

Although Western discourses of masculinity tend to take as given the mater-iality of the male sexed body upon which a male gender is inscribed, the very materiality of the body can be seen to be an artifact of the modern discourses through which it is represented. 'Masculinity', conceived as a bodily quality or condition that defines a person, and that can be distinguished from 'fem-ininity', is a historically recent concept. Although the origins of the word 'masculine' (derived from the French, *masculin*, and the Latin *masculinus*), meaning simply 'male', can be traced back to the fourteenth century, the word 'masculinity' first appeared only in the mid-eighteenth century (Simpson and Weiner, 1989). It appeared at that very moment in history when efforts were beginning to be made to define manhood and woman-hood in terms of distinct bodily criteria.

In his book, *The Image of Man: The Creation of Modern Masculinity*, George Mosse (1996) argues that the construction of modern masculinity, involving an emphasis on the physical body, was closely linked with the rise of the new bourgeois society towards the end of the eighteenth century. This is not to say that there was an abrupt break with older, aristocratic ideas of manhood. As Mosse points out, medieval ideas such as chivalry and insti-tutions such as the duel, which were closely connected with ideals of manhood, lasted well into modern times. The adjustment of such ideas to middle-class sensibilities, and their institutionalisation in moral imperatives, was an important step in the construction of modern masculinity. However, increasingly from the end of the eighteenth century an ideal version of (masculinity began to emerge that encompassed the whole personality and 'set a definite standard for masculine looks, appearance, and behaviour' (Mosse, 1996:19):

> Chivalry and manly honor, in the modern age, meant not only moral but also general physical toughness. Physical skill and dexterity had always been prized as necessary to defend one's honor, but now the new society in the making looked at the entire male body as an example of virility, strength and courage expressed through the proper posture and appearance. We hear much about knightly conduct in earlier times but rarely about physical appearance and never – except perhaps for the darkest of villains – of how the human body itself set a standard for judging conduct. To be sure, looks had always counted; thus in the medieval and early modern period dress had been a sign of rank and status often fixed by royal ordinance. Comportment had been important as well, a certain manly bearing and courtesy. But what had been present earlier in a fragmented manner was now systematized, formed into a totality in which not merely dress and bearing but the male body itself became the focus of attention, judged . . . according to a set standard of beauty. A stereotype was fashioned that would determine the perceptions of manhood in the modern age, when earlier times knew no such method of classification. (Mosse, 1996: 23)

The construction of the 'ideal' male body involved reference to its complementary opposite: the female body. More and more, the emphasis was on defining *natural* differences between men and women which became the foundation for explaining and legitimating *social* differences. I have already referred to the work of Thomas Laqueur (1990) and Londa Schiebinger (1989) in Chapter 2. As both writers have argued, beginning with the Enlightenment, bodies came under increasing scrutiny for what they revealed about the essential characters of men and women, employing an assumed idealised European male body as the standard for comparison and evaluation. Although since the time of the ancient Greeks it had been recognised that there were differences between the sexes, before the Enlightenment these differences were seen as being a matter of *degree* rather than of a fundamental nature. As I also pointed out earlier, it is Laqueur's view that there existed a 'one-sex/one-flesh' model of sexual difference. A woman had the same organs as a man, except they were inverted, and hence were imperfect (Laqueur, 1990). Woman's inferiority was explained in terms of the theory of humours (women had lesser heat than men) or the Judeo-Christian account of creation (Schiebinger, 1989: 160–5).

However, in the late eighteenth century, these theories gradually gave way to the anatomy and physiology of sexual difference; to the detailed analysis and differentiation of flesh and bones. This concentration on biological sex difference has been referred to by Laqueur as the 'two-sex' model. Both Laqueur and Schiebinger see the development of the two-sex model as being a response to the threat posed by the increasing demands of women to the dominant relations of gender following the rise of liberal democracy. Just as women were beginning to question the imperatives of marriage and motherhood, male political philosophers were beginning to argue that differences in women's and men's roles were rooted in immutable 'natural' differences. The philosophical doctrine of complementarity posited that women and men were perfect in their difference. Increasingly, this doctrine drew support from anatomy and physiology (Laqueur, 1990: 194–207; Schiebinger, 1989: 216–27). In the eighteenth century doctors began to define and redefine sex differences in every part of the human body, and anatomy turned to the comparative study of skulls and pelvises, emphasising women's 'natural' adaptation to child rearing and their inherent inferiority to men (Schiebinger, 1986, 1989: 190–213).

These developments did not go unchallenged. Following the revolutionary fervour of the 1790s, there were incessant calls in England, France, and Germany for equality for women in society. However, even egalitarians shared the Enlightenment faith in science, and the (mostly male) anatomists fell mostly in the complementarist camp (Schiebinger, 1989: 227). The ideas of sexual complementarity and of natural difference continue to hold sway in discourses of gender, and either implicitly or explicitly inform the work of many contemporary feminists, including both those who valorise this difference (the so-called 'sexual difference' feminists) and those who call for the resocialisation of the sexes ('egalitarian' feminists). One of the tasks of this chapter is to show just how enduring and widespread these ideas have been. However, at the outset, I wish to emphasise the profound impact of the categories of 'race' and 'sexuality' on the regulation of sexed bodies – themes that will re-emerge in later chapters.

Racialised and sexualised bodies

Recent work in the social sciences and humanities has underlined the point that categories of difference are rarely constructed along single axes of differentiation. The categories of 'sex', 'sexuality', 'gender', and 'race' interact in various and complex ways in different contexts and at different times, and are mutually constitutive, and it is dangerous to assume that one category of regulation is more significant than another. Recently, some scholars have begun to pay closer attention to the interactions of 'gender', 'race', 'sexuality' and 'sex' in the context of nineteenth-century colonialist discourse (for example, Bleys, 1996; Gilman, 1985, 1989, 1993a, 1993b; McClintock, 1995; Schiebinger, 1993). This work shows that these categories coexist, each helping to constitute the others, while at the same time serving to marginalise or exclude those who are not white, European, middle class and male. The anatomists whom Schiebinger studied tended to confine their research to middle-class Europeans, and when they did make comparisons with non-Europeans these were made in order to confirm the normative value of the white European male body. Schiebinger has found that the anatomical portrayals of distinctly female skeletons that began to make their appearance from the mid- to late-eighteenth century were all Europeans. Both women and non-European men and women were regarded as deviations from the European male norm, and theories about 'race', like theories about 'sex', were developed by examining male bodies (Schiebinger, 1993: 146). 'Women and Africans were seen as sharing similar deficiencies when measured against the constant norm – the elite European man' (1993: 158).

'Race' was the major division of bodily classification and evaluation, and the female sex was considered to be a sub-set of their 'race' so that any unique female traits were taken as confirmation of their racial standing. Both Gilman and Schiebinger have described in some detail how the Hottentot female became a central icon for sexual difference between the Europeans and 'blacks' in the nineteenth century: she was seen as more primitive, indeed ape-like, and sexually intensive. Like European women, the Hottentot did not fit comfortably within the great chain of being – the monogenetic view, referred to in the last chapter – whereby species were laid out in a fixed and vertical hierarchy, with God at the apex, through to the lowest creature. There was a fascination with the size and shape of Hottentot genitalia and buttocks, and particularly with the so-called 'Hottentot apron' (the elongation of the labia minora, or inner vaginal lips) which were seen as providing evidence that 'blacks' were a separate and 'lower' race (i.e. the polygenetic view) (Gilman, 1989: 291–5; Schiebinger, 1993: 160–72). Evaluations of non-Europeans were made according to European notions of aesthetics and beauty. The famous sexologist, Havelock Ellis, for instance, believed that there was an objective standard for beauty derived from the advanced aesthetic of the European which could be applied in evaluations of the different 'races'. This objective element in beauty, Ellis argued, 'is confirmed by the fact that it is sometimes found that the men of the lower races admire European women more than their own race', and added that 'it is among the more intelligent men of lower race – that is to say those whose aesthetic feelings are more developed – that the admiration for white women is most likely to be found' (Ellis, 1911: 153).

In his analyses of nineteenth-century constructions of the Jew, Gilman has underlined the ways in which theories of sex and race may interact to construct, marginalise and stigmatise *particular* male bodies (1985, 1989, 1993a, 1993b). The image of the 'black Jew' – particularly the Eastern European Jew who was seen to have 'black' skin, or was at least 'swarthy' – held a central place within nineteenth-century theories of racial difference, but the body of the male Jew had a special status. Although the association of the Jew with 'blackness' has a long history in Christian iconography, involving the juxtaposition of the 'black' image of the 'synagogue', of the 'Old Law', with the 'white' of the church (Gilman, 1985: 30–31), in the nineteenth century theories of race and sex operated together to construct the Jew as 'other'. As Gilman explains, although a wide range of physiological and psychological markers of difference were employed to document the difference of the Jews from all other 'races' (for example, skull capacity, size and shape, skin and hair colour, and so on), it was in the arena of the ritual practice of infant male circumcision that the pathological nature of the Jews was thought to be most clearly manifest.

> The centrality of the act of circumcision in defining what a Jew is made the very term 'Jew' in the nineteenth century come to mean the male Jew. Thus there was an

immediate dichotomy – all Jews, male and female, are different from the 'neutral' scientific observer (who is male and Aryan in his ideology), but male Jews are uncanny, in that they superficially appear to be males but are not because of the altered form of the genitalia (Jewish women are different too – different in a manner other than that in which Aryan women are different from Aryan men.) (Gilman, 1993a: 49)

Elsewhere, Gilman has described how, in the ethnographic writing of the period, Jews were seen as possessing qualities usually ascribed to women, and to homosexuals and other 'deviant' sexual categories (1989: 281). The unique form of their genitalia marked them off as different from the sexual norm, and it was not uncommon for them to be compared with prostitutes, who were believed to embody the degenerate and diseased female genitalia. Jews were seen to bear their diseased sexuality on their skin – as 'blackness' –which identified them as being part of a marginal category of male who, like women, were the potential source of corruption for both the individual and the collectivity (Gilman, 1989: 255–61; see also Mosse, 1996: 63–70). As Gilman's work so clearly shows, *both* 'race' and 'sex' have been important in the historical and social construction of the 'ideal' male body, each category reinforcing the regulatory power of the other through their association with existing signifiers of difference. Both these categories have, in turn, been profoundly shaped since the late nineteenth century by the context of social Darwinism.

The impact of Darwinism on the disciplining and shaping of male bodies

With the advent of Darwinism after 1859, competition and 'survival of the fittest' became dominant metaphors for thinking about categories of difference and how they develop. As McClintock notes, social Darwinism gathered 'race', 'class' and 'gender' into a single narrative by the image of the Family of Man: 'the evolutionary "family" offered an indispensable metaphoric figure by which often contradictory hierarchical distinctions could be shaped into a global genesis narrative' (1995: 44). Darwin's theory of natural selection challenged the notion that 'Man' was created exactly in God's image, and the body began to be seen to play a decisive role in the two basic goals of life: survival and reproduction (Kern, 1974: 252). Bodies were increasingly evaluated in terms of their adaptability and robustness, and some bodies were viewed as naturally more adaptive than others. However, in line with post-Enlightenment modernist ideals, it was also believed that bodies could be made more adaptable and robust through education and the application of science. The idea that some bodies are naturally more adaptable or 'flexible' than others, but that one can develop a body more able to survive, continues to have a powerful influence in contemporary discourses on the body. Emily Martin (1994) has found that scientists frequently make reference to a version of the Darwinian notion of the survival of the fittest to explain variations in the immune responses of different people. For example, ethnic differences in susceptibility to disease are explained in terms of natural, genetic variations. It is argued, however, that through practice and training one can develop an immune system better able to survive threats (Martin, 1994: 229–40).

As Anthony Rotundo (1993) has shown, the cultural forms that have come to shape 'manhood' in the twentieth century began to emerge in the second half of the nineteenth century at that very point in time when Darwinism was beginning to provide the master narrative for thinking about the social world. More and more, masculinity was defined in terms of vigour, competitiveness, bodily strength, and assertiveness, and such institutions as athletics, scouting, clubs and societies came to be recognised as sites for disciplining and cultivating male bodies and 'building manly characters' (see also Bourke, 1996: 137–44; Warren, 1987). The valorisation of qualities such as competition, physical strength, and physical aggression – inversions of 'feminised' Victorian society – can be explained in part as a response to the growing penetration of the public sphere by women (Rotundo, 1993: 253). There was a new regard for distinctly 'boyish' virtues that had for the first three-quarters of the century been negatively evaluated – exuberance, spontaneity, a love of free play. 'Men embraced boyhood at the same time that they were learning to value savagery, passion, and the embodied manhood of the athlete and the soldier' (1993: 256). Organised sport, schools and colleges took on a particular significance in nurturing those qualities seen as 'manly', and in sorting out men into hardy, masculine types who would succeed in a competitive world and gentle, feminine types who would be less likely to succeed. A vogue for physical culture gained momentum during the century's final third, and the findings of modern biological science were used to support theories about health through exercise and character development through sport.

It was during this time that the nature of the mind and its relationship to the body began to be debated. It was believed that by strengthening the body, one could also strengthen the will. Intensive and detailed work on the body became a means of demonstrating one's ability to discipline and master the self, and in the process demonstrate one's 'manliness'. The benefits of vigorous exercise for male character formation were promoted by educationalists and scientists, and sport came to play a central role in both strengthening bodies and 'building characters' (Park, 1987: 9–14). The effort to 'build characters' through sport and athletics was bound up with the effort to counteract those qualities seen as effeminate, such as luxury and self-indulgence, and to claim a new social and cultural terrain away from women, who were seen as no longer fulfilling their duties in instilling appropriate moral training in young males. Team sports became the basis for a new moral training, and were believed to offer benefits in every aspect of life. Indeed, sport became a metaphor for life, and was seen to instil those qualities needed in life because they were competitive endeavours (Rotundo, 1993: 242). Although the institutionalisation of organised games and athletics appears to have originated in the public school system, the ethos linking 'manliness' with games playing was popularised through such channels as clubs and publications. In Britain, for example, sports and athletics gradually became compulsory in public schools between 1860 and 1880, and attempts were made to extend the public school ethos through the Boys' Brigade to working-class boys in large urban areas (Springhall, 1987).

The belief in the value of sport and athletics for building 'manly' character that emerged during this period has an earlier antecedent with the ancient Greeks, who believed in the value of the gymnasium for marshalling the powers in the naked bodies of boys and making them into 'good' citizens. As Richard Sennett explains, the Greek gymnasium was a place where the boy learnt how to use his body, how to be naked sexually, how to use his muscle power, and how to exercise the oratorical skills which he would need to participate in the city's democracy. Like the football oval or cricket pitch in the modern period, the Greek gymnasium taught boys how to compete with one another and how to become good warriors. 'It was in the gymnasium that a boy learned that his body was part of a larger collectivity called the *polis*, that the body belonged to the city' (1994: 46). There is, however, a point of difference between the ancient Greeks and the moderns in their views on the effect of games on the body's physiology, which reflects differences in their conceptions of the sexed body. Consistent with their belief that boundaries between male and female were of degree and not of kind, and were defined by amount of body heat (with men being hotter than women), the Greeks saw the gymnasium as a means of marshalling the body's heat permanently in muscles at a critical point in their development, namely, in middle to late adolescence (Sennett, 1994–6). In the late nineteenth century, however, sport and athletics came to be seen as ways of developing the basic body chassis – a body that was already largely sex differentiated – to make it more pliable. Nevertheless, it would seem that the link between physical exercise and male character formation, which became a strong theme in the late nineteenth century, had an earlier manifestation in the practices of the ancient Greeks.

The modern Western ideal of physical development and the work ethic

As Dutton (1995) has explained, the bodily ideal that has come to dominate modern discourses of masculinity is the developed or muscular ideal. Dutton has traced the evolution of the muscular body as the emblem or metaphor of perfection, power, and pleasure in Western cultures, from the time of the ancient Greeks through to the contemporary period (Dutton, 1995). His research indicates that there is nothing inevitable about the association of muscularity with perfection or physical beauty. In many non-Western societies, and even in earlier periods in the West, beauty is seen, or has been seen, to reside not so much in the body itself, but rather in body displays, body decorations or even mutilations (1995: 16). The body may be viewed as a canvas: as providing the foundation for a work of art, with the skin and flesh providing the artist's medium rather than their inspiration for painting, tattooing, scarring, or mutilation. In the eighteenth century, men (and women) of the aristocracy, and of the upper bourgeoisie who emulated it, adorned their bodies with lace, rich velvets, fine silks and embroideries, wigs and hats of rococo embellishment, and routinely used scented powders, rouges, and other cosmetics (Los Angeles County Museum of Art, 1983, cited in Davis, 1992: 38). Even as recently as the nineteenth century, Western men regularly adorned their bodies with powders, paints, and scented ointments. A late nineteenth-century American book on male etiquette, for example, advises the use of hair dye, paint, face powder and eye shadow (Brain, 1979: 45). From this period onwards, however, the muscular body increasingly came to signify sexual potency and power, and bodybuilding and sport provided the means and the occasions for nurturing and celebrating this bodily ideal.

The muscular ideal has undoubtedly been shaped by the Protestant work ethic and the cultural link, increasingly evident in the late nineteenth and early twentieth century, between strenuous physical work and prevailing ideals of 'manliness'. With the industrial revolution, there emerged a new regard for the developed body and a great deal of interest in the means of its realisation. The post-Enlightenment concern for scientific method, coupled with a view of the body as a machine that was subject to control through scientific regimes, was now joined by modern notions of progress and development leading to a new understanding of the human body as an object capable of being perfected by advances in human knowledge and by physical training and hard work (Dutton, 1995: 99). With the rise of industrial capitalism, work came to provide the major occasion and opportunity for exercising those self-disciplines associated with the masculine virtues of control, competitiveness, aggression, and conquest. It is significant that, according to the dominant definitions of work in the modern Western world at least, the only work that has any substantial value is that which is paid and seen to occur in the public domain. A 'real' man not only undertakes hard work, but has to be *seen* to be *at work*.

The concept of the working body/body-at-work is a heavily gendered one, although it has been increasingly politicised through feminist efforts to make visible the non-visible, unpaid work undertaken mainly by women in the private sphere, and to make men take a greater share of domestic labours. There is now a substantial literature exploring the importance of work for male identity and the significance of the public/private division of labour for the domination of 'men' over 'women' (see, for example, Connell, 1987: 6–10, 99–106; Edley and Wetherell, 1995: 96–130; Hearn, 1992). The idea of 'success' for males in the modern West is bound up with paid labours, and with being the breadwinner and head of the household. The idea that men sacrifice themselves or 'do it all for their families' is strongly rooted, and has provided a powerful support for the institution of reproductive heterosexuality, while serving to relieve men of a major responsibility for child care and domestic labour (Pahl, 1995: 190). Although the notion of male-as-breadwinner is coming under threat in the late twentieth century as a result of the casualisation in employment and changing gender definitions, among other trends (see Chapter 6), 'successful' masculine identity continues to be strongly connected with paid labour.

The 'division of labour' ushered in by industrial capitalism involved gendered, sexualised, and racialised sub-divisions, with different types of bodies seen as suited to different kinds of work. The bureaucratisation of work in the late nineteenth century involved the increasing separation of physical and mental labours, with the former kinds of labour seen to demand a more muscular development. According to Jeff Hearn, the office provided an important site for the developing division of labour *in the public sphere* in the late nineteenth century, and provided an 'archetype form of the general bureaucracy' (1992: 150–53). Although Hearn's primary focus is on the gendered division of labour, and the office as a site of men's domination of women, the appearance of the office/bureaucracy can be seen to correspond to the development of a broad range of social and corporeal divisions based on the distinction between manual and mental labours, represented by the factory and the office respectively. These divisions have provided the foundation for the class divisions of capitalism and for the emergence of a range of different bodily ideals and types. Labouring or 'blue-collar' work, associated with the factory and with the outdoors, became increasingly associated with the ideal of physical toughness, robustness, and invulnerability, and with an instrumental view of the body. The routine physical risk-taking and demonstration of one's ability to push oneself to one's physical limits that has been observed among male manual workers, for instance in the building industry (see Carter, 1993: 33–44), can be seen as evidence of the persistence of this bodily ideal.

While the muscular body has come to provide a dominant metaphor for such masculine virtues as physical strength, rugged individualism, and mastery over one's environment, it is important to recognise that its significations vary through time and across contexts. The representation of muscular, working-class men in the public artworks studied by Barbara Melosh (1993) in Washington, DC, in the United States, can be seen as emblems of the enduring values of 'manhood' and work in the face of economic depression, as statements of the proper place of men and women, and as allegories of the nation's history and future. (The state funded 1,400 artworks for federal buildings across the nation during the period of the New Deal of the 1930s and early 1940s.) However, the depiction of the muscular bodies of young black men in some contemporary photography and artwork, such as that of Robert Mapplethorpe, can be seen to signify not so much the owners' possession of power, or even physical strength, as their positioning as sexualised and dominated objects. As Mercer explains, 'regardless of the sexual preferences of the spectator, the connotation is that the "essence" of black male identity lies in the domain of sexuality' (Mercer, 1994: 174). The representation of black male nudes as beautiful 'things'

> reveals more about the desires of the hidden and invisible white male subject behind
> the camera, and what 'he' wants to see, than it does about the anonymous black
> men whose beautiful bodies we see depicted. . . . [This representation can be]

characterized in terms of a masculine fantasy of mastery and control over the 'objects' depicted and represented in the visual field, the fantasy of an omnipotent eye/I who sees but is never seen. (Mercer, 1994: 175–6)

Mapplethorpe's work reflects the strong cultural association of male muscularity, and particularly black male muscularity, with (homo)erotic fantasy. In this case, the representations can be seen to be for the gaze of other men, particularly white gay men, as much as for women. As Mercer observes, 'Mapplethorpe appropriates elements of commonplace racial stereotypes in order to regulate, organize, prop up and *fix* the process of erotic/aesthetic objectification in which the black man's flesh becomes burdened with the task of symbolizing the transgressive fantasies and desires of the white gay male subject' (1994: 176). Within the culturally available frameworks of representation, the muscular male body can be variously positioned and 'read', depending upon the particular configuration of relationships existing between the body/object, the reader/audience, and the mode and context of representation. It is clear, however, that the sexualised, muscular male body is increasingly positioned as an object of consumption in the late twentieth century, aided by the advertising industry which presents the body as a 'vehicle of pleasure' and as a site for constant self-improvement (Featherstone, 1991: 174–5).

The valorisation of the idealised perfectible body has arguably generated intolerance for non-normative body types – a situation which has profound implications for the subjectivities of men, and for relations between men and between men and women. It may help explain, for instance, the findings of one study that homosexual men show more body dissatisfaction than heterosexual men and that heterosexual men who rate themselves as underweight may experience poor self-concepts (Silberstein et al., 1989). The effort to achieve the ideal body implies the need for the objectification of, and an instrumentalist view towards, one's own body. The evidence that exists suggests that there is a gendered dimension to this process of self-objectification. One study, which explored the phenomenological, embodied aspects of health among white, middle-class men and women, aged 35–55, found that men were more likely than women to speak about their bodies in the language of ownership. (Women tended to refer to their bodies as though their bodies had a momentum or subjectness of their own.) For this particular group of men, their experience of 'healthiness' was defined in terms of 'keeping' or 'being in control' and 'minding' one's body (Saltonstall, 1993: 9). That the striving after bodily perfection may involve oppressive, life-denying effects, can be seen in the experience of Nazi Germany, when the Western conception of physical development was turned to blatant political ends. In the period leading up to and during the Second World War, the ideal of bodily perfection (the young, muscular Aryan male) was extensively exploited by the Nazis, and their propagandist filmmakers such as Leni Riefenstahl, and eventually led to the persecution and extermination of all kinds of 'foreign' bodies: homosexuals, Jews, Gipsies, and blacks (Dutton, 1995: 207–8; Grau, 1995, Kern, 1974: 255).

Games, military training, and the shaping of male bodies

Organised games and military training have been important techniques deployed for the shaping of male bodies in the modern period. As Rotundo has argued, towards the end of the nineteenth century, both sportsfield and battlefield were seen to provide the opportunity for nurturing and proving manly, fighting virtues. War, in particular, was widely believed to develop those martial qualities in men that were seen to be needed in the struggle for life, and it was widely thought that there was an inseparable link between the fulfilment of martial ideals for the individual man and imperialism abroad (1993: 232–9). War provided the opportunity to nurture the individual's ability to endure pain and even mutilation, and to control the emotions. Military discipline developed such character traits as honesty, trust, loyalty to comrades, 'toughness', and heroism (Mrozek, 1987). The idea of the heroic soldier has been central in modern nationalist discourse, both underpinning and reproducing conceptions of gender and nation as unchanging 'essences', as Graham Dawson (1994) has shown in his study of the imagining of 'masculinities' in adventure stories. War has provided the opportunity for the shaping and demonstrating of those virtues (for example, masculine prowess) seen as definitive of 'real' 'manhood' and as expressive of national character. According to Joanna Bourke, in her book, *Dismembering the Male: Men's Bodies, Britain and the Great War* (1996), the First World War played a decisive role in shaping male bodies, making them more useful while helping to confirm particular masculine norms. War intensified state surveillance and discipline of the body, and encouraged a proliferation of regulatory institutions – developments that were to have an enduring legacy. New techniques for sorting and classifying bodies, evident in the grading of recruits according to their level of fitness, were brought into play. For British recruits, in 1917, for instance, four grades were adopted, ranging from grade one (or 'fit') through to grade four ('unfit'). Military definitions of fitness were widely adopted in the civilian population. Nearly all young adult and middle-aged men in Britain had their bodies surveyed and categorised by medical officers at least once between 1914 and 1918. Military drill was also applied to the civilian population and, with the onset of war, organised games began to be promoted for all boys as a means of moulding their bodies (Bourke, 1996: 172–5).

Racist, sexist, and chauvinistic values and practices have been evident in the promotion of the martial arts. In the First World War, military drill was seen as a means of developing a 'perfect race of men', while at the same time promoting the welfare of nation and empire. It was seen as a means of counteracting perceived racial 'degeneracy' – a fear increasingly confirmed by scientific studies of the general population. Joanna Bourke has described how, in Britain during the First World War, the British body was presented as competing with other – 'foreign' – bodies (1996: 177). In times of war and peace, 'foreign' bodies have included the bodies of homosexual men (and women). Military restrictions on the service of gay men (and lesbians), long in force in some countries (for example, the United States), underline the institutional and cultural privileging of a heterosexual masculine ideal. Heterosexual norms have been policed in the military through such mechanisms as barring entry to 'homosexuals', discharging those deemed to display homosexual 'intent' and 'desires', the privileging of the traditional family among officers and career-enlisted men, and a general intolerance for behaviours seen as characteristically 'homosexual'. Within the military, any sign of weakness, vulnerability, or even sensitivity, can be interpreted as a sign of homosexuality, and hence of failed 'masculinity' (Britton and Williams, 1995: 3–4, 11, 14). On the other hand, the expectation of heterosexuality – 'of a particularly violent and virulent form' – can be seen in the tolerance (if not encouragement) of prostitution and in forms of sexual discrimination, harassment and exploitation (for example, sexist jokes and rape) (1995: 12). War and other male-exclusive quasi-military arenas (for example, the Scouts) are believed to provide the opportunity for the development of male solidarity and mutual support away from women. This bonding and solidarity is encouraged by military leaders as an essential element in forging effective fighting units, and is seen to be threatened by homoeroticism. The military's exclusion and persecution of homosexual men can be understood 'as an attempt to suppress the homoerotic "buddy bonding" and other highly sexualised elements of military life' (Britton and Williams, 1995: 13).

Historically, there have been intimate links between nationalism, racism, and constructions of heterosexual masculinity. Defence of the nation, and especially the military, have been defined as masculine and heterosexual in character. As Kinsman (1993) explains, the system of sexual regulation has been closely bound up with the broader class, gender, and racial organisation of society. Sexual regulation has been a crucial aspect of 'nation-building' (Kinsman, 1993: 10). Thus, the heterosexual family has played a central role in the nation's public imaginings, with motherhood being seen as a national service while female non-reproductive sexuality and female-female eroticism were constrained to operate within the private domain (Parker et al., 1992: 7; see also Dawson, 1994: 2). Alongside the 'ideal' of 'manliness' which provided the foundation for the nation and society, there existed an ideal of the woman as guardian of the traditional order. In the first decades of the nineteenth century, nationalism assimilated new ideals of womanhood, and new symbols of the nation such as Germania, Britannia, and Marianne, stood for both respectability and the collective sense of national purpose (Mosse, 1985: 90–113). 'Nationalism and respectability assigned everyone his [sic] place in life, man and woman, normal and abnormal, native and foreigner; any confusion between these categories threatened chaos and loss of control' (Mosse, 1985: 16).

Rudi Bleys (1996) has examined how definitions of, and responses to, homosexuality have been shaped by late nineteenth-century concerns about the degeneration of the nation. National decline and loss of empire were seen to be a consequence of the spread of 'perverse' and 'degenerate' social practices. Through a process of analogous reasoning, which was an essential part of Enlightenment and post-Enlightenment ideology, 'homosexual' minorities in Europe were compared with 'endemic' forms of sexual perversion outside Europe. As Bleys explains,

> Since all non-Western peoples were considered as occupying an inferior position on the evolutionary scale, same-sex praxis was seen merely as an integral part, an obvious sign of their lower status. But it could not be seen as originating from an innate impulse, shared by virtually every man, as this would have led to the extinction of the race. Presenting indigenous homosexuality as a 'minority trait', on the other hand, would acquit a majority, which went against the imperatives of racialist rhetoric. In the end, same-sex praxis, though not labelled 'genuine homosexuality' was depicted as a characterizing trait of non-western people, whose sexuality was considered distinct from and inferior to the white race's superior sexuality. (1996: 191–92)

Consistent with the search for a single vocabulary and principle that would explain any variety of 'mankind', difference was seen to reside in 'nature', and thus great authority was ascribed to the anatomy and physiology of bodies. Thus, the Enlightenment debate on the natural status of non-European 'races' was marked by an ascription of sexual qualities. For example, 'feminine' characteristics were ascribed to the people of America, Asia and the Pacific, while Sub-Saharan Africans and Arabs were commonly accredited with an exaggerated and 'uncivilized masculinity' (Bleys, 1996: 90).

The processes of body regulation and exclusion that I have sketched above reached their most extreme form under fascist militarism. In his work, *Male Fantasies* (Volume 2) (1989), Klaus Theweleit describes how the male body both organises and expresses the politics of gender and sexuality in a fascist context, specifically the period of the German *Freikorps* preceding the rise of Nazism. As Theweleit explains, the male warrior ideal of the fascist imagination – the controlled, emotionally bereft body – expresses revulsion and fear of the soft, fluid, and liquid female body which is seen to be the quintessentially negative 'other' lurking inside the male body. This body is the source of pleasure or pain which must be sealed off and kept separate from the hard, organised, phallic body devoid of internal viscera. In this psychoanalytic account, masculine identity is seen as a flight from the feminine, as fear of ego dissolution, and as an expression of a longing for fusion with the military machine and legitimate explosion in the moment of battle (Benjamin and Rabinbach, 1989: xvii). The male self needs to be organised in a way which protects it from the constant threat of disintegration, a feat which is accomplished by the mechanisation of the self through military drill, countenance and training. The soldier is expected to show allegiance to the military machine, and to keep all feelings 'tightly locked in steel armor' (Theweleit, 1989: 159).

> The 'new man' sired in the drill (the drill as organised battle of the old men against himself) owes allegiance only to the machine that bore him. He is a true child of the drill-machine, created without the help of a woman, parentless. His associations and relationships bind him instead to other specimens of the new man, with whom he allows himself to be united to form the macro-machine troop. All others belong only 'under' him – never alongside, behind, or in front . . . [He] is a man whose physique has been machinized, his psyche eliminated – or in part displaced into his body armor, his 'predatory' suppleness. We are presented with a robot who can tell

the time, find the North, stand his ground over a red-hot machine-gun, or cut wire without a sound. In the moment of action, he is devoid of fear as of any other emotion. His knowledge of being able to do as he does is his only consciousness of self. (1989: 160–62)

Although Theweleit's study is historically limited – it is based largely on 250 *Freikorps* novels and memoirs of the 1920s – many of the masculinist values and regulations associated with fascist militarism can be seen to be in evidence, to varying degrees, in all modern military and sporting endeavours. Furthermore, the fascist flight from the feminine and the fear and revulsion of homosexuality, described with such poignancy by Theweleit in Volume 1 of his book (Theweleit, 1987), are implicit in relationships in non-military/sporting contexts. This is not to say that the modern military and sports, and fascist militarism in particular, shape the male body in any simple, direct way. The body is not passive and, in the case of the military, as David Morgan (1994) argues, the nexus linking masculinity, violence, and the military is more complex than is sometimes represented in the literature on men and their identities. The links should be seen as a cultural achievement that is frequently brought into question through changes in military technology and forms of conflict and in the broader culture; for example, the growing participation of women in the services and the influence of the peace movement. Indeed, following Shaw (1991), Morgan has suggested that, in the West at least, there has been a weakening of some of the strong linkages between gender constructions and war and the military associated with the rise of the nation-state, industrialisation, and state bureaucracy in the nineteenth and early twentieth century – the period of 'classical militarism' (1994: 173). Nevertheless, military drill and competitive sports have played, and continue to play, a significant role in shaping and disciplining male bodies and identities in the modern period. And this influence can be seen to extend outside military and sports contexts, for example in organisational culture where military and warlike metaphors are used by managers, of at least the post-war generation, to describe their work experiences (Roper, 1994: 111–17).

The naturally aggressive male

Male competitiveness, toughness, and desire to control – values that are instilled in the military, competitive sports, and organisational life – are taken as indicative of a natural male aggressivity. The idea that men are biologically predisposed to fight, as a survival mechanism, and in defence of their 'property' (for example, women), has been an enduring one in the twentieth century, having gained credence with the development of Darwinian-inspired instinct theory in the late nineteenth century. The hydraulic metaphor has been commonly used in instinct theories to suggest that pent-up aggression, in the absence of an outlet, is likely to explode with destructive effects (see Petersen and Davies, 1997: 312). In the emerging psychology of aggression, male aggression was seen to be a consequence of the frustration of the 'fighting instinct' or 'hunting instinct' which, when aroused, was likely to burst forth, often in unpredictable ways, and to override other instincts such as 'sympathy' and even the 'paternal instinct'. For instance, in his book, *The Principles of Psychology*, originally published in 1890, William James argued that the fighting and hunting instincts often found an outlet in cruelty towards other animals, in aggression towards human rivals, in games and sport, and in the exercise of property rights. James observed that boys who 'are brought up naturally' take great pleasure in acts of cruelty or acts of destruction of other species of animals, for example by pulling out the wings and legs of flies, by plundering birds' nests, or by tormenting them (James, 1901: footnote, 411–12). Women, although equally if not more likely to get angry than men, were seen to be inhibited by 'fear and other principles of their nature from expressing itself in blows'. As James explained, this was because 'the hunting instinct proper is decidedly weaker in them than in men' (James, 1901: 415; see also Thorndike, 1921: 84–5). Instinct theory laid the groundwork for the development of a range of new psychological theories of aggression in the twentieth century based on the idea that observed sex differences in aggression have a biological basis. Some of these theories had obvious direct links to the early instinct theories, and particularly to the work of Freud (1930). For example, the so-called 'frustration-aggression hypothesis', as articulated in the works of Dollard et al. (1949) and Durban and Bowlby (1939), proposed that male aggression is a logical and expected product of 'frustration' when the attainment of a desired goal is blocked. Instinct theory continues to enjoy widespread favour in the psychological literature on aggression. However, the idea that the origins of male aggression, and even the origins of war, could be explained in terms of biochemical processes or genetic factors began to gain increasing currency after 1920 with developments in hormonal theory and human genetics, respectively.

Hormonal theories have been invoked to explain a whole range of personal and social problems involving conflict, and have frequently led to calls to castrate men who have a history of violent or antisocial behaviour. Endemic to the writings on the biology of aggression, as Anne Fausto-Stirling observes, is the consistent confusing and interchanging of social and biological concepts. This is especially apparent in writing about war, where the term 'aggression' (conceived as an individual intent or attempt to inflict harm) is often used synonymously with 'war' (which is part of a spectrum of political processes) (Fausto-Sterling, 1992: 129). Although biological explanations for male aggression are believed by some commentators to have been largely displaced in the 1970s and 1980s by the idea that male aggression is 'learnt' (and, by implication, can be 'unlearnt'), learning theory can be seen to coexist and overlap with a range of contending discourses on male aggression. In the event, learning theory, at least as it has been articulated by some theorists, is also underpinned by biological determinism. One of the tenets of social learning theory is that men and women are differently equipped in *preparedness to learn* different behaviours. In the Male Sex Role Identity Paradigm (MSRI) of Joseph Pleck (*The Myth of Masculinity*, 1981) the individual is 'pre-programmed' to develop sex role identity as part of 'normal' psychological development. There is, in other words, an innate predisposition to seek appropriate role identity which, for men, includes expressions of aggressive behaviour. In another version of learning theory, the supposed lower incidence of female aggression is explained by the fact that females are disadvantaged in size and strength, and so any physical aggression in which they do engage is less likely to meet with the reinforcement of success (Petersen and Davies, 1997: 316–17).

The heterosexual male body and the 'natural' sex drive

Darwinism was important in laying the foundations for the development of a male sex-drive discourse that began to emerge from the 1860s. The key principle of this discourse is that men's sexuality is directly produced by a biological drive, which functions in the reproduction of the species (Hollway, 1984: 231). The sex-drive discourse has had a profound and enduring influence on thinking about sexuality and gender, at least in much of the Western world, and, as I will explain, has been manifest throughout much of this century in research and policy on 'homosexuality' as well as in contemporary academic and 'popular' writings on 'masculinity'. From its inception, this discourse has constructed homosexual desire as oppositional and abnormal. Writers such as Richard von Krafft-Ebing, Carl Westphal, Karl Ulrichs, and Havelock Ellis, who contributed to a new 'sexual science' in the late nineteenth and early twentieth centuries, helped define the norms of heterosexual desire. The idea that male desire for the opposite sex was an innate 'fact of nature' was underpinned by a growing body of instinct theory. It was even suggested, by Havelock Ellis, that men might have a natural, weekly, 'menstrual sexual rhythm' not unlike the female menstrual cycle, characterised by a heightened sexual desire (1900: 73–87). According to instinct theory, normal male sexuality is characterised by an attraction towards, and the active pursuit of, the opposite sex – a disposition which has been contrasted with normal female restraint and passivity.

As I pointed out in the last chapter, heterosexuality and heterosexual desire were 'invented' late in the last century, when it came to be widely acknowledged that there existed a normal, essential opposite-sex eroticism. Although there was an increased emphasis during this period on female pleasure, a natural, stronger male desire was seen to provide the basis for male initiative in opposite-sex sexual relations. Krafft-Ebing's thoughts, from *Psychopathia Sexualis*, which made its first widespread British appearance in an 1892 translation, are not uncharacteristic of the period:

Man has beyond doubt the stronger sexual appetite of the two [sexes]. From the period of pubescence he is instinctively drawn towards woman. His love is sensual, and his choice is strongly prejudiced in favour of physical attractions. A mighty impulse of nature makes him aggressive and impetuous in his courtship . . . Woman, however, if mentally and physically normal, and properly educated, has but little sensual desire. If it were otherwise, marriage and family life would be empty words. As yet the man who avoids women, and the woman who seeks men are sheer anomalies. (1953: 14)

Up until the early twentieth century, women were characterised by 'passion-lessness' and seen to be guided more by maternal instinct than sexual desire *per se*, and were expected to dampen men's obsession with sex (Simmons, 1993: 20). Although as Simmons indicates, this characterisation began to be challenged somewhat by a sexual revisionism in the 1920s and 1930s – involving recognition of the value of sexual expression for both sexes other than for reproductive purposes (1993: 20–5) – the belief in the stronger male sex drive has remained reasonably constant throughout the twentieth century. A survey of gynaecological texts published between 1943 and 1972 found, for instance, that despite shifts and fashions in theories of sexuality over the period (for example, Kinsey, and then Masters and Johnson), the enduring view has been that the male sex drive is stronger (Scully and Bart, 1973).

The association between male physiological desire for sexual release and the psychological desire for conquest has been a central theme in twentieth-century discourses of sex and sexuality. In psychoanalytic theory, for example, a certain amount of sadism is seen as an essential part of male sexuality, as masochism is of female sexuality Stember has noted that, although writers after Freud have been less inclined to see the need for conquest in the male as anything other than a neurosis common to many men, 'so institutionalised has become the association of conquest with masculinity that one rarely finds any sense of shame attached to such behaviour' (Stember, 1976: 145). As he observes, language itself reveals the component of conquest in male sexuality:

> The words 'fuck' and 'screw' are synonymous in popular parlance with 'doing injury to' or 'conquering over'. One 'lays' a woman which is to say one renders her prostrate in the position of a conquered victim. If she is not 'layed', she is 'had' or 'made' – in terms clearly denoting achievement in the act. (Stember, 1976: 145)

The quest ('the hunt') and conquest are, in turn, integral to the modern Western notion of romantic love, as Giddens (1992) explains. Romantic love fastens upon and idealises a particular other and it anticipates a course of future development, involving a 'meeting of souls' or the coming together to create a 'wholeness' (generally through marriage). This presumes a degree of self-interrogation: 'How do I feel about the other? How does the other feel about me? Are our feelings "profound" enough to support a long-term involvement?' (1992: 44). The subjects of modern romantic love are active subjects, who seek to produce love, often through devious scheming and setting elaborate 'traps' for their beloved. 'Falling in love' entails the desire for possession and sexual exclusivity, as is reflected in the following definition appearing in John Money and Patricia Tucker's *Sexual Signatures: On Being a Man or a Woman* (1976):

> Falling in love is a state characterized by an intense preoccupation with the loved one. His or her every feature becomes a source of minor raptures. There is an urgent need to be close to, a yearning to touch and fondle, the loved one, although the expression of these yearnings may be inhibited by moral code, cultural pre-scription, or circumstance. Reciprocation intensifies the phenomenon. . . . Falling in love inspires a jealous protectiveness that brooks no competitor. It is monogamous to the extent that it excludes the possibility of simultaneously falling

in love with another person, although not the possibility of having sexual relations with another or others. . . . Falling in love is not a one-time thing; the experience can be repeated again and again. Onset may be sudden or gradual. It's quite possible to fall in love at first sight, or at a distance (1976: 160).

As this quotation so clearly shows, 'falling in love' is seen to involve an attraction that is overwhelming, in that the individual is 'swept up' by intense emotion. It is also seen as characterised by a degree of unpredictability, which suggests that it is driven by some natural force. Indeed, according to Money and Tucker, 'falling in love' is part of 'nature's design', the purpose of which was 'to draw the human male and female together as soon as their sex organs matured for reproduction, and keep them together long enough to insure the next generation' (see Money and Tucker, 1976: 160). Given the strong historical and cultural connections between romantic love and monogamous reproductive sex, it is hardly surprising that 'falling in love' is rarely used to describe attraction between same-sex couples.

In male sex-drive discourse, 'normal' opposite-sex attraction and conquest has been defined in contrast to 'perverse' sexual desires and behaviours, particularly those of 'the homosexual'. In his *Three Essays on the Theory of Sexuality*, originally published in 1905, Freud argued that the disposition to 'perversions' (among which he included same-sex love) was an original and universal disposition of the human sexual instinct, which was normally held in check by various organic changes and psychical inhibitions in the individual. In his view, 'normal' opposite-sex attraction was inherently unstable and, as he sought to show in his analysis of the 'psychoneurotic', there always existed the potential for one to shift one's gaze from one sexual object to another (Freud, 1962). Attempts to define and 'fix' 'normal' opposite-sex desire and behaviour in the late nineteenth and early twentieth centuries resulted in the delineation of a whole new range of 'perverse' sexual identities – the exhibitionist, the fetishist, the sadomasochist, the paedophile, and the 'sexual invert' or homosexual. The male 'homosexual', in particular, came to signify the antithesis of the 'normal' male 'heterosexual', and was seen to possess an effeminate body having its own distinct desires and pathologies.

The effeminate body of the male homosexual

In his analysis of shifts in the discursive production of normative male heterosexuality, employing a case study of newspaper reports of the trials of Oscar Wilde in 1895 on the charge of 'acts of gross indecency', Ed Cohen (1993) argues that the criminalisation of sexual acts between men in the later part of the nineteenth century was predicated on the assumption that there existed a 'type' of person who had a 'tendency' towards certain sexual offences. This study clearly shows the emergence of new representations of normative masculinity based upon the 'natural' determination of the opposition between the male and female. Homosexuality was constructed as an 'inversion' – a pathology – as the binary half of the heterosexual/homosexual dualism that has served since the 1890s to define that which is other than the 'healthy', 'manly man' (Cohen, 1993: 17–18). It was around this time that writers like Krafft-Ebing and Ulrich began to propagate the idea of the 'female soul in a male body', and some suggested the existence of a 'third sex'. More and more, 'manliness' was defined as *non*homosexual (Hekma, 1994: 223–9). By the early twentieth century, the notion that the homosexual male body could be distinguished from the heterosexual male body on the basis of its effeminacy was well established in expert and 'popular' writings, and homosexual men began to be routinely derided and persecuted as a result.

By the 1930s, it was widely accepted in medical and scientific circles that homosexuality was pathological, and systematic inquiries into the lives of homosexuals were undertaken with the view of detecting markers of 'deviance'. One well-known study in the United States was the so-called Sex Variants study conducted between 1935 and 1941, which involved the physical examination of, and interviews with, individuals from New York's homosexual community. This investigation aimed to learn as much as possible about homosexuality in order to assist physicians in identifying and treating 'sexually maladjusted' persons, and help prevent the spread of sexual variance throughout the rest of the population (Minton, 1996: 452; Terry, 1995: 138). These studies were often taken with the support and active involvement of 'homosexuals' who believed that such scientific study would serve the cause of homosexual rights (Minton, 1996: 437). In the early 1930s, medical professionals took a particular interest in physical appearance and body type – what they called 'constitutional factors' – and in corresponding personality characteristics, as the basis for their theories on gender and homosexuality. According to Karin Martin, the medical profession's efforts to define homosexuality according to physiological factors were part and parcel of its efforts to move away from 'unscientific' psychoanalytic claims and to consolidate the boundaries around its expertise (1993: 252). In the attempt to delineate constitutional factors, these researchers measured all sorts of body proportions, examined the pitch of voice, when men started shaving, and menstruation began in women. In her analysis of medical articles on homosexuality published between 1934 and 1942, Martin found little discussion on sexual behaviour, with most focusing on 'deviant' gender behaviour. A common conclusion was that

> The homosexual male is characterised by a feminine carrying of angle of the arm, long legs, narrow hips, large muscles, deficient hair on the face, chest and back, feminine distribution of pubic hair, a high-pitched voice, small penis and testicles and the presence of a scrotal fold. Not uncommonly there is an excess of fat on the shoulder, buttocks and abdomen. Occasionally the penis is very large and the hips are unusually wide. (Henry and Galbraith, 1934: 1265, cited in Martin, 1993: 253)

In their well-known study on 'sex differences in personality and temperament' published in 1936, Terman and Miles (members of the expert committee overseeing the aforementioned Sex Variants Study) describe a category which they identify as 'passive male homosexuals' in the following way:

> The behaviour of these male homosexuals . . . is as different from that of a group of

average men as one could possibly imagine. It is well known that the average boy makes every effort to keep from appearing effeminate. The passive male homosexual, on the contrary, takes advantage of every opportunity to make his behaviour as much as possible like that of a woman. He not only accentuates any feminine qualities which he may already possess, such as high-pitched voice, but also attempts to imitate women in his speech, walk, and mannerisms. Practically every subject has adopted a 'queen' name by which he is known among his associates. They constantly refer to themselves as 'the girls'. Their behaviour often seems exaggerated and ridiculous, although in some cases the inversion of behaviour is remarkably complete. (Terman and Miles, 1936: 248)

The inference here is quite clear: 'real men' avoid appearing feminine and, since this group of homosexuals are seen to actively adopt 'feminine' mannerisms, behaviours and forms of self-address, they cannot be considered 'real men'. Indeed, the use of the adjective 'passive' in the description of this group of men reinforces the association of homosexuality with femininity since, as indicated earlier, women have been defined by their passivity. In an effort to confirm the view that these homosexuals are more like women than men, Terman and Miles go on to explain that their subject preferences when in school were 'strikingly feminine' (language studies, history, art, and music), that their favourite childhood games were 'more feminine than masculine' (especially 'playing house'), and that they preferred 'female' playthings and toys (for example, dolls) (1936: 249–50). These 'true inverts', as they are referred to elsewhere in the report, are compared to 'active male homosexuals', who were found to be 'masculine' in their subject preferences in school and childhood play, although still described as 'male[s] of feminine personality' (Terman and Miles, 1936: 256).

With the development of the new science of sex endocrinology in the early decades of the twentieth century, biomedical science began its search for biological markers of 'femininity' and 'masculinity' in homosexuals. Some scientists hypothesised that the effeminacy of male homosexuals could be explained by the presence of female sex hormones. Although most studies failed to find any difference between 'heterosexuals' and 'homosexuals' in the amount of sex hormones in their bodies, hormonal tests began to be routinely employed in the 1930s and 1940s, and were used both as the basis for subsequent hormonal treatment of mainly male homosexuals and in homosexual criminal trials to determine the 'true nature' of people suspected of the criminal act (Oudshoorn, 1994: 56–9; Oudshoorn and Wijngaard, 1991: 462). Eventually, however, the lack of supporting evidence for the hormonal theory of homosexuality led scientists to develop a theory on sexualisation of the brain as an explanation of homosexuality in humans, building upon evidence obtained in animal studies (Doell, 1995: 34). In one version of this theory, first proposed in the 1970s, the 'natural', causal relationship between anatomical sex, on the one hand, and both gender and sexual orientation, on the other, is seen to be altered by an abnormal hormonal influence on the brain *in utero*, resulting in the development of 'masculinised women' (lesbians) and 'feminised men' (gays) (1995: 348). In a more recent version, homosexual behaviour is explained by differences in the size of particular parts of the

brain, namely a small cluster of neurones in the hypothalamus, which is
alleged to be slightly larger in heterosexual men than in homosexual men (see
LeVay, 1994). Although the role of this part of the brain in sexual behaviour
has not been demonstrated, these differences are assumed to be causally
related to the sexual orientation of the subjects in research that has been
undertaken (Doell, 1995: 348).

A sissy gene?

More recent research into the so-called 'gay gene' reflects the continuing
association between homosexuality and effeminacy and efforts to find a biological basis for behaviour. The existence of the gay gene is, according to its
supposed finder, Dean Hamer, confirmed by studies showing that a high pro-
portion of gay brothers share the same small quantum of genetic
information – their DNA, 'the long threadlike molecule that contains both
the blueprints of life and the instructions for carrying them out' (Hamer and
Copeland, 1994: 21). Drawing on previous scientific research into child
development, Hamer hypothesised that the 'gay gene' is really a 'sissy gene'
that provides the biological blueprint of effeminate behaviour. In order to
test this hypothesis, Hamer undertook interviews with gay and heterosexual
men in order to determine childhood experiences of masculine identity. He
found that the gay participants recalled substantially more 'gender-atypical'
experiences and behaviours than the straight subjects. For example, when
they were children, homosexual men were less likely than heterosexual men
to consider themselves masculine compared to other boys their age, and
were less likely to enjoy sports such as baseball and football (which are, pre-
sumably, typical 'masculine sports'). This information was then used to test
the 'sissy gene hypothesis' by seeing whether those brothers who shared part
of the chromosome harbouring the 'gay gene' were 'more gender atypical'
than brothers who did not (1994: 167). Although Hamer was unable to confirm his hypothesis, he nonetheless noted that 'there are some intriguing
observations that suggest there may yet be a connection between the "gay
gene" and gender-atypical behaviour'. He cites, for example, a study of twins
undertaken by another researcher, Bailey, showing the gay-gay pairs had
more similar gender 'atypicality scores' than did gay-straight pairs (1994:
169–70).
　There seems to be no end to the interest in biological explanations of
homosexuality, despite many damning critiques of the research. Among other
things, critics have pointed to the 'lack of scientific rigour' in research
methodology, including: doubts about the applicability of the findings of
animal studies to human populations, and (in research on human populations) problems with the use of non-representative samples and of samples
that are too small to draw statistically-significant conclusions; the limitations of using questionnaires to elicit information on subjects' sexual
histories; the inadequacy of methods for determining the genetic relatedness
of individuals (in behaviour-genetic studies), and the dangers of drawing

conclusions from simplistic genetic models (see, for example, Byne, 1995; McGuire, 1995). Biological theories of homosexuality are based on the belief that biology is a value-free science. This denies the ways in which cultural assumptions about gender and sexuality, and causality in human behaviour, shape the definition of research problems, the research process, and the publication and reception of findings (Byne, 1995; Haumann, 1995).

The idea of a genetic or biochemical basis for homosexuality has had a somewhat mixed response from the gay population: some seeing it as serving to affirm 'difference', while others see it as potentially providing a basis for legitimising unequal treatment of gay people. In his recent book *Queer Science* (1996), Simon LeVay – a gay scientist who is well known for his research on differences in brain structure between gay and heterosexual men (see LeVay, 1994) – outlines some of the arguments for and against biological research into homosexuality. On the negative side, he points to the possibility that, in the future, scientific findings might find application in tests for sexual orientation based, say, on gene markers or brain imaging, which will then be used to unfairly discriminate against gay people, or that efforts might be made to 'convert' gay people to heterosexuality, for example through genetic therapy (1996: 257–62). However, against this, LeVay believes that such research will serve to 'strengthen the identity of gays and lesbians as a discrete group within the larger society, independent to a considerable extent of the actual sexual behaviour they may engage in' (1996: 284). In his view, science is an ally in efforts to improve relations between straight and gay people by strengthening gay people's status as an objective category of human beings. It can help shift the focus of public debate away from behaviour ('what we do') – and the assumption that homosexuality is simply a matter of choice and, therefore, can be and should be changed – to identity ('who we are') (1996: 284–95).

The point that is overlooked by LeVay, and by others who follow this line of argument, is that biological research into homosexuality begins from the premise that an identity based on same-sex desire is problematic. As in the past, research continues to be inspired by efforts to confirm that the homosexual is 'other' (Herrn, 1995: 49). One of the key assumptions underlying research is that behaviours and desires falling outside the norms of the dominant heterosexuality should be corrected or 'normalised'. It is significant that there has been no research into the biological basis of *heterosexual* behaviour, for it is seen as 'natural', and therefore as not needing to be changed. Feminist philosophers of science have offered many critiques of research such as that described, drawing attention to the regulatory and exclusionary implications of the dualistic thinking which it so obviously reflects (see, for example, Bleier, 1984; Haraway, 1991). Nevertheless, biology – oriented as it is to describing, and sometimes altering, the very makeup of the material body – continues to have a powerful influence on thinking in the area of sexuality and gender, and provides an implicit or explicit point of reference in most contemporary analyses of 'masculinity' and 'masculine identity'. In the following section, I examine the ways in which biology has been deployed in some of these analyses, and may even inform the work of those who claim to reject biological determinism.

Biological determinism in some contemporary analyses of 'masculinity'

An example of the explicit and liberal use of biology, and more specifically sociobiology and genetic science, to explain the acquisition of 'masculine identity', male behaviour, and social differences between men and women can be seen in the work of Yves Christen, in her book *Sex Differences: Modern Biology and the Unisex Fallacy* (1991). Christen is an unapologetic biological determinist, arguing against those who would claim that gender identity is a product of 'socialisation' and in favour of the view that gender identity is genetically programmed but reinforced through cultural practices. The biological 'facts' of reproduction – differences in reproductive organs and cells (eggs versus spermatozoa) – are seen to explain male- (and female-)specific sexual behaviours. The fact that the sex act involves copulation, and that the female has a limited number of eggs (400 in the course of a woman's life) whereas the male 'expels around 100 million sperm cells in each ejaculation', is seen to have profound consequences for the respective behavioural dispositions of men and women. Reproductive success means that 'for one partner more than the other [i.e. the male] copulation is a conquest, a dissemination' and that 'the male opts for quantity' (of sexual encounters) whereas 'the female opts for quality' (1991: 31). Note how this explanation reflects the premises of the sex-drive discourse, described above; namely, that the male has a stronger sexual desire underpinned by the biological imperative to reproduce, and that conquest is part of this imperative. Biological factors, including sex differences in brain structure, are seen to explain such phenomena as male aggression, male-perpetrated infanticide, polygamy (noted in '80 per cent of human societies'), male superiority in spatial and mathematical abilities, the psychological fragility of males (for example, mental illness, behavioural difficulties, learning disabilities), and the disproportionate representation of men in science. (The popularised view that sex differences in the brain determine men's behaviours is discussed in more detail later.) Biology is also seen to explain the mother–child bond (which 'clearly constitutes the greatest difference between man and woman'); female territorial behaviour and competitiveness; women's emotional responses; girls' precociousness and overall superior performance in school; patterns of male–female cohabitation; nymphomania; and women's political subordination (1991: 37–48, 65–79, 87–100).

Christen's biological determinist argument might seem extreme, but is shared to varying degrees by a growing number of other feminists – the so-called feminists of difference, referred to earlier – who have become disillusioned with egalitarian feminism and have begun to develop a theory and practice based upon the recognition of the irreducible, embodied differences between men and women (see, for example, Diprose, 1994; Grosz, 1994; Irigaray, 1993). Whereas feminists of equality see both sexes as having analogous biological or natural potential which is unequally developed because of unequal 'socialisation', feminists of difference point to the inherent uniqueness of women's and men's standpoints in the social world, which tends to be obscured by 'patriarchal' social arrangements. Feminists of difference call for, among other things, transformation in the social and symbolic order, which involves the universalisation of the singular (male) identity, and resistance to the homogenisation of separate political struggles, such as those against racism, and those against 'patriarchy' (Grosz, 1990a: 339–40). Recognition that women are subject both to material oppression and lack of symbolic representation has led these feminists to advocate the strategy of 'speaking the/from the body' (Braidotti, 1991: 218). Writers such as Luce Irigaray, Hélène Cixous, Judith Butler, and Elizabeth Grosz argue that discourses are often presented in gender-neutral form, but in fact have a male gender bias – for example, the law, discourses on the body. These writers argue for the creation of new forms of representational practice or (to use Irigaray's term) a 'new ethics of sexual difference' outside the patriarchal frameworks which 'provide women with nonpatriarchal terms for representing themselves and the world from women's interests and points of view' (Grosz, 1994: 188; see also Irigaray, 1993: 169–206).

Irigaray invokes this concept of difference, for example, in her *Sexes and Genealogies* (1993). In this book, she argues that there is a need to develop a cultural and political ethics based upon sexual difference which is undervalued in modern societies. She refers to legal discussions about the relationship between the male and female sexes, particularly in so far as the family and its relation to reproduction are concerned, which she sees as premised on a code of morality that collapses male and female genealogies into a single genealogy: that of the husband. This genealogy is one that obliges women to submit to their husbands and to reproduction. Irigaray believes that the rights of both the male and the female need to be written into the legal code to 'offer justice to *two genders that differ* in their needs, their desires, their properties' (Irigaray, 1993: 4; emphasis in original). Irigaray believes that a new ethics of sexual difference also requires, among other things, a change in language, which appears to be gender-neutral but is in fact heavily marked by the masculine gender; the revaluing of the mother-daughter couple which once 'formed a paradigm for nature and for society' and was a great source of individual and collective identity for women, but has been usurped by 'patriarchal regimes'; and recognition of the specific nature of the relationship that men and women have with their mothers and how this affects the development of male and female identities (Irigaray, 1993: 169–206). This particular account can be criticised on the grounds not only of its romanticisation and idealisation of a supposedly original, ideal, pre-patriarchal femininity, but also for its essentialism in the use of the categories 'women' and 'men', and its positioning of a universal, all-dominating 'patriarchy'. Although they have developed a complex and challenging body of ideas, it is evident that in their attempts to develop a sex-specific perspective, feminists of difference seem unable to avoid charges of essentialism, universalism, and naturalism – those very same tendencies that are seen to be characteristic of 'masculinist' discourses (Braidotti, 1991: 248; Grosz, 1990a: 341).

Christen criticises egalitarian feminism for its supposed failure to redress inequalities in economic and social spheres and entrenched gender stereotypical attitudes evident among the population, arguing instead for a position (what she calls 'feminitude') which recognises the 'values proper to each sex' (1991: 117). However, her work (like that of many other feminists of difference) shares an affinity with that of the nineteenth-century complementarians who argued that women's bodies are perfect in their difference – an argument which, as I explained in Chapter 2, has been used to legitimate women's exclusion from the public sphere. Her case rests strongly on the evidence drawn from the modern biological and natural sciences and, indeed in developing her theory of difference, she argues the need to 'bring together the evidence of embryology, genetics, ethology, primatology, evolutionary theory, endocrinology, neurophysiology, ethnology, etc.' (Christen, 1991: 115). Christen seems not to recognise the extent to which the sexual specificity of which she speaks in arguing the case for a positive theory of difference is a product of historically and culturally specific configurations of power and knowledge. It is significant that issues of 'race', ethnicity, sexuality, and class are totally absent from Christen's analysis. As is common with many such feminist analyses of sexual difference, while it is claimed that the aim of analysis and political practice should be to affirm the specificity of 'embodied experience', the specificity that is referred to pertains only to women who are white, European, heterosexual, and middle class.

The work of Elisabeth Badinter, *XY: On Masculine Identity* (1995), provides another recent example of the influence of biological determinism on thinking about 'masculinity'. This work is of particular interest here because Badinter *explicitly* distances herself from the biological reductionist accounts of the feminists of difference, whom she refers to as 'differentialist feminists'. She characterises differentialist feminists as 'the latest heirs of Darwin', and sees their work as necessarily leading to the valorisation of one sex at the expense of the other. Differentialist feminism, she says, shares the same belief as sociobiology in the existence of an immutable sexual essence, and carries the same conservative implication that everything is pre-determined so that there is no possibility of change or creation. Its biological reductionism and essentialism 'necessarily ends in separation and worse: oppression' (1995: 25). However, Badinter's theory of masculinity, based as it is on the premise that 'a boy's development is governed by a natural, universal, and necessary given: the fact that he is born of a mother', involves a similar kind of essentialism and determinism (1995: 45).

Drawing on a combination of psychological, psychoanalytic, cross-cultural, and biological sources to support her claims, Badinter argues that 'masculinity' develops as a response to the developing boy's need to separate himself from his mother's 'femininity'. Like some other feminists before her (for example, Nancy Chodorow 1978, 1988), Badinter inverts Freud's claim that 'masculinity' is the original, natural mode of gender identity in the two sexes, and that it results from the first relationship with a heterosexual object of the boy with his mother, in favour of the argument (originally proposed by Robert Stoller) that 'femininity' is primary since it is shaped in 'the very first stage of life, consisting in the fusion that takes place in the mother – baby symbiosis' (1995: 46). Badinter draws on a 'discovery' of genetic science – 'that the male gene XY develops within the female XX – to explain the natural disadvantage of the male body and men's lifelong struggle to differentiate themselves from women. She claims that since 'masculinity' 'comes second' it must be 'created' and that, in acquiring 'masculinity', 'a man's first duty is: not to be a woman' (1995: 47). The fear of women and of feminine qualities ('tenderness', 'passivity', 'caregiving to others', etc.), and of homophobia are seen as 'defense maneuvers' that define 'appropriately masculine' behaviours (1995: 47). Thus, 'in most societies, becoming an adult man is problematic', and is acquired at a great price, often involving (for the boy) painful initiation rites which serve symbolically and physically to separate the boy from his mother (1995: 67ff). However, Badinter contends that achieving masculine identity has become especially problematic in modern Western societies, since the 'rites of masculinity' have lost their meaning, and feminism has critiqued traditional notions of 'masculinity' (1995: 75, 124–5). Consequently, there has emerged the concept of the 'mutilated man' who has 'lost his identity' and has responded by becoming either a 'tough guy', involving 'the amputation of a man's femininity', or a 'soft man' (typically a fatherless child), who renounces male privileges and power (1995: 127–60). Badinter sees neither model, nor a synthesis of them, as satisfactory, and proposes instead the concept of the 'reconciled man' who is reunited with his early 'femininity' and is able to combine male and female in an androgynous way of being – an ideal which presupposes, among other things, a 'revolution in fatherhood' involving a greater role for fathers in the parenting and nurturing of children (1995 161–85).

Like Christen, above, Badinter fails to recognise the extent to which those bodily qualities, abilities, and practices that have come to be seen as quintessentially 'masculine' in the modern West, and which she describes in part in her work ('virility', homophobia, mastery of the self, etc.) are a product of historically and socially specific relations of power. Her theory of male identity formation involves reference to a natural, fixed body whose workings are seen to be explained by the 'facts of biology' as constructed by modern Western rational science (genetics). She seems unaware of feminist arguments and evidence that scientific knowledge is itself a product of power/knowledge and is implicated in the 'naturalisation' of gender relations, particularly through reference to genetic evidence (see, for example, Bleier, 1984: 40–60; Fausto-Sterling, 1992; Rapp, 1995: 69–86). In her use of genetics to bolster her argument, Badinter shares the very same assumption of the sociobiologists, whom she criticises, that gender-stereotypical dispositions and behaviours can be explained by biology. Indeed, her argument lends support to those who would justify inequalities of power by reference to natural sex differences. Although in various places in her argument Badinter acknowledges that 'masculinity' is a historically and culturally relative concept (see, for example, 1995: 9, 142–3) and that it is wrong to view behaviours (for example aggression) as exclusive to one sex (1995: 153), she nevertheless makes generalisations about 'masculinity' on the basis of a historically and culturally specific set of observations and understandings about male physiology and behaviour. Consequently, a diverse range of practices ('initiation rites') occurring in a wide variety of societies and contexts, from the tribes of New Guinea through to English public schools and 'certain military units', are seen to perform the same 'cruel' and 'dramatic' function of physically and symbolically separating boys from 'maternal femininity' and allowing them to develop a male identity (1995: 48–54, 69–77).

Sex in the brain

Recently, there has appeared a new biological discourse involving reference to the physiology of the brain to explain the origins of male (and female) behaviours and the acquisition of masculine (and feminine) identities. This has prompted Anne Fausto-Sterling to speculate that the 1990s may be the decade of sex differences in the brain (1992: 223). While one might wonder why there is this current level of academic interest, it is clear that philosophers and scientists have long been preoccupied with studying and measuring sex differences in the brain. In fact, one can see the origins of a theory of sex in the brain in the work of Aristotle (384–322 BC), who postulated that a woman's defect in heat resulted in her brain being smaller and less developed than man's (Tuana, 1989: 148). It was in the nineteenth century, however, that scientists – first, the phrenologists, and then later, the craniologists – began to systematically focus on sex (and race) differences in the sizes, shapes, and structures of brains as part of a broader effort to establish a material explanation for social difference (see, for example, Russett, 1989: 16–38). Overturning the Christian and metaphysical postulate that 'the mind' was independent of 'the body', these new sciences posited that 'the body – more specifically, the head and brain – determined 'the mind'. It was hypothesised that women and non-Europeans had different (smaller) brain sizes, shapes and structures that reflected their natural intellectual inferiority. While the idea of sex and racial differences in the brain went out of favour for a period in the twentieth century – having being replaced by the notion that sex-specific hormones define male and female realities – it has recently been revived in the conservative context of the 1990s, giving rise to new research into brain sizes, structures, and functioning (Fausto-Sterling, 1992: 223–59).

Science has 'discovered' that sex-specific behaviours and abilities are controlled by particular areas of the brain. More specifically, it has found that there are differences between men and women in the brain region known as the corpus callosum, the mass of nerve fibres connecting the right and left cerebral hemispheres, and that this accounts for male–female differences in various behaviours and levels of skill, such as mathematical skills, and verbal and visual abilities. One of the key researchers in this area is Sandra Witleson, who has argued that women have a less asymmetrical brain than men, and consequently have 'a bi-hemispherical representation of emotion' (Witleson, 1978: 298, citing Christen, 1991: 68). That is, the left and right sides of the female brain are more intensively interconnected resulting in more information being exchanged, which accounts for women's greater verbal dexterity and emotional responses. Women's biological wiring, it seems, makes them less able than men to separate their emotional response from their rational analytic behaviour – 'facts' that have been cited by a number of recent writers in support of their natural difference arguments (Christen, 1991: 67–8; Moir and Jessel, 1991: 47–8; Nicholson, 1993: 103).

In their book, *BrainSex* (1991), for example, Anne Moir and David Jessel have used the argument of difference in brain organisation to explain what they describe as 'the real difference between men and women'. Drawing on evidence of psychology and brain sex research, including the work of Witleson, cited above, they argue that men's brains are 'more specialised'. That is, whereas for women, language and spatial abilities are controlled by centres in both sides of the brain, for men they are more specifically located – the right side for spatial skills, the left for verbal ones. This 'difference in the layout of the average male or female brain is found to have a direct effect on the way men and women differ in their ways of thinking' (1991: 44). The specialisation of function in the male brain means, among other things, that 'men are not so easily distracted by superfluous information' and that it is 'easier for men to perform two different activities at once', such as talking and map reading. Evidently, for women, having the visual and spatial activities controlled by areas on both sides of the brain can lead to confused messages: 'the two activities can interfere with each other and she will not be as good at talking and map reading at the same time' (1991: 45). Differences in brain organisation are also seen to account for men's superior mathematical abilities; their inferior language skills; and, as noted above, their weaker verbal expression of emotions (1991: 45–8).

Anne Fausto-Sterling (1992) and Judith Genova (1989) have provided extensive critiques of research into sex differences in the brain. As they have pointed out, such studies suffer from logical, methodological, and ethical-political problems, and reflect dominant, culturally specific assumptions about how men and women think. Issues of power relations and power/knowledge are effectively obscured by reference to objective, rational science. If differences in ability and behaviours of men and women are shown objectively to be a result of immutable, natural differences, then the corollary is that there is little that can be done to change the status quo. Such arguments and evidence have long been used for justifying inequitable social policies, although at different times different parts of the body have been the focus of enquiry. Thus, it is not surprising that Moir and Jessel conclude by arguing that gender differences in occupational representation (they cite fewer female than male architects, scientists and mathematicians, and more female musicians than composers) might be largely explained by sex differences in 'preferred cognitive strategies' (1991: 49). Although they acknowledge the impact of culture and history on occupational differences, they make no effort to evaluate this contribution, and they seem not to recognise the historical and cultural specificity of the scientific knowledge to which they defer. (For a more complex version of the sex in the brain argument – which at least gives some acknowledgement to social context – see Nicholson, 1993: 86–114.)

Conclusion

This chapter, which draws extensively on the insights of recent work in postmodern feminism, poststructuralism, and feminist philosophy of science, among other sources, has analysed the ways in which the male body has been discursively fabricated. I have argued that biology and its categories of difference – 'sex', 'sexuality' and 'race' – have played a central role in 'normalising' particular male bodies – specifically the bodies of white, European, heterosexual men – and constructing them as naturally different from female bodies, homosexual bodies, and 'black' and non-European bodies. I have shown how Darwinian theory has provided the master metaphor for thinking about, acting upon, and shaping the male body, and how this metaphor has been applied in different discourses on the body; for example, the sex-drive discourse. Biology has had a profound influence on contemporary thinking about 'masculinity' in the modern West, as can be seen from the diverse array of discourses of gender and sexuality, including sexual difference feminism and recent research into sex differences in the brain. Although recent developments in the social sciences and humanities have highlighted the fact that 'the body' is historically and socially constructed, analyses of 'masculinity' within many strands of feminism and 'men's studies' share the assumption that the body is a biological given; that it has a natural sex upon which gender is inscribed. Much, if not most, of this work can be criticised for its biological reductionism and for its emphasis on an essential difference between men and women that is in fact socially constructed.

To argue that the body is socially constructed is not to deny its materiality, as some writers have claimed, but simply to recognise the fact that its specific materiality is a product of shifting relations of power/knowledge. It also involves appreciation of the fact that the different significations that are attached to different male bodies at different times have material effects for the 'owners' of those bodies – for example, exclusion and/or persecution. Although there has been a proliferation of writings on the body within the social sciences and humanities, there has been little systematic exploration of the relationship between the materiality of bodies and subjectivity. Within this literature, the body often appears as a malleable substance without subjectivity and agency. As Chris Shilling (1993) has pointed out, theoretical work on the body has been dominated by two major approaches: the naturalistic approach, which broadly describes the dominant approach in the writings on 'masculinity' outlined in this chapter, and the currently influential social constructionist approach, which, as I mentioned in Chapter 1, actually includes a vast variety of perspectives, but can be simply and crudely characterised as viewing the body as an 'invention' of society. Within neither tradition is much credence given to the corporeal body as integral to subjectivity and human agency (Shilling, 1993: 99). This shortcoming reflects the dualistic split between 'mind' and 'body', and between 'culture' and 'nature', that is widely seen to be characteristic of modern 'masculinist' thought. Feminists and some pro-feminist male scholars have sought to expose, and transcend, dualistic and rationalist thinking. However, as I explain in the next chapter, they have not found it easy to do this in their own work.

4

Mind over matter: 'masculinity' and reason

> The opposition of reason and passion or emotion is paralleled by the opposition of male and female. Men are seen as rational and women as emotional, lacking rationality . . . Maleness is associated with order not disorder, with the mind not the body, with knowledge and the subjection of nature. (Crawford et al., 1992: 17)

The connection between 'masculinity' and rationality, and the opposition of 'masculinity' and emotionality, are central themes in contemporary Western thought. As Genevieve Lloyd (1984) argues, rationalism is deeply embedded in Western philosophy and has provided the foundation for thinking about sexual difference and the complementarity of the sexes. Thus, as I pointed out in Chapter 2, maleness is seen to involve the privileging of the mind over the body, rational control, and the domination of nature (which is implicitly coded feminine). This dualistic and hierarchical ordering operates not only as a popular assumption but also as an established academic 'truth'. It provides the basis for much contemporary discussion about men and their preoccupations, values and experiences. Critical commentators have noted that the pursuit of impartial knowledge, or the development of a 'view from nowhere' requires that the human body and all subjective qualities be set aside in the process (see, for example, Young, I.M., 1990: 96–121). This disembodied view of the process of knowledge production denies the fact that what passes as reality, knowledge and 'truth' is produced by embodied subjects and is mediated by power, language, and history. Identity movements have sought to expose the extent to which they are omitted from prevailing theoretical models. They have revealed the biases behind knowledge hitherto regarded as objective, showing that all epistemology is discourse-specific and involves narratives which 'are often posed as dichotomies in which the master term (e.g. male, reason, self, heterosexual) is defined as possessing certain qualities which its opposing term lacks' (Domenici and Lesser, 1995: 5).

This chapter critically examines some recent critiques of so-called masculinist rationality and the mind/body dualism, deriving from feminist psychoanalysis, feminist theories of moral development, ecofeminism, and 'pro-feminist' male writers' analyses of male emotionality, respectively, focusing on the works of a number of key contributors. These diverse areas, which often share overlapping concerns and perspectives, have strongly shaped contemporary discourses on gender, and all have something important to say about the mind/body dualism, the formation of male psyches and/or the manifestations or implications of 'masculinist' rationality. Each area can be seen to be concerned with one or more aspects of the link between mind and body, and/or rationality and 'masculinity'. It is important to see these works as more than discrete exposés or deconstructive analyses of the mind/body dualism or of what has been posited as 'Western masculinist rationality'. In different ways, and to varying degrees, they can be seen to articulate and contribute to the very discourse on 'masculinist' rationality which writers claim to challenge. A close examination of these works underlines the difficulty of escaping the dichotomies, hierarchies and essentialisms that are seen to be characteristic of Western rationality. The emergence of the idea of the social construction of 'masculinity' has created the opportunity for a systematic analysis and critique of the historical and cultural links between 'masculinity' and rationality, and the associated mind/body dualism. The chapter asks: what kinds of critiques of these links have thus far been proposed? How exactly do they seek to challenge dualistic, hierarchical and essentialist thinking, and how ' successful' have they been in this challenge? What implications for further critical deconstructive work can be drawn from this analysis? This chapter provides the background for the next chapter, where I discuss the queer critique of the idea of the authentic, essential self and of impartial or disembodied knowledge, specifically in relation to the question of sexual identity.

The diverse critiques of 'masculinist' rationality

In feminist analyses, the privileging of the mind over the body, or the rational over the affective, has long been identified as a defining feature of 'phallogocentrism' and as implicated in the domination of women in the public and private spheres, in the inexpressiveness of men in relationships, and in the domination of 'nature' and of non-European peoples. Recently, however, other groups have also begun to systematically question the premises of Western rationality: especially those of marginalised sexualities (for example, 'gay', 'lesbian', 'transsexual', 'bisexual'), black people, 'Third World' people, and sections of what is a highly diverse environmental movement. Even when critiques do not establish direct links between 'masculinity' and rationality, these links have been often implicit. There has consequently emerged a growing number of deconstructive analyses of the rationality informing thinking and practice in such areas as: law and justice, medicine, biology, psychology, psychoanalysis, technology, caring work, and environmental philosophy, to name but a few. Many deconstructive strategies have been employed: some writers have sought merely to make visible through description that which has been largely invisible, while others strive to develop new perspectives, and a new language and politics, sometimes drawing on or reworking established, 'malestream' traditions of thought (for example feminist psychoanalysis) while at other times developing a radically new theory, language and practice (ecofeminism). These efforts serve to unsettle the dominant logic, variously referred to as the 'logic of identity' or the 'metaphysics of presence', which involves the urge to find the universal single principle, or law, covering the phenomena to be accounted for (Young, I.M., 1990: 98). As many critics have pointed out, this logic has generated a vast number of mutually exclusive oppositions (subject/object, mind/body, culture/nature) which correspond to other dichotomies and hierarchies such as good/bad and pure/impure.

Feminist critiques of rational science

Given science's drive to produce universal, 'total', explanations, it is hardly surprising that scientific institutions, methods and practices have been a target of sustained criticism by feminists and other critical scholars. Many of the insights of the feminist critics of science have informed the arguments of this book, including those of Donna Haraway, Londa Schiebinger, Nelly Oudshoorn, Ruth Bleier, Anne Fausto-Sterling, and Rosi Braidotti. Science has been identified as an important mechanism for legitimating women's exclusion from the public sphere, including scientific practice, by declaring them as unfit for the usage of reason, and as being synonymous with nature, feelings and emotions, and caring for others. As Braidotti et al. explain, 'the very definition of "the scientific mind" is coterminous with rationality, masculinity and power', and it is for this reason that 'feminists have criticized scientific discourse as an account of the world that systematically devalues every category that is "other" than the male, Western, bourgeois self: women, children, other races, foreign cultures, lower classes, handicapped people and nature' (1994: 31). The idea of impartiality that underpins science and notions of justice has been extensively critiqued by feminists such as Donna Haraway and Iris Marion Young on the grounds that it denies the particularities of situation and embodied experience. As Young notes, the ideal of impartiality is an impossibility, a fiction, in that 'no one can adopt a point of view that is completely impersonal and dispassionate, completely separated from any particular context and commitments' (1990: 103). Feminism does not represent a single, homogeneous position, however, and, as in other areas of social analysis and critique, there are a number of competing feminist perspectives on science and scientific rationality.

In what has become something of a classic reference in feminist epistemology, Sandra Harding (1986) has identified three broad feminist theories of knowledge: feminist empiricism; feminist standpoint; and feminist postmodernism. Feminist empiricists believe that it is possible to gain unmediated access to an objective 'truth', but that sexism and androcentrism are identifiable biases of individual knowers. These biases, it is believed, can be eliminated by a more rigorous adherence to scientific method. Feminist standpoint theorists reject the notion of an unmediated truth, and argue that knowledge is always mediated by 'race', class, and gender in particular sociopolitical formations and at certain points in time. However, even they do not reject the notion of truth altogether. Other social positions, such as those specific to women, can overcome ideological bias and attain a valid knowledge free of 'masculinist' bias. Only feminist postmodernists seek to challenge the claim of any perspective on knowledge and access to impartial 'truth'. Knowledge is seen to be 'invented' rather than 'discovered', and to be a product of relations of power, however, this does not deny the importance of the position of the knower. Although postmodernist theory is often criticised for falling into complete relativism, as Braidotti et al. explain, one should not confuse relativism with the stress on the relativity of different positions and corresponding 'truth' claims. At least in principle, postmodern feminists (among whom many of the feminist philosophers of science cited above may be counted) acknowledge the existence of a multiplicity of 'truths' and seek to develop a politics based on respect for differences (Braidotti et al., 1994: 45).

These different feminist perspectives on science, and variations on these perspectives, are all represented in recent critical analyses of the natural sciences and social sciences, including biology, primatology, biomedicine, anthropology, sociology, psychology, psychoanalysis, and political science. None, however, seems able to completely escape the dualistic and essentialist thinking that dominates Western thought. This can be seen in a large variety of analyses, but perhaps most clearly in the reworking and application of psychoanalysis to the study of psychosexual development. Psychoanalysis has been highly influential in many areas of feminist enquiry over the last two decades – implicitly or explicitly informing views on the mind, the body, and the self – as well as in contemporary writing on 'men' and 'masculinity' (see McMahon, 1993), and so this seems a logical place to begin the present discussion. How exactly has psychoanalysis been seen to be useful? How has it been applied? And, how effective has it been as a form of analysis and critique?

In search of the irrational: feminist psychoanalysis

Psychoanalysis is seen by many feminists as offering the potential to overcome the mind/body dualism and 'masculinist' rationality by giving space to the expression of the *irrational*. That is, it is seen to emphasise *embodied* subjectivity, and 'the complex ways in which psychosexuality is bound up with unconscious processes' (Rowley and Grosz, 1990: 176). Its challenge to the cultural correspondence between the biological body and gender identity (biology-as-destiny) resonates with the particular concerns and projects of many contemporary feminists. Unconscious forces are seen to impinge on 'rational' thought and behaviour, perpetually disrupting 'rational reconstructions' of reasons for a choice or belief which may turn out to be nothing but an elaborate rationalisation of an irrational wish or fear. This is not to say that feminists have been uncritical of psychoanalysis. As Rowley and Grosz point out, many psychoanalytic formulations, including Freud's own work, have been seen by feminists to reflect a 'masculinist' bias and to be overly scientistic. Until the early 1970s, most feminists were hostile to Freudian psychoanalysis, which was seen as misogynist, ahistorical, and acultural, and as rationalising and justifying relations of domination and subordination between the sexes (Rowley and Grosz, 1990: 180–3). However, from this time onwards, feminists began to reform, 're-read', and reinterpret psychoanalytic theory as part of the effort to describe and explain the acquisition of sex roles and concomitant psychical attitudes and structures.

Particularly influential in post-Freudian feminist thinking have been the Lacanian and the object-relations psychoanalytic theories. (The influence of these theories on the development of feminist psychoanalytic theory is discussed in detail by Flax, 1990; Henriques et al., 1984: 203–26; and Rowley and Grosz, 1990.) It cannot be said that all problems associated with Freud's work have been satisfactorily resolved by feminist psychoanalysts, even after they have addressed glaring omissions concerning gender. In her detailed critique of psychoanalysis, Jane Flax (1990) has identified a number of enduring gendered dualisms 'pervading virtually all psychoanalytic discourse', beginning with Freud's own work, and including feminist reworkings of Lacanian and object-relations theories. These include the body/mind dualism which is seen to correspond to the female/male dualism, where women are believed to be more determined by and subject to the body and its drives, and the nature/culture dualism, which again corresponds to the female/male dualism, and reflects the gender-based division of labour in Western society whereby women have primary responsibility for care. The cultural dichotomy between the public, 'masculine', realm of production, in which 'instrumental' relations are seen to be the norm, and the private, 'feminine', realm of reproduction, in which 'affective', 'natural' relations prevail, is replicated in both feminist and non-feminist psychoanalytic work (Flax, 1990: 76–88).

The replication of this dichotomy is clearly evident in feminist reworkings of the so-called object-relations psychoanalytic theory. As Flax (1990) explains, feminists, like object-relations theorists, have emphasised the importance of sustained intimate relations with other persons or the repression of such relations in the constitution and ongoing experiences of the self. The self is presented as complexly structured with its own 'inner world' and its own system of internal relations, and as constituted through networks of social relations. Unlike other object-relations theorists, however, feminists have paid attention to the location of people within networks of relations which extend beyond the family, and the structuring of these relations through domination (Flax 1990: 229–30). Thus, the construction of the gendered self, and the perpetuation of gendered relations is seen to be explicable in terms of the dominant child-rearing arrangements, and more specifically women's greater involvement in childcare. This assumption provides the starting point for the work of such influential theorists as Juliet Mitchell, Dorothy Dinnerstein, and Nancy Chodorow – writers who have been closely associated with analyses of mothering, child-rearing, and the acquisition of gender identity. In formulating their arguments and claims and visions of justice, however, these feminists still rely on the notion of an innate or essential property of the self, and on categorical and essentialist distinctions such as 'mind' and 'body', 'self' and 'other', and 'men' and 'women' (Flax, 1990: 230).

Nancy Chodorow, whose book, *The Reproduction of Mothering*, has attained the status of a seminal text on feminist object-relations theory, relies heavily on such essentialist and dualistic distinctions in her work. For example, she assumes that there are gender-specific 'relational capacities', which are seen to be explained by the fact that the mother is the child's primary caretaker, socialiser, and 'inner object', and that the father is a 'secondary object' for boys and girls. As Chodorow explains,

> This process [attachment to the mother] entails a relational complexity in feminine self-definition and personality which is not characteristic of masculine self-definition or personality. Relational capacities that are curtailed in boys as a result of the masculine oedipus complex are sustained in girls . . . Because of their mothering by women, girls come to experience themselves as less separate from boys, as having more permeable ego boundaries. Girls come to define themselves more in relation to others. Their internalized object-relational structure becomes more complex, with more ongoing issues. These personality features are reflected in superego development. (1978: 93)

In this account, there are two basic gender-specific styles of relating: the feminine and the masculine. There is no recognition of a complexly structured, constituted and differentiated self and of the potential for the subject to 'relate' in diverse, non-gender-specific ways. In his book *Men's Silences* (1992), Jonathan Rutherford identifies a number of problems with Chodorow's account which come to light when one attempts to apply her work to an analysis of masculine identity. Included among these are its failure to account for differences between men and the effects of class and 'race' upon the formation of male subjectivities, and its psychological reductionism and 'functionalism' – i.e. the tendency to explain a phenomenon by its apparent use value (1992: 37–40). In his review of the impact of object-relations theory on 'men's studies', Anthony McMahon has pointed to a diverse array of evidence of male nurturance which, he concludes, is 'extremely problematic for Chodorow's position'; for example, data showing that fathers were neither inept nor uninterested in interacting with their children and that 'quite unexceptional men' routinely provide primary care of others (1993: 679). Dimen has also commented that although 'object-relations' theories seek to avoid the notion of an essential self through the avoidance of biological determinism (i.e. instinctively-driven behaviour), they have succeeded merely in displacing the naturalisation of sex with the naturalisation of attachment. When one asks who it is who is doing the relating, what one finds is the pre-social, atomised Western self (Dimen, 1995: 142–3,147).

In the effort to avoid essentialist notions of the self, many feminists have turned to the work of Jacques Lacan for inspiration. Lacan has been seen by many feminists, especially French feminists, as offering the most powerful critique of the notion of the unitary self. His popularity can perhaps be explained in part by the fact that in his own work he continually attacked the orthodoxy of psychoanalysis, and of other theoretical and therapeutic

developments, including object-relations theories, which in his view romanticised 'the myth of missed experience in babyhood' (Henriques et al, 1984:
212). For Lacan, the acquisition of sexual identity is explicable not in terms
of the effect of nature or anatomy, or even attachment, but rather in terms of
the child's entry into language which provides the pre-condition for becoming aware of oneself in respect to social relations and cultural laws. The
resolution of the Oedipus complex, whereby the child resolves problems
associated with desire for the mother or father by identifying with the same-
sex parent, marks the point at which the child becomes a subject according
to the cultural laws, and more specifically the Paternal Law, which preordain
it (Henriques et al., 1984: 215). Lacanian feminists have been critical of
object-relations theorists for their failure to account for the unconscious
and the discontinuities which characterise the psyche *prior* to the formation
of the ego and a separate sense of self. In her summary of this position,
Butler notes that 'by claiming certain kinds of identifications are primary,
"object-relations" theorists make the relational life of the infant primary to
psychic development itself, conflating the psyche with the ego and relegating
the unconscious to a less significant role' (1990b: 328). However, Lacanian
theories, like object-relations theories, can be criticised for instituting a concept of gender coherence in their narrative of infantile development. The use
of the categories 'men' and 'women' and '*the* boy' and '*the* girl' obscures differences based on class, colour, age, ethnicity, and so on. Furthermore,
although the unconscious is seen as a locus of subversion, it is unclear how
far the workings of the unconscious can be understood through rules of
language, and what changes the unconscious can provide given the rigidity of
the structuralist frame (Butler, 1990b: 329; Henriques et al., 1984: 217).
Lacan's theory is, arguably, no less deterministic than Freud's. He relies on a
universalist analysis (specifically the work of Lévi Strauss) whereby the terms
of the debate are already fixed around the Law of the Father (Henriques et
al., 1984: 216). The immutability of the rules that constitute and regulate sexual identity raises questions as to the usefulness of the Lacanian theory for
social and cultural transformation. Both forms of psychoanalytic discourse,
in fact, can be seen to employ essentialist narrative strategies in that gender
meanings are circumscribed within a story that both unifies certain legitimate sexual subjects and excludes others. Both are Utopian in that it is
assumed that there is an original sexuality without power, which is then cor-
rupted by the arrival of power which creates a culturally relevant sexual
distinction (gender) as well as gender hierarchy and dominance (Butler,
1990b: 330).

   Many feminist psychoanalysts, it would appear, remain committed to
Freud's vision of creating a science. They seem not to recognise the political
implications of their adherence to the universalising, objectifying gaze of
psychoanalytic discourse. Psychoanalysis is seen to offer an account of patriarchal culture as a trans-historical and cross-cultural force. That is, it
conforms to the feminist demand to provide a theory that can explain
women's subordination across specific cultures and different historical

periods (Butler, 1990b: 326). Herein lies the source of much of the difficulty with the use of the psychoanalytic model for the acquisition of gender identification: the failure to take account of itself as a narrative. As Butler argues, psychoanalysis reproduces the coherence in the story-line about infantile development when it ought to be investigating the historical formation of those exclusionary practices that shape that particular narrative of identity formation (1990b: 332). Feminist psychoanalysts seem inattentive to the insights offered by the growing number of critiques of psychoanalysis and its power/knowledge relations, which draw on Michel Foucault's work and that of other postmodern and poststructuralist thinkers (for example, Foucault, 1980; Donzelot, 1980; Rose, 1989; Domenici and Lesser, 1995). Such work emphasises the fact that psychoanalytic knowledge is not only historically and culturally specific, but that it has prescriptive, 'normative' power, producing particular sites for intervention and regulation – for example, the establishment of sexual norms (Henriques et al., 1984: 206). Gay and lesbian theorists have recently joined other theorists in exposing the ways in which psychoanalysis's claims to objectivity have masked its role in the regulation of subjects, particularly through the medicalisation of homosexuality (Domenici and Lesser, 1995). One of the enduring limitations of psychoanalysis, from the gay and lesbian perspective, is its failure to distinguish between gender and sexuality, which tend to be 'conflated and reduced to the gender of our "object choice"' (Jackson, 1996: 27). As Jackson notes, while psychoanalysis calls normative heterosexuality into question by insisting that it is not innate, heterosexuality is nevertheless reinstated as the norm through the linkage between gender and desire (1996: 27). It is not clear that attempts to combine the perspectives of psychoanalysis and poststructuralist feminism, such as in the work of Henriques et al. (1984), overcome the objections to psychoanalysis that have thus far been raised. The psychoanalytic belief in science and the drive to posit a total theory of the acquisition of *gender* identity (i.e. *a* feminist viewpoint) that is not only different from, but more 'true' than, the previous 'masculinist' ones, rests upon many assumptions uncritically appropriated from Enlightenment thinking (Flax, 1990: 227).

Gender and morality

The critique of 'masculinist' reason, and of the separation of mind and body, has been articulated with particular force in discussions about the relationship between gender and morality. As part of their effort to dislodge 'masculinist' notions of morality based on abstract rules, as embedded in the legal justice system and social convention, many feminists have proposed alternative or complementary, women-specific notions of morality based on relationships and care. Reflecting the profound influence of the psychoanalytic imagination on Western thought, a common starting point for many such analyses is the assumption that the distinction between men's and women's subjectivities is founded on fundamental differences in early experiences of intimate relations. This assumption has arguably been the source of many tensions within feminist theorising on gender and morality. On the one hand, feminists seek to expose the 'detached', 'uncaring' dimension of 'masculinist' rationality by establishing a contrast with the 'feminine' virtues of 'relationship' and 'care'. This tends to involve a reversal of what is posited as the existing hierarchy of gender-specific moral values, so that women are seen to have the superior moral voice. However, in emphasising the association of 'femininity' with care and relationships, feminists can be seen to reinforce a kind of naturalisation of female attachment and empathy whereby women are seen as naturally more suited to care and to be concerned with the needs of others. These and other tensions are evident in the work of a number of different strands of feminist thought, including ecofeminism, which is discussed later. However, they are perhaps nowhere more evident than in the work of Carol Gilligan, whose ideas have had a profound influence on thinking about gender and moral development in the 1980s and 1990s. Because Gilligan's ideas have been so highly influential and her assumptions implicitly or explicitly inform the work of many other feminist theorists, her arguments are worth examining in some detail.

A different voice?

In her book, *In a Different Voice*, published in 1982, Gilligan articulates a response to what she identifies as the 'masculinist' bias in theorising about moral development, whereby women have been consistently defined as deficient. Gilligan takes particular issue with the work of male theorists such as Sigmund Freud, Jean Piaget, and Lawrence Kohlberg who, she claims, employ an interpretive framework of moral development which assumes that maturity in moral development is marked by the formation of a separate self. This conception of maturity is derived from the study of men's lives, and reflects the importance of individualisation in their lives. Those very traits that have been traditionally defined as the 'goodness' of women, such as their care and sensitivity to the needs of others, she claims, are those which mark them out as deficient in the theory of moral development. Drawing on Chodorow's object-relations theory, above, Gilligan seeks to emphasise the importance of early relationships in the formation of the self. Female identity formation takes place in a context of ongoing relationship with the mother, Gilligan argues, whereas male identity formation involves early separation from the mother and the consequent development of firmer ego boundaries. This results in different, gender-specific, constructions of moral development, with women tending to develop a conception of morality around the understanding of responsibility and relationships, and men developing a conception of morality based upon notions of rights and rules. Because girls mature in a world dominated by the morality of men, they find it difficult to 'listen' to their own 'voice', with the result that there is a 'disconnection between mind and body, thoughts and feelings, and the use of one's voice to cover rather than to convey one's inner world, so that relationships no longer provide channels for exploring the connections between one's inner life and the world of others' (1993: xxi). The psychological exclusion of girls from the public world at the time of adolescence sets the stage for both 'a kind of privatization of women's experience' and the underdevelopment of 'women's political voice and presence in the public world' (1993: xxii).

In the introduction to her book, Gilligan points out that the 'different voice' that she describes is characterised not by gender but by theme – that there is an interplay of voices within each 'sex' – and that contrasts between male and female voices are used 'to highlight a distinction between *two modes of thought* and to focus a problem of interpretation rather than to represent a generalization about either sex' (1982: 2). This seems to be an attempt by Gilligan to forestall any charge that she is developing a reductionist account of the gender–morality relation. In her subsequent discussion, however, she paints a gender-specific and -exclusive picture of moral development, with little acknowledgement of the complexities and ambiguities of gender constructions and of the mediations of other, non-gendered identities. In her descriptions, it is exclusively women who speak in the different voice (Hekman, 1995: 8). That Gilligan assumes to a gender-specific rationality and 'way of knowing' is evident, for example, in her 'Letter to readers, 1993' in a reprint of her book, when she states that

> The differences between women and men which I describe center on a tendency for women and men to make different relational errors – for men to think that if they know themselves, following Socrates' dictum, they will also know women, and for women to think that if only they know others, they will come to know themselves. Thus men and women tacitly collude in not voicing women's experiences and build relationships around a silence that is maintained by men's not knowing their disconnection from women and women's not knowing their dissociation from themselves. Much talk about relationships and about love carefully conceals these truths. (1993: xx)

Although Gilligan argues that 'no claims are made about the origins of the differences described or their distribution in a wider population, across cultures, or through time' (1982: 2), her data, which are based on interviews with college students in the United States, are used to develop a general theory. There is no reference to how the *particular* experiences she describes are mediated by culture and history and by different subject positions. Her primary focus is on the dualistic orderings of gender. It is apparent from the preamble of her book that one of her aims has been to address what she sees as a lacuna in the psychological literature on the relationship between *gender* and moral development. For example, in her introduction, she states that 'My goal is to expand the understanding of human development by using the group left out in the construction of theory to call attention to what is missing in its account', and that 'the discrepant data on women's experience [will] provide a basis upon which to generate new theory, potentially yielding a more encompassing view of the lives of both of the sexes' (1982: 4). She does not concern herself with the *multiple* exclusions associated with the dominant 'masculinist' morality – i.e. those that include, but are not limited to, gender.

This point should be kept in mind when assessing the significance of Gilligan's work.

As Susan Hekman (1995) argues, in her recent and extensive review of Gilligan's contribution to feminist moral theory, assessments of the significance of *In a Different Voice* have varied widely among feminists. While some writers praise Gilligan for 'ushering in a new era of feminist thought', others are less complimentary, condemning her for 'subverting the gains made by previous feminists' (Hekman, 1995: 21). This lack of unanimity of assessment of Gilligan's work can perhaps be explained in part by the fact that there are many ambiguities in her arguments, including those pertaining to science, which make her especially liable to be 'read' in very different ways. Her stated aim to provide a 'more encompassing view of the lives of both of the sexes', noted above, and to find 'the truth of women's experience' (1982: 62) and thus of human experience (1982: 63), can be seen to reflect a commitment to empiricist methodology (Hekman, 1995: 4). Gilligan's uncritical appropriation of object-relations psychoanalytic theory, whose premises were unpacked earlier, can be seen to involve the appropriation of a conventional, modernist view of self and social relations. This view of self is clearly revealed in her comment (again, in her 'Letter to readers, 1993') that womanhood requires 'a dissociative split between experience and what is generally taken to be reality' (1993: xxi), which suggests that there is a 'real' 'inner self' or 'core self' which can be distinguished from a socially constructed 'outer self'. Reference to a split self appears at various points in her discussion.

In defence of Gilligan, Hekman argues that it is possible to make a more critical, reflexive 'reading' of Gilligan's work which, she says, 'departs significantly from the methodological assumptions that inform the work of the theorists she examines and that her concepts of "truth" and "method" differ significantly from theirs' (1995: 4). For example, she observes that Gilligan acknowledges recent developments in the social sciences that call into question the 'presumed neutrality of science' and that 'the categories of knowledge are human constructions' (1982: 6, citing Hekman, 1995: 4). Hekman argues that in her more recent work, Gilligan has moved away from the attempt to define the universal parameters of morality, evident in *In a Different Voice*, and towards the acknowledgement of a more complex relationship between gender and moral voice. Although she continues to identify gender as a significant factor in the expression of moral voice, Gilligan now asserts that 'differences cannot be reduced to questions of gender' (Gilligan et al., 1988: 54, citing Hekman, 1995: 10). Hekman argues that in her book with Lyn Brown, *Meeting at the Crossroads*, Gilligan emphasises the particular, and the complexity of moral voices (Hekman, 1995: 10). This other 'reading' of Gilligan's work is the one preferred by Hekman, who suggests that what Gilligan is proposing 'is a different interpretation of the same moral experiences' (1995: 7). As Hekman explains, Gilligan cannot *add* the different voice to the theory, since her definition of morality and the moral subject (as constructed through relationship) is incompatible with conventional moral theory (1995: 9). That is, unlike the male theorists whom she critiques, Gilligan is not claiming to discover the 'truth' about moral development, but rather to 'interpret women's stories as genuinely moral narratives, distinct from, but every bit as moral as, those based on abstract principles' (1995: 7). Such a 'reading', Hekman argues, allows one to acknowledge 'the range of factors, including but not limited to gender, that constitutes these voices' (1995: 10).

I believe this is a rather generous 'reading' of Gilligan, that fails to recognise fundamental problems inherent in her argument and methodology. In the 1993 Preface of the reprint of *In a Different Voice*, Gilligan seeks to clarify what she claims is a misunderstanding of her arguments:

> When I hear my work being cast in terms of whether women and men are really (essentially) different or who is better than whom, I know that I have lost my voice, because these are not my questions. Instead, my questions are about our perceptions of reality and truth: how we know, how we hear, how we see, how we speak. My questions are about voice and relationship. And my questions are about psychological processes and theory, particularly theories in which men's experience stands for all of human experience – theories which eclipse the lives of women and shut out women's voices. I saw that by maintaining these ways of seeing and speaking about human lives, men were leaving out women, but women were leaving out themselves. In terms of psychological processes, what for men was a process of separation, for women was a process of dissociation that required the creation of an inner division or psychic split. (1993: xiii)

Despite Gilligan's protestations about being cast as an essentialist, her comments reveal her adherence to essentialist and dualistic categories, and her belief in the possibility of an 'unbiased' science. She makes no attempt to repudiate the arguments outlined in her 1982 book. In fact, Gilligan takes the opportunity in her Preface to confirm the validity of her approach, emphasising that it is 'grounded in listening' and more specifically in 'listening' to the 'voice' of women which is lost in relationship (1993: xv–xxvi). 'A new psychological theory in which girls and women are seen and heard', she argues, is 'an inevitable challenge to a patriarchal order that can remain in place only through the continuing eclipse of women's experience' (1993: xxiv). Her repeated references to 'voice', to which she refers as 'something like what people mean when they speak of the core of the self' (1993: xvi), and to 'women's experience', reflect her view of an essential self. Her assumption that there is a stable, core 'experience' that is shared by women – and is quite distinct from that of men – is evident in the repeated use of phrases such as 'divisions that are familiar to many women' (1993: xxi), 'the conventional feminine voice' (1982: 79), and 'the truth of the women's perspective' (1982: 98). The further assumption that 'women's experience' can be 'discovered' through 'listening' to women shows that she subscribes to the positivist scientific belief that there is indeed an authentic, 'true' knowledge of the self that can be 'discovered' given the appropriate scientific method. It is significant in this regard that Gilligan employs the conventional empiricist strategy of interviewing 'women' in order to 'hear' their 'voices', which she seems to assume is unmediated by relations of power and knowledge. Although Gilligan claims to be critical of the scientific method that underlies 'masculinist' psychological theories of moral development, she does not extend her critique to the methodology upon which her own work relies. She seems not to recognise how her own narrative reinstates the very dualistic distinctions which she claims to critique.

Ecofeminism and the feminine ethic of care

A number of the criticisms that I have raised about feminist psychoanalysis and about Gilligan's work, particularly the inclination towards essentialist thinking, can be seen to apply also to many, if not most, ecofeminist analyses. From the ecofeminist viewpoint, the dualism between humans and nature, reason and emotion, mind and body, etc., is an important source of the domination of both 'nature' and women by men. Although ecofeminism encompasses a highly diverse array of perspectives, 'a basic assumption common to all ecofeminist positions is the rejection of the assumed inferiority of women and nature and of the superiority of reason, humanity and culture' (Plumwood, 1992: 13, cited in Murphy, 1994: 87). As part of their effort to break with dualistic thinking, ecofeminists have proposed a new, 'holistic', worldview and a new ethics of care based upon the revaluing of traditionally feminine characteristics and activities. As Mies and Shiva explain,

> An ecofeminist perspective propounds the need for a new cosmology and a new anthropology which recognises that life in nature (which includes human beings) is maintained by means of co-operation, and mutual care and love. Only in this way can we be enabled to respect and preserve the diversity of all life forms, including their cultural expressions, as true sources of all well-being and happiness. To this end ecofeminists use metaphors like 'reweaving the world', 'healing the wounds', and re-connecting and interconnecting the 'web'. This effort to create a holistic, all-life embracing cosmology and anthropology, must necessarily imply a concept of freedom different from that used since the Enlightenment. (1993:6)

This new 'holistic' worldview, with its emphasis on 'connection', 'healing', 'care', and 'love' is seen to embody values and practices that are distinctly *feminine*. Ecofeminists use the metaphors of 'weaving' and 'quilt-making' – activities that are coded 'feminine' in many societies – to characterise their process of theory-building and to distinguish it from the more conventional, 'masculinist', view of theory-building which is seen to employ abstract, ahistorical terms that apply to all individuals irrespective of their position within the dominant–subordinate structures (Warren, 1994: 180–1). A key assumption held by many ecofeminists is that women are 'closer' to the biological and natural processes of child-bearing and birth and therefore embody the relational capacities required to sustain 'nature'. That ecofeminists seek to revalue the feminine should not be taken to imply that they necessarily espouse a separatist, 'anti-male' philosophy. Rather, the ecofeminist vision is for a world which is more 'feminised', which means a feminine stress on relationships and care (Martell, 1994: 155–6). Furthermore, ecofeminists are not necessarily saying that feminine values are *biologically* inherent to women, and therefore immutable. In fact, the argument that femininity needs to be generalised throughout society suggests that they do not assume that feminine values are fixed and exclusive of one biological sex. It is considered, however, that women's special experience of child-bearing makes them 'closer' to natural and biological processes of reproduction (Martell, 1994: 155).

Many ecofeminist arguments, however, ultimately rest upon determinist and essentialist premises. This is most clearly the case in relation to the assumption that 'women are closer to nature'. Even if one accepts that 'nature' has a universal and relatively stable essence – a highly dubious assumption, as I will argue below – the argument that because 'women' bear children they are somehow 'closer' to 'nature' clearly involves biological determinism and essentialism. Men may not bear children, but even according to ecofeminist 'holism', they are still 'part of nature' and live within the materiality of their bodies. As Murphy notes in his critique of ecofeminism, men, like women, proceed through the lifecycle of birth, growth, puberty, ageing, and eventually death, and their bodies depend upon the same 'natural' elements of clean air, unpolluted water, sunlight, and so on (1994: 89). It is true that male and female bodies are differently constituted in discourse, with the consequence that the lived experiences of men and women will tend to differ in certain key respects. However, to conclude that because men and women have different reproductive experiences they will have a different understanding of, or empathy with, 'nature' involves not only the confusing of individual and societal levels of explanation but gross generalisation and determinism. Those writers who argue that 'women are closer to nature' show a lack of appreciation of the historical connections between constructions of gender, 'race' and sexuality, on the one hand, and constructions of 'nature', on the other. Historically, women, like many non-Europeans and homosexuals, have been marked as closer to 'nature', or as more 'primitive' than men (and Europeans, and heterosexuals), and this assumption still prevails today (see, for example, Mies, 1993: 150–2). This connection has been used to subordinate all that is 'other', that is, that which falls outside the normative standard of white, European, heterosexual 'masculinity'. Some groups, such as gay males, have been seen as perversions of 'nature', and have been persecuted for 'crimes against nature' (see Chapter 3). Ecofeminists who argue that 'women are closer to nature' tend to overlook the fact that many women cannot, or choose not to, have children. How do they figure within this particular ecofeminist schema? Are they, like men 'remote' from 'nature'?

A number of ecofeminists, including Karen Warren and Val Plumwood, reject those versions of ecofeminism which propose that 'women are closer to nature' than men on the grounds that they involve biological determinism. Warren argues that the problem with biological determinism is that it presupposes the very nature–culture dichotomy that ecofeminist philosophers seek to challenge. Plumwood notes that such accounts fail to explain how dichotomies are constructed and naively believe that valuing 'nature' over 'rationality' while retaining dichotomies is an effective strategy for change (Buege, 1994: 51). They rely upon the assumption that 'nature' is separate and distinct from 'culture', an assumption that is seen as central to 'patriarchal domination'. These critics point out that biological determinist accounts need to be distinguished from other ecofeminist work which questions the very basis for the nature–culture dichotomy. Many ecofeminist accounts of the women–nature connection, however, are not so much proposing biological determinism as *social determinism*. That is, 'feminine nature' is seen to be shaped by socialisation which constructs 'women' and 'nature' as 'other' within the patriarchal social order. This socialisation argument is, nevertheless, essentialist in that it still presupposes the existence of some universal concept of nature that attaches to a certain group of beings. Socialisation arguments rely upon a notion of the pre-social individual who, in many accounts, rapidly reduces to the biological (Henriques et al., 1984: 20–1). Ecofeminism's focus on 'feminising' society implies a resocialisation strategy, and suggests the existence of gender-specific attributes that are unvarying across time and place. This downplays the complexity and cultural variability of gender ascriptions, and the many possible ways in which subjects may engage with prevailing constructions of gender. As I argued in Chapter 2, the resocialisation strategy of feminism is built upon an implicitly rationalist view in that it posits the body as neutral and passive with regard to the formation of consciousness, and denies the social and historical specificity of the network of relations obtaining between the female body and 'femininity' and the male body and 'masculinity'. The relationship between gender ascriptions and actual practices is complex, with men and women each exhibiting a variety of traits and sharing attributes that are generally associated with the other gender, with some men being more caring and some women being less caring than cultural norms might suggest (Murphy, 1994: 89). It is important to recognise that the linking of 'femininity' and 'nature' is a historical and cultural construction that has been employed extensively to justify the subordination of *many* different groups. The strategy of valorising those activities and traits defined as 'feminine' – nurturing, care, empathy, etc., – serves to reverse the dualistic ordering of masculine/feminine activities and traits while leaving unquestioned and intact those relations of power and knowledge that have created that ordering in the first place.

Ecofeminists' appeal to the abstract, feminised concepts of 'connection', 'healing', 'care' and 'love' and to unity reflects an idealised and romanticised vision of social relations, and can be used to conceal fundamental differences of viewpoint and to dispose of minority dissent. Terms such as these have superficial attraction, but what do they mean in practice? Peta Bowden (1995) has warned of the dangers of an uncritical appropriation of 'the ethic of care' in her discussion of the ethics of nursing care. As she observes, there has been a tendency to posit this ethic as a universal principle that expresses a unitary and generalisable ideal distinct from more conventional, 'rationalist' constructions involving reference to general rules and concepts. Such a tendency works against the radical potential of the ethic of care which resides in the acknowledgement of the complex, diverse, ambiguous and *context-specific* nature of ethical understanding (Bowden, 1995: 11). Some scholars attempt to quell the charge that ecofeminists claim to speak with 'one voice' by referring to ecofeminists' concern with 'diversity' and 'difference'. Thus, it is claimed that ecofeminism is formed by a 'collage' of different viewpoints that reflect the diverse experiences of particular women in their particular circumstances (Buege, 1994: 53). The naive belief in 'global sisterhood' has been replaced with 'strength in diversity', and many writers advocate a politics of coalition requiring as its pre-condition the acceptance and valuing of 'differences' among women (Braidotti et al., 1994: 55–8). However, this position is also naive in that it assumes that a united political movement can be forged on the basis of highly diverse, and often diametrically opposed, feminist and ecopolitical positions. Despite their claims for tolerance of 'difference' and 'diversity', ecofeminists often simply assume, rather than demonstrate, that women have shared interests and experiences that unite them and divide them from men. Like many other feminists, they invoke the concept of 'patriarchy' as a universal and trans-historical phenomenon. Patriarchy is assumed to exist in all cultures and in most, if not all, historical periods, while little or no attempt is made to explore the limits of the concept in different situations and its relationship to other forms of oppression and domination. A question that needs to be asked is how useful is the concept of patriarchy for those seeking to develop historically and culturally grounded analyses of the gender–nature relation? Like theorists of the gender–technology relation, ecofeminist writers often move between different terms such as 'men', and 'males', 'patriarchy' and 'masculinity', often conflating these categories and overlooking their diverse meanings rather than seeking to explicate their specific meanings and relations (Gill and Grint, 1995: 12, 14).

The source of many problems in ecofeminist writings is the tendency to posit 'nature' as an unproblematic, fixed, and separate unity, rather than as a site for culturally constructed and contested meanings. Writers often adhere to a modernist, romanticised concept of 'nature' that is seen to exist independently of 'humanity', as is evident in references to 'nature's' original unspoilt, pristine beauty (Mies, 1993: 152–6). They fail to critically examine the particular ways in which the humanity/nature dualism has been drawn in modernist discourses of nature. This dualism connects with other dualisms such as the mind/body, subject/object, and heterosexual/homosexual dualisms. Although most ecofeminists acknowledge that the modern industrial period has brought about a change in the conception of nature – from an 'ensouled' organism to inorganic matter to be mastered – discussion often implicitly assumes a prior and fixed distinction between 'humans' and 'nature'. Our ideas of 'nature', however, as Kate Soper reminds us, reflect 'changing conceptions as to who qualifies, and why, for full membership of the human community' and, as such, are inherently political (1995: 73). As mentioned, different groups at different times have been associated with functions and attributes that place them nearer to 'nature' and render them less than human. What is considered proper to humanity is defined in relation to a number of excluded dimensions – for example, the primitive, the animal, the corporeal and the feminine, among others. However, as Soper argues, although 'humanity' has tended to define itself in opposition to these relegated 'others', it never quite manages to confine them to their supposedly

natural realm (1995: 74). The politics of 'nature' became increasingly trans-
parent with the onset of AIDS, when assumptions about the 'unnaturalness'
and 'unhealthiness' of same-sex behaviour, particularly among men, was used
to construct boundaries between heterosexual selves and 'deviant' 'homosexuals', and led to controls over this 'at risk' group (see Chapter 5). However,
'nature' has long been used for policing sexual practices and bodily behaviours and for condemning 'deviants' and 'perverts' who fail to conform to the
sexual or social norms of their culture (Soper, 1995: 32, 140–1). Clearly,
ecofeminists who uncritically use the concept of 'nature' run the risk of
unwittingly reinforcing sexism, heterosexism, racism, and an instrumentalist
view towards non-human forms of life.

In examining the politics of the idea of 'nature', it is useful to adopt a distinction, drawn by Soper (1995), between 'nature-endorsing' and
'nature-sceptical' positions. In the former case, '"nature" is appealed to in val-
idation of that which we would either seek to preserve or seek to instigate in
place of existing actuality'; in the latter, the focus is on the 'oppressive use of
the idea to legitimate social and sexual hierarchies and cultural norms'
(Soper, 1995: 3, 34). These are by no means mutually exclusive political positions, and there is in actuality much overlap and blurring between the two.
However, in their appeals to 'feminising' society many ecofeminists are
inclined towards the 'nature-endorsing' end of this spectrum. That is, 'nature'
is seen to need 'protection' from the rampant exploitation of 'masculinist'
rationality. It is further assumed that because only 'women' have not become
disconnected from 'nature' it is their historic role to lead society to the
promised ecosystem (Murphy, 1994: 89). This involves a form of van-
guardism, not unlike that practised by socialists in Marxism. Assuming that
women are the special custodians of 'nature' because of their closeness to it
not only absolves men from any responsibility towards 'nature', but also
effectively denies the validity of the many other ecopolitical positions that
have emerged over recent decades in the context of global concerns about
'ecocrisis', resource depletion, and the loss of biodiversity (Petersen and
Lupton, 1996: 139–44). References to images of ecofeminist harmonisation
serve to obscure the divisions and ambiguities of position within and across
feminist and ecological camps, and the potentially reactionary aspects of
ecological naturalism (Soper, 1995: 124). (For a recent overview of feminist
debates about the relationship between women and 'nature', see Braidotti et
al., 1994: 59–76.)

Uncovering the male emotions

The cultural links between 'masculinity' and rationality, and 'femininity' and
emotionality have been seen by many recent writers to have an empirical
manifestation in the emotional lives of men and women. 'Men' are typically
seen as emotionally inexpressive, 'selfish', and 'calculating', while 'women'
are seen as emotionally expressive, 'selfless', and intuitive. This discourse on

gender and the emotions connects with a number of other contemporary gender discourses, such as those discussed above, which posit 'women' as more 'caring' or more 'in touch with their feelings'. In the 1980s and 1990s, there has been a growing number of writings – undertaken mainly by men who identify themselves as 'pro-feminist' – examining the implications of the 'masculinity'–rationality connection for the emotional lives of men, and calling upon men to uncover their 'true feelings'. The emotional life of men has come to occupy centre stage in contemporary sexual politics. It is widely believed that by paying greater attention to their emotions, and by talking 'openly and honestly' about their relationships, men can change both themselves and society.

The notion that there are gender-specific temperaments, or emotional realms, is not an entirely new idea. It has earlier antecedents in theories of the eighteenth and nineteenth centuries that postulated that women were guided by feelings and men by the intellect. However, recent thinking has been profoundly shaped by developments ushered in by Darwinism. The advent of Darwinism in the late nineteenth century heralded the beginnings of a psychology of sex differences (Russett, 1989: 18–19, 40–4) that laid the groundwork for detailed enquiries into the specificities of the male and female emotions. Psychology and psychoanalysis have helped shape the construction of the male subject as alienated – alienated from his body, his 'true feelings', and his significant others. This alienated male subject appears in the work of many contemporary male writers on men and 'masculinity', but perhaps most clearly in that of Victor Seidler, who has contributed a great deal to recent discussions on men and rationality, in articles (see, for example, Seidler, 1987, 1988, 1995) and books such as *Rediscovering Masculinity* (1989) and *Unreasonable Men* (1994). His work therefore deserves close and critical attention.

Seidler sees the connection between 'masculinity' and rationality as providing not only the basis of heterosexual male privilege, but as being the source of difficulty in the lives of *individual* men. As Seidler argues,

> the very identification of masculinity with reason has tended to blind men to their masculinity as something that has been socially and historically sustained. We are so used to identifying our interests with the universal interests of others that we have often blinded ourselves to the tensions and contradictions in our experience . . . we end up speaking for others before we have really learnt to speak for ourselves. This has become part of the contemporary crisis of masculinity, as the very masculinist conceptions of science, progress, medicine and psychology made in the image of the Enlightenment identification of reason, morality and masculinity are being challenged both in theory and practice. (1989: 17)

In his references to the identification of self-interest with the universal interest of others and to men being 'blinded' to the conditions shaping their experience, Seidler seems to be suggesting a version of the so-called dominant ideology thesis. Like the worker in Marxist theory, the male subject is alienated from himself and from others by historical and social conditions not of his own making. But in place of exploited labour power, we find repressed emotion. As Seidler points out elsewhere in his book, the identification of 'masculinity' with reason has meant that men have found it difficult to share their individual feelings and emotions, and that they have learnt to become dependent on women to interpret their needs, desires, and feelings for them. Seidler argues that men's dependence on women means that they are able to have their emotional needs met without really having to show their vulnerability. Unfortunately, this has meant that men have not developed an 'emotional language' in which to articulate their feelings 'without feeling immediately exposed and vulnerable'. The identification of 'masculinity' with reason means that men believe that there is always something they can do to better and rectify a relationship. As Seidler puts it, men are 'control freaks'. They assert their 'masculinities' and define their sense of identity by controlling themselves as well as controlling the world around them, a process assisted by their instrumental use of language. Feminist demands to have their own values recognised in the institutions of society, and for more equal relationships, has forced men to realise the pain that their insensitivity and power have created. This has created something of a 'crisis' for men who had never learnt to express their feelings outside their relationships with women. Men have sought redemption through constant activity, and fear giving more time and space to themselves. Consequently, they have little ongoing relationship with their somatic processes. The body is used as an instrument to serve ends, rather than to be 'listened to' (Seidler, 1989: 61–5).

The idea that men have an instrumental relationship with their bodies is a common theme in much recent writing by men about 'masculinity', and reflects the view that the mind/body dualism of Western thought has its correlate in the psyches of individual men. The Cartesian tradition, in which bodies are part of a separate 'nature' and hence separate from selves, is seen to provide the basis for a mind/body split within men whereby the body is seen to be a threat to masculine identity and therefore in need of control by the mind. Part of 'learning to be a man', and proving one's 'manliness', is learning to suppress emotions and desires that do not fit with the ideal of rational detachment (1994: 13–22). As Seidler comments in a recent article:

> Learning to think of the body within dominant white masculinities in mechanistic terms as something that needs to be trained and disciplined, men are often left with little inner connection to their bodies. We often give up whatever authority we might have in relation to our bodies, accepting that our bodies have little connection with our identities as rational selves. We learn that the body has to be subordinated to the mind and that we have to exert a rigorous control in relation to it. This helps to shape not only the ways we learn to think of ourselves as men but the relationship we can have to different aspects of our experience. The body as part of a disenchanted nature has no voice of its own. If it has desires of its own they have to be 'animal' and have to be externally regulated and controlled. There is no sense of the possibilities of developing a dialogue with different parts of our bodies, for instance giving the pain in our lower back some kind of voice of its own. (1995: 173)

An essentialist view of identity and of the emotions is clearly evident in this passage. Seidler's discussion of the disconnection of mind from body suggests the existence of a pre-social, fixed subject and self, on the one hand, and a stable domain of bodily 'desires' and 'feelings', on the other. In his *Unreasonable Men*, he refers to the need for men to learn to 'take greater responsibility for their emotional lives, rather than leaving it to their partners to interpret their emotions and feelings for them' (Seidler, 1994: 41). This is based on the premise that there is a stable, gender-specific, emotional realm, unmediated by history, culture, and the specificities of situation, and that the self operates as a fully autonomous, rational ego. Essentialist thinking is apparent in his discussion of men's relationship to the 'softer' emotions 'like sadness, tenderness, fear' which, he argues, 'are often displaced into anger because this can be seen as affirming rather than threatening our masculine identity' (1994: 41–2). Seidler's suggestion that men are alienated from the 'softer emotions' because they have learned to displace their emotions from an early age, and hence 'never learn to discern and name the other emotions and feelings', implies that there is a fixed realm of the 'emotions' waiting to be 'discovered'. And, his argument that men need to 'take greater responsibility for their emotional lives' reflects a cognitivist and rationalist view of the self.

Seidler's analysis of men's disconnection from their bodies presupposes the existence of a natural realm outside relations of power and knowledge. By failing to recognise the different constructions of bodies and body–'nature' connections, and the complex and varied social relations and self relations that result, Seidler unwittingly reinforces the very dualistic distinction between 'mind' and 'body' that he sets out to critique. In his 1995 article, above, he argues that 'the dualities between what is 'natural' and what is "constructed" are asserted too readily before we have fully understood what is at issue' (1995: 170). However, Seidler himself seems not to recognise the extent to which assumed dualistic distinctions inform his own argument. Given Seidler's acknowledgement of the existence of multiple 'masculinities', and of the regulatory power of the dominant heterosexual masculinity, in his own work he is surprisingly quiet about the regulations and exclusions that have applied historically to non-dominant groups of men, such as 'homosexuals'. As mentioned earlier, the view that homosexuality is a perversion of 'nature', and that homosexuals have committed crimes against 'nature', has a long history in the modern West. Seidler generalises from his own particular experience, while paying inadequate attention to the specificities of different male bodies and their different culturally established connections with 'nature'. His emphasis on 'consciousness-raising' among men, and various forms of work on the self ('self-care', the striving for 'intimacy', making oneself 'vulnerable', etc.) is characteristic of discussions among many contemporary scholars and activists in Western societies, and reflects a rationalistic emphasis on changing psyches. The confessional style of writing adopted by Seidler in the above excerpts reveals his indebtedness to the psychoanalytic approach, and is also typical of that found in a growing number of books and articles about men and 'masculinity' published in the 1990s (see, for example, Biddulph, 1995; Cohen, 1990; Jackson, 1992; Keen, 1992). (See Chapter 1.) The constant references to 'we' and 'our' reflects an assumed commonality of experience and viewpoint among men, uncomplicated by time, place, social location, and so on. This assumption is evident in his particular use of the term 'the body', which implies there is a fixed, generic male body which is unmarked by 'race', ethnicity, sexuality, age, physical ability, and so on.

The implicit heterosexism, essentialism, and rationalism evident in Seidler's approach can be seen in many recent articles written by men on male emotionality, appearing in such magazines as the British magazine, *Achilles Heel*, and the Australian magazine, *XY*. These two magazines espouse the belief in the link between reflection on personal identity and personal and social change, and claim to be 'pro-feminist' and 'gay affirmative'. Given their philosophy, one would expect that they would be a source for critical commentary on 'masculinist' rationality and the mind/body dualism. However, they tend to focus narrowly on experiences of emotional trauma, on personal identity, and on the personal search for 'new models of masculinity'. Articles are written predominantly by the respective editorial groups, readers, members of men's groups, and academics with a specialist interest in men and 'masculinity', and reflect the particular concerns of this group (for example, work, sport, fatherhood, father–son relationships, heterosexual relations). Topics discussed in the 1990s include:

- the expression or control of male emotions in general: for example, the expression of anger, the 'repression of rage', problems with intimacy; fear of failure, loneliness, vulnerability, rejection, etc. (see *XY*, Summer 1995/96; *Achilles Heel*, Winter/Spring 1997; *Achilles Heel*, Winter 1995/96).
- the emotional and other costs of competitive endeavours such as sport and work: for example, physical and emotional pain, reinforcement of aggression (see *XY*, Spring 1995; *Achilles Heel*, Spring/Summer 1996).
- feelings about fatherhood: for example, as a 'male crisis', concerns about responsibilities, the experiences of being a separated father (see *Achilles Heel*, April 1990, Autumn, 1994).
- feelings, including sexual feelings, towards women: for example, abuse, fear and hate of women; concerns about accountability to women (see *Achilles Heel*, Winter 1993/94, Summer 1995).
- feelings about their own health problems, including the implications of 'emotional silence': for example, depression (see *Achilles Heel*, Summer 1991).

In seeking to relate their 'feelings' and experiences, the writers of these articles make liberal use of dichotomies seen to be connected with the masculine/feminine dichotomy, such as emotional control versus emotional expression, detachment versus relationship, 'selfishness' versus 'selflessness', and aggressivity versus passivity. Many writers suggest or imply that men should reject 'masculinist reason' in favour of 'feminine feeling'. However, few have critically interrogated this dualistic ordering, or sought to explore its historical and cultural origins. In fact, these writings are characterised, by and large, by a near total silence in respect to the epistemological foundations of male power and privilege. Although there are a significant number of references to sexism, and some acknowledgement of the links between 'masculinity' and racism and homophobia, discussions about personal identity and experiences of personal 'crisis' tend to be given priority over discussions about relations of power. There is little or no acknowledgement of the profound challenges to the idea of a stable male identity posed by recent developments in the social sciences and humanities, such as postmodernism, poststructuralism, and deconstruction. Discussions are rife with generalisations about 'men' and 'women', and 'feminism'.

The emphasis on emotion in this literature can be, and has been, criticised on a number of grounds. For a start, much of the writing engages uncritically with the concepts of intimacy and emotion, which are assumed to have universal applicability. The meanings of 'emotion', although gender-laden, are also always context-specific. For example, although the meanings of the 'emotional labours' performed by airline attendants and corporate managers are deeply gendered – the former being coded feminine, and the latter, masculine – the content of each is specific to the occupation in question. In the former case, one is expected to be 'deferential' and 'polite', in the latter case one is called upon to be 'in control' and 'tough' (see Hochschild, 1983; Roper, 1994). A growing body of anthropological research on gender and sexuality has emphasised that the content of 'emotion', and expressions of male emotionality, are highly variable cross-culturally. For example, the concepts of 'aggression' and 'machismo' are connected to culturally specific discourses about gender and sexuality, and do not necessarily have cross-cultural salience (see, for example, Cornwall and Lindisfarne, 1994a: 14–16; Gilmore, 1990; Moore, 1994a, 1994b). Writings by men on male emotional life, such as *The Sexuality of Men* (Metcalfe and Humphries, 1985), compiled by contributors of *Achilles Heel*, draw heavily on feminist reworkings of object-relations theory, particularly Nancy Chodorow's work, and can be seen to exemplify a number of the theory's problems that I identified earlier. A major problem is the tendency to explain male domination as an effect of the non-relational nature of masculine psychology, rather than in terms of material and political practices (McMahon, 1993: 677–8). According to Middleton, the appeal of this perspective to men in the men's movement is that it accepts the premise that men grow up emotionally suppressed (Middleton, 1992). However, it fails to account for differences among men and the effects of class, 'race', ethnicity, age, sexuality, and so on, upon the formation of masculine subjectivities. As Roper comments, it is assumed that all men – regardless of age, social class, ethnicity, and 'race' – find it difficult to establish intimacy, a problem which arises from the child's need to reject his original closeness with his mother (1994: 7; see also Rutherford, 1992: 37–8). Male writers on 'men's emotions' can be accused of neglecting power relations and the construction of social differences. Robinson has argued that in so far as the issue of male violence to women is addressed at all, its source tends to be located in the psyches of men rather than in social arrangements, and that critiques of heterosexuality are too narrowly concerned with heterosexual men's insecurities about their own sexual identities and fail to examine the structural manifestation of both the contradictions around 'masculinity' for men and how the attendant male power and privilege is connected to women's oppression (Robinson, 1996: 116–18). In short, efforts towards changing men's emotions are far from unproblematic, and it should not be assumed that they are compatible with the goals of feminism and the gay, lesbian, and queer movements, which are basically about changing relations of power.

Beyond the 'masculinity'–rationality connection

One of the key points that I have sought to emphasise in this overview of some recent and influential critical analyses of 'masculinist' rationality and the mind/body dualism, is just how difficult it has been for critics to escape rationalism, essentialism, universalism, and hierarchical distinctions in their own work. Although critics acknowledge the limitations and implications of the logic of Western rationality, particularly dualistic thinking, few have extended their deconstruction to *all* categories and dualisms. Essentialism and reductionism are evident in the uncritical use of categories such as 'men' and 'women' and the 'rational' and the 'irrational'; in the persistent failure to recognise or explore the operations of the regulations of identity apart from 'sex' or 'gender', such as 'race', 'sexuality', and 'nature'; in references to an assumed atomised, rational self, and in the tendency to confound and interchange categories such as 'masculine' and ' male'. Rationalism can be seen in the appeal to resocialisation strategies which imply that 'the mind' (the rational ego) exists separately from 'the body', and that each, and their relations, are unaffected by power, and in the continuing strong adherence to scientism, evident especially in feminist psychoanalysis and theories of moral development. Individualistic and, indeed behaviouristic, tendencies are strongly apparent in a number of the above analyses, especially in the more psychoanalytically inclined writings. Critics have consistently failed to recognise the complexity of interconnections between different dualisms – women/men, heterosexual/homosexual, nature/culture, mind/body, individual/society, and so on – and the fact that these dualisms are historically and culturally contingent. Thus, while writers acknowledge that some categories and dualisms are constructed – generally those seen as most immediately relevant to their own particular analyses – they often fail to extend their criticism to other related categories and dualisms.

The drive to achieve a 'total' viewpoint is implicit in many of the above analyses, despite critics' avowed claims to reject universalism, and is the source of many of the problems that I have identified. The idea that knowledge is always 'situated' or 'embodied' is seen by an increasing number of feminists as a prerequisite for avoiding normative, regulative and exclusionary forms of thought (see, for example, Braidotti et al., 1994: 56–8; Haraway, 1991: 183–201; Young, I.M., 1990: 96–121). In her critique of the ideal of impartiality in moral theory, Iris Marion Young has discussed at length the ways in which the dualism between rationality and affectivity, or the bodily realm, has operated to privilege certain groups – predominantly, 'white Anglo nominally heterosexual men' – while excluding women and other groups (1990: 100). The ideal of impartiality, argues Young, is a regulative ideal that legitimates bureaucratic, hierarchical authority, while suppressing the particular (1990: 115–17).

> Because of their particularity, feeling, inclination, needs, and desire are expelled from the universality of moral reason. Dispassion requires that one abstract from the personal pull of desire, commitment, care, in relation to a moral situation and regard it impersonally. Feeling and commitment are thereby expelled from moral reason; all feelings and desires are devalued, become equally irrational, equally irrelevant to moral judgement. . . . (1990: 103)

Young's critical deconstructive approach differs from those discussed because she critically interrogates the historical and cultural origins, and the context of the operations, of the ideal of impartiality, and recognises the manifold exclusions involved in the modern urge to 'totalisation'. An important point that is also emphasised by Young, and that tends to be overlooked by most other critics, is that impartiality is an *ideal* that is prone to failure. This point is emphasised perhaps most forthrightly by queer theorists, whose contributions provide the focus of the next chapter.

5

'Queering' sexual identity

> To be 'oriented' toward a particular sex as the object of one's sexual expressivity means, in effect, having a sexuality that is like target practice – keeping it aimed at bodies who display a particular sexual definition above all else, picking out which one to want, which one to get, which one to have. Self-consciousness about one's 'sexual orientation' keeps the issue of gender central at precisely the moment in human experience when gender really needs to become profoundly peripheral. Insistence on having a sexual orientation in sex is about defending the status quo, maintaining sex differences and the sexual hierarchy; whereas *resistance* to sexual-orientation regimentation is more about where we need to be going. (Stoltenberg, 1989: 106)

The idea that men and women have a natural 'sexual orientation' is one that is deeply inscribed in modern Western thought. Sexuality is seen as so intimately bound up with the modern individual's sense of self that it is difficult for many people to imagine that sexuality is a category that is arbitrary or historically contingent. As I explained in Chapter 2, social constructionist research has challenged the belief that human beings have a natural, invariant sexuality, and has revealed the ways in which 'sexuality' serves to regulate identity and to define an ideal of relations between the 'opposite sexes'. It has become evident that there are close interconnections between social constructions of 'gender' and of 'sexuality' each helping to constitute the other, but in historically and socially specific ways. As I also pointed out in Chapter 3, 'normal' masculine identity has been historically and socially constructed as 'heterosexual', and defined in opposition to the sexual 'other', particularly the male 'homosexual', who is seen as effeminate. These associations continue to be strong and can be seen, for instance, in recent research into the 'gay gene' and in discrimination against those who are not heterosexual. The idea that there are, and can be, fixed and mutually exclusive sexual desires and identities has been challenged on a number of fronts, however, but most insistently by those who have been marginalised by the dominant discourses of sexuality.

This chapter focuses on the queer critique of sexual identity and identity politics that has emerged in a number of contemporary societies, particularly the United States, Great Britain, and Australia. According to its proponents, queer theory has been a response to dissatisfaction with gay liberation politics, which is seen to have proved ineffectual in the effort to create a democratic culture and oppressive of those who identify themselves as neither 'gay' nor 'straight'. It is seen to reinforce a binary opposition between the categories of homosexuality and heterosexuality, while leaving intact the frameworks of knowledge and practice that support the dominance of heterosexuality. In the same way that postmodern and poststructuralist feminists have turned a critical gaze on the identity politics of 'second-wave' feminism (see Chapter 2), queer theorists, influenced by poststructuralist approaches, have questioned the identity politics of 'the gay and lesbian movement'. This work presents important challenges not only for political activism in relation to gay identity, but for all theoretical and political work in relation to issues of identity, including that focusing on masculine identity.

As I will explain, queer theory and politics is a highly contested and politically charged field. There is a lively debate regarding the objects of enquiry and the most appropriate forms of intervention. Even the use of 'queer' as an identity label is a point of contention. Nevertheless, there is a great deal of agreement among 'queer' commentators about the dangers of essentialism in theory and practice, and about the need for a more critical use of identity categories. Queer theory questions the 'naturalness' of basic concepts and categories, particularly 'sex', 'gender' and 'sexuality', and dualistic distinctions such as homo/heterosexual and sex/gender which are seen as pervasive in the modern West and as operating as mechanisms for regulating identity and reinforcing heterosexism. I begin this chapter by examining the context of the emergence of queer theory before moving on to outline its particular challenges for gay theory and politics and its implications for thinking about, and research on, the question of masculine identity

A crisis in the epistemology of sexuality

The emergence of queer theory can be seen to reflect a crisis in the epistemology of sexuality. This epistemology is defined by heterosexual dominance, an entrenched hetero/homosexual dualism, and the prevailing assumption that there exists some single definable 'truth' to our sexual being that provides the basis for our sense of self or 'identity'. Queer theory and politics question the dominant socio-sexual arrangements, but especially the identity politics of 'the gay movement', the deployment of the gay/straight binarism and the use of 'gay' and 'lesbian' identity categories. A growing number of scholars and activists have argued that 'lesbian' and 'gay' are employed by 'straights' as administrative labels for the management of sexual difference and by gays and lesbians themselves to police personal identities and individual behaviours. This has served to deny differences among gay people and the fluidity of sexual identifications which are not limited to the gay/straight binarism – for example, bisexuality, transvestism, transgenderism (see, for example, Elkins and King, 1996; Epstein and Straub, 1991; Garber, 1995; Nataf, 1996). Within gay culture, the proliferation and fragmentation of groupings, organised by gender, 'race', ethnicity, religion, workplace, and cultural and recreational interest, is seen to defy easy categorisation of political positions and to call into question the idea that there is, or could ever be, a single, unified 'gay and lesbian movement' (Adam, 1995: 146, 157–61). According to queer theorists, gay politics has been, and continues to be, inattentive to, and intolerant of, diverse sexual constituencies and fails to acknowledge the regulations of identity.

The conservative backlash against homosexuality and the AIDS crisis underlined the limits of a politics of minority rights and inclusion, and the need for new theoretical and strategic directions (Seidman, 1996a: 10). With the onset of AIDS, the extent of homophobia – manifest in media representations of risks posed by 'homosexuals' to 'heterosexuals' and to 'the family' (see Watney, 1997) – and the implications of conceiving 'the problem' according to the hetero/homosexual division, became apparent. The onset of the AIDS crisis highlighted the implicit assumption of masculine heterosexuality in official policies and the limitations of the modernist concept of a fixed sexual identity. As Jagose (1996) notes, the initial governmental and medical response to AIDS was to treat AIDS and homosexuality as discursively synonymous, which resulted in gay males, and to some extent lesbians, being identified as sources of pollution. That is, in line with the discourse of homosexuality, AIDS-education policy focused on *identities* rather than *acts*. There was, for example, a failure to recognise the necessity for targeting safe-sex information at men who have sex with other men but who do not identify themselves as 'gay'. The AIDS-education strategies served to demonstrate the limits of the paradigm shift which is widely understood to distinguish modern from pre-modern sexualities – that is, the shift from acts to identities (Jagose, 1996: 19–20).

Internal developments within gay and lesbian subcultures, particularly the critique of the idea of a unitary gay identity by lesbian and gay people of colour and lesbians who were marginalised by mainstream gay culture, also prompted a rethink of gay theory and politics. The concept of a gay and lesbian identity that provided the foundation for the building of community and for organising politically had come to be seen to reflect a white, middle-class experience (Seidman, 1996a: 10–11). According to Watney (1994), in Britain, as well as in the United States, it was the 'sanctimonious moralism' of much of the gay and lesbian culture that gave rise to queer politics in the first place. For example, the emphasis in gay culture on the so-called objectification of the body in visual representation is based on the questionable values and beliefs of radical feminism and denies that 'sexual desire and fantasy could not even exist without some degree of psychic objectification' (Watney, 1994: 18). By the early 1980s, many people believed that Gay Liberation had lost sight of its goal to contest the classificatory schemes of sexuality and seemed to regard lesbian and gay issues as though they were relevant only to lesbians and gay men, who were imagined as a discrete minority, evident in the use of such notions as 'the homosexual community' (Watney, 1994: 18–19). By the early 1990s, there appeared to be a basic conflict 'between those who think of the politics of sexuality as a matter of securing minority rights, and those who are contesting the overall validity and authenticity of the epistemology of sexuality itself' (Watney, 1994: 19).

The crux of the queer critique centres on the question of the essentialism of identity – an issue preoccupying many scholars in diverse fields of thought in the 1990s. According to some accounts, this essentialism is a direct consequence of the tendency for gay males and lesbians to organise themselves along the lines of an ethnic group, using the civil rights and Black Power movements of the 1960s as models for political organisation. The 'gay and lesbian movement', along with the feminist movement, appropriated not only the arguments of civil rights and group pride, it is argued, but also the metaphors and descriptions of position; 'gay pride' became the equivalent of 'black pride', as did 'global sisterhood' of 'brotherhood', in black political discourse (Phelan, 1994: 60). As Phelan points out, treating sexuality as ethnicity inevitably leads to essentialism. That is, sexual object choice is seen as given and stable over the lifetime of the individual. People 'really are' heterosexual or homosexual, and there is little scope for 'deviant' combinations of physical sex, social gender, personal desire, and social identity – or ambiguity in identity (1994: 61–2). Defining one's 'sexual orientation' according to the hetero/homosexual divide has come to be seen as the primary basis for self-identity, excluding other possible self-identifications. A growing number of people have come to recognise that the identity politics of gay and lesbian mobilisations involves the 'fixing' of identities, and serves to marginalise those who do not subscribe to gay and lesbian self-identifications.

The search for authenticity of self that has been integral to Gay Liberation and to the politics of other new social movements, queer theorists argue, never leads one to interrogate the Western epistemology of sexuality which is structured by the homo/heterosexual division and its related binarisms. The 'queer' critique of identity politics is closely linked to the critique of the essentialism of the self – the assumption that identity can be defined by a core set of attributes which are unvarying across time and space, such as 'natural' sexual desire or gender-linked propensity to aggress or to care (see Chapters 3 and 4). Many theorists eschew essentialist strategies on the grounds that these serve to construct an identity, and a supporting ideology, that is white, heterosexual, middle class, and male. Queer theorists and activists have advocated tactics which promote social transformation supportive of difference while seeking to avoid the essentialism of identity. Groups such as Queer Nation, which is the most visible and notorious of the new queer movements, have aimed to achieve just that through, among other things, exposing the 'straightness' of public spaces and seeking to 'reterritorialise' them (see Richardson, 1996b: 15; Slagle, 1995: 86–8).

The contentious politics of 'queer'

The use of the term 'queer' as an identity label has been a highly contentious issue in academic debates in the 1990s, a point which underscores the centrality of naming practices in contemporary politics. As Simon Watney (1994) points out, some gay and lesbian people in Britain and the United States have questioned the adoption of 'queer' as an identity label because it has been long used as a term of abuse. However, the point that tends to be overlooked in many discussions is that it had also been used as a term of self-identification between the 1950s and the 1970s before the emergence of Gay Liberation. Gay politics rejected the use of words such as 'queer' and 'homosexual', along with the values they were seen to represent (Woods, 1995: 30). Watney argues that resistance to the use of the word 'queer' would seem to be more widespread among an older generation of lesbians and gay men who 'came out' in the sixties and seventies than among those who have 'come out' since the beginning of the AIDS epidemic (1994: 14). Clearly, the conditions giving rise to queer politics and theory in the 1980s and 1990s were/are different from those confronting an earlier generation. The refusal of the authorities to acknowledge young gay people's needs and entitlements in the context of the AIDS epidemic, a pervasive institutional backlash against virtually everyone who does not self-identify as heterosexual, combined with growing disenchantment with traditional Left and gay politics, created the climate for the development of a loose alliance between various marginalised groups around the term 'queer', and for the emergence of 'queer' activist organisations such as Outrage! (in Britain) and Queer Nation (in New York) in the early 1990s (de Lauretis, 1991: v; Watney 1994: 15).

In seeking to make visible and to validate sexual difference in a heterosexual-dominant society, such groups have made a political play on the word 'queer', employing it as one of a series of 'reverse affirmations' in which categories constructed through medicalisation are turned against themselves (Stein and Plummer, 1996: 134). As Warner (1993) argues, the question of how one names oneself needs to be taken seriously, specially within a liberal-pluralist context:

> The problem of finding an adequate description is a far from idle question, since the way a group is defined has consequences for how it will be mobilized, represented, legislated for, and addressed. Attempts have been made to use 'nation', 'community', even 'ethnicity', just as 'sexual orientation' has often been used as though it were parallel to 'race' or 'sex'. But in each case the results have been partly unhappy, for the same reasons. Among these alternatives the dominant concept has been that of a 'gay and lesbian community', a notion generated in the tactics of Anglo-American identity politics and its liberal-national environment, where the buried model is racial and ethnic politics. Although it has had importance in organizational efforts . . . the notion of a community has remained problematic if only because nearly every lesbian or gay remembers being such before entering a collectively identified space, because much of lesbian and gay history has to do with noncommunity, and because dispersal rather than localization continues to be definitive of queer self-understanding ('We are everywhere'). Community also falsely suggests an ideological and nostalgic contrast with atomization of modern capitalist society. And in the liberal-pluralist frame it predisposes that political demands will be treated as demands for the toleration and representation of a minority constituency. (1993: xxv–vi)

It is partly as an attempt to avoid this problem, argues Warner, that many people have shifted their self-identification from 'gay' to 'queer'. The preference for 'queer' represents, among other things, a rejection of 'a minoritizing logic of toleration or simple political interest-representation in favor of a more thorough resistance to regimes of the normal' (Warner, 1993: xxvi). The term 'queer' has consequently come to be widely used as a noun, adjective, and verb in the work of those sexuality theorists who take their major cue from the postmodern/poststructuralist turn in theory and politics (Namaste, 1996).

This is not to say that 'queer' signifies a unified field of thought and practice, and that it is totally distinct from 'older' lesbian and gay culture, for there are many continuities between the two. (On this latter point, see Watney, 1994: 23.) In the academic literature, there has been a great deal of debate about what 'queer' actually designates and the extent to which the theoretical and practical projects of different sexual-political groupings overlap or conflict. Sometimes queer is used as a synonym for 'gay and lesbian', while at other times as an umbrella term for 'a coalitional group of anti-normative sexual self-identifications' (Berry and Jagose, 1996: 6). According to some writers, it is useful to conceive of queer as 'less a new identity than a critique of identity' (see, for example, Berry and Jagose, 1996: 11; Jagose, 1996: 131). There has been concern among a number of scholars that 'queer' may become institutionalised and lose its 'critical edge'. For example, Teresa de Lauretis, the theorist who is often credited with coining the phrase 'queer theory', abandoned the term three years later because of concerns that it had been co-opted by the mainstream forces and institutions (Jagose, 1996: 127). The overall impact of queer theory on identity politics has yet to be determined. Nevertheless, queer theorists have had an undoubted influence in moving the focus of theoretical and critical concerns about sexuality and sexual identity.

The queer critique

'Queer' is difficult to define. Some writers have argued that its definitional indeterminacy is one of its constituent characteristics (Jagose, 1996: 1). According to Jagose, queer 'has no interest in consolidating or even stabilising itself' and 'it is always an identity under construction, a site of permanent becoming' (1996: 131). Nevertheless, its broad outlines are often sketched and debated. As one summary has it, queer theory is characterised by the following hallmarks: (i) a conceptualisation of sexuality which recognises the ubiquity of sexual power, and its discursive expression and enforcement through boundaries and binary divides; (ii) the problematisation of sexual and gender categories, particularly the foundational category of both homophobic theory and gay affirmative theory: the homosexual subject or identity; (iii) the deconstruction of 'identity' and recognition of the inherent instability of identity constructs; (iv) a rejection of civil rights strategies in favour of politics of transgression and parody connected with strategies of deconstruction, decentring, revisionist readings, and anti-assimilationist politics; and (v) a willingness to interrogate areas not usually seen as the terrain of sexuality, and to undertake 'queer readings' of ostensibly heterosexual and non-sexualised texts (Stein and Plummer, 1996: 134). Queer theorists have sought to put issues of representation (particularly in respect to the hetero/homosexual and normal/abnormal divisions), language, difference, diversity, and subject position firmly on research and political agendas. They opt for 'de-naturalisation' as their primary strategy (see Jagose, 1996: 98) – that is, they approach sexuality as a discursive effect rather than as a natural given. Arguing for the impossibility of any natural sexuality, they call into question even such taken-for-granted terms as 'man' and 'woman' (Jagose, 1996: 3). As part of the deconstructive impulse that has been evident also in many other areas of contemporary scholarship, queer theorists have begun to rethink the utility of basic concepts and the politics of identity politics. In the rapidly changing context of late twentieth-century society, it has become increasingly evident to many people that identity categories are, as Gamson puts it, both 'necessary and dangerous distortions' (1996: 410); that the effort to define 'who we are' inevitably involves regulations and exclusions.

Academic writers such as Eve Kosofsky Sedgwick, Diana Fuss, Teresa de Lauretis, and Judith Butler are considered key figures in the development of a new 'queer movement'. Sedgwick's (1994) insight that the modes of thought and knowledge of twentieth-century Western culture have been profoundly structured by the hetero/homosexual definition dating from the end of the nineteenth century has been highly influential in queer theory debates in the 1990s. Sedgwick sees the hetero/homosexual divide as affecting Western culture through its marking of other categories and distinctions such as masculine/feminine, secrecy/disclosure, majority/minority, natural/artificial, domestic/foreign, health/illness, same/different, active/passive, in/out and voluntarity/addiction. It is Sedgwick's view that 'there currently exists no framework in which to ask about the origins or development of individual gay identity that is not already structured by an implicit, trans-individual Western project or fantasy of eradicating that identity' (1994: 41). As Sedgwick argues, both constructivist and essentialist accounts of the origin of sexual preference and identity carry dangers. While the former takes its premises from a history of other nature/culture debates which assume that culture is malleable relative to nature and that it is the thing that can, and indeed should, be changed, the latter gives credence to medical fantasies of preventing homosexuality through the alteration and reform of bodies. In Sedgwick's view, gay-affirmative work should aim to minimise its reliance on any particular account of the origin of sexual preference and identity in individuals, especially one prefigured by the constructivist versus essentialist views of homosexuality (1994: 41–3).

The critique of gay historiography

Sedgwick's work signals growing disquiet among many scholars and activists with the objectives and methods of gay historical work and the recognition that it has the potential to reinstate the very normalising regimes that gays have sought to resist. As Bravmann (1995) points out, historical work has been considered crucial in the gay effort to reveal the constructed and arbitrary regimes of the normal and in providing political lessons and strategies for present struggles. (See also my comments on gay history in Chapter 2.) Gay and lesbian historiographers have believed that it is important to emphasise that 'the homosexual' and 'the heterosexual' were 'inventions' in the latter half of the nineteenth century that were linked to changes in regulatory regimes (for example, medicine and law) accompanying the emergence of capitalist society. In the process, however, they have tended to present these changes as a grand, universalising process in which differences and complexities tend to be underplayed. Although social constructionist accounts have been highly provocative, they have not been very successful in terms of recognising 'race', ethnicity, gender, age, and other aspects of 'identity'. In foregrounding the differences between the social constructions of 'homosexuality' in different historical periods, gay historical studies have reified gay and lesbian identity and neglected contemporary differences among social constructions of homosexuality and their respective specific histories. There has been a tendency to take the white, male, middle-class homosexual as the prototype for the 'homosexual role' (Bravmann, 1995: 56–62).

Sedgwick has referred to the tendency in gay historical work (as undertaken, for example, by Michel Foucault and David Halperin) to adopt a 'unidirectional narrative' in which one model of sexuality supersedes another model, which then 'drops out of the frame of analysis'. Such narratives are based upon assumptions about 'homosexuality as we know it today', and present a danger in terms of reinforcing the dominant epistemology of sexuality. As Sedgwick argues, the most potent effects of modern homo/heterosexual definition derive from the inexplicitness or denial of the disparities between long coexisting discourses of same-sex relations (1994: 47). Sedgwick's aim is not to cast aside existing work, or to construct alternative historical narratives, but rather to 'denaturalize the present' by giving greater emphasis to the varied, plural, and contradictory understandings of history (1994: 47–8). Bravmann, too, has argued the need for gay historians to develop many complementary and competing versions of the past if they are to avoid the totalising impulse of historiography. They need to remain sensitive to the fact that 'historical understandings are always subject to questions of interpretation, representation, authority, textuality, and narrative' and that stories that gay people tell about themselves are powerful social practices in the construction of identity, community, and politics (Bravmann, 1995: 53, 60).

As Donna Penn (1995) has pointed out, the presumption of identity in gay male and lesbian histories has led scholars to overlook the challenges posed to the sex/gender system by various subjects. The privileging of identity over behaviour has made it difficult to recognise the existence of multiple and deviant subjectivities. Among these one can include bisexuals, transsexuals, transvestites, and hermaphrodites, some of whom have already begun to speak out against the notion that sexual identities are fixed, mutually exclusive and of only two kinds (Nataf, 1996). As Penn asks: how does one recognise the histories of men and women who may or may not have identified as gays or lesbians; who may or may not have lived exclusively as 'homosexuals'; who may or may not have associated with local or national gay or lesbian subcultures, organizations or communities; but whose lives nevertheless give credence to the idea of homoerotic desire among men and among women? (1995: 25). The shift in focus away from 'homosexuality' *per se* to an exploration of the production and maintenance of the so-called 'normal', has created the opportunity for the retelling of sexual histories, with an emphasis on describing how, where and when the line is drawn between acceptable and unacceptable sexual practices, and by whom. As Penn notes, this is 'a decidedly political task' since, although 'the line itself may be inevitable . . . where it is drawn is not'. As a politics of sexual deviance, it is imperative that queer attend to the shifting of the line, and historicise the politics of drawing the line. In other words, attention must be given to analysing the diverse ways in which deviance is mapped, contested, and remapped, so that one can identify the specific conditions and contexts under which normative heterosexuality is challenged (Penn, 1995: 39).

The politics of 'coming out'

The queer critique of identity politics has brought into question the gay tactic of 'coming out of the closet'. In the late 1960s and the early 1970s, 'coming out' became a key tactic of gay politics and fundamental to assumptions about 'being gay'. It 'represented the adoption of an identity in which the erotic became emblematic of the person, rather than an isolated act, and in which identity was chosen rather than imposed as a medical label of deviance' (Freedman, 1995: 44). The ability to exercise choice in 'coming out' has been crucial in the politics of the liberal assimilationist strand of the gay movement since it is seen as a personally 'empowering' tactic and as a form of resistance to the imperatives associated with the historically and socially constructed 'homosexual role'. The voluntary articulation of one's personal identity, in other words, has been seen to be a prerequisite to elaborating one's personal politics. This is reflected in the slogan: 'the personal is the political'. Although, originally, 'coming out' was a discreet and highly informal process, involving 'frank acknowledgement to oneself, and to one's gay peers, that one was homosexual', Gay Liberation turned it into 'a politicised ritual of public avowal' (Miller, 1993: 255).

> To proclaim, defiantly, that one was gay was to reject, dramatically, the idea that one's sexuality ought to be regarded as shameful or sick; it was to flout social taboos and to prove the courage of one's convictions at the risk of losing friends, the support of one's family, and even one's job; it was to cross a critical line, and to wager on the success of a public movement of protest. In the process, gay activists hoped to demonstrate their own freedom from self-hatred – and their resistance to the institutions of an oppressive society. As a Gay Liberation Front slogan exhorted, 'COME OUT FOR FREEDOM! COME OUT NOW! . . . COME OUT OF THE CLOSET BEFORE THE DOOR IS SHUT!' (Miller, 1993: 255–6)

The production of homosexuality in medical and legal discourse produced a paradox: although it allowed for the development of an identity which guaranteed civil rights, it brought with it the notion of 'the closet' and the idea that some people are 'visible' about their sexualities while others remain silent (Namaste, 1996: 199). As Sedgwick explains, '"the closet" has been the defining structure for gay oppression in this century', and the metaphor of 'coming out of the closet' reveals the relationship of homosexuality to the concepts of secrecy and disclosure, and of the private and the public, that have structured thought and knowledge about sexuality and gender in the modern West (1994: 71). While the concept of 'coming out of the closet' can be, and has been, employed in relation to the public revelations of other oppressed groups, such as racial groups and groups of overweight people, the 'epistemology of the closet' (Sedgwick's phrase) has a special salience in the lives of gay people, as Sedgwick notes:

> Vibrantly resonant as the image of the closet is for many modern oppressions, it is indicative for homophobia in a way it cannot be for other oppressions. Racism, for instance, is based on a stigma that is visible in all but exceptional cases (cases that are neither rare nor irrelevant, but that delineate the outlines rather than coloring the centre of racial experience); so are the oppressions based on gender, age, size, physical handicap. Ethnic/cultural/religious oppressions such as anti-Semitism are more analogous in that the stigmatized individual has at least notionally some discretion – although, importantly, it is never to be taken for granted how much – over other people's knowledge of her or his membership in the group: one could 'come out' as a Jew or Gypsy, in a heterogeneous urbanized society, much more intelligibly than one could typically 'come out' as, say, female, Black, old, a wheelchair user, or fat. (1994: 75)

As this suggests, 'coming out' can only occur where there is the possibility of secrecy and of disclosure, and where there is the potential to exercise discretion. It does not have salience in cases where one displays physical markers of identity that are already available for all to see, such as skin colour, or body shape or size, and where discretion is missing. 'Coming out' involves the 'voluntary' disclosure of the 'private' self. It is premised on the existence of a demarcation between public and private spheres, where heterosexuality is associated with the public and homosexuality with the private. The strength of these associations becomes apparent when one considers the possibility of 'coming out' as 'a heterosexual'. Within a heterosexual-dominant society, it makes sense to 'come out' only if one is *not* 'heterosexual'.

Foucault, among others, has been critical of the gay tactic of 'coming out' for its assumption that one had a more or less stable sexual identity (see, for example, Miller, 1993: 256). 'Coming out' can be seen as a means of 'fixing' one's identity; of consolidating the boundaries between the self and the other. To publicly declare oneself as 'gay' or 'lesbian' suggests that this identity is exclusive of other sexual potentialities; that it defines some essential difference from others. It involves the reification of sexuality, giving it primary, trans-situational significance and primacy over other aspects of identity. As important as sexuality might be for self-identity, we are not purely sexual creatures whose experiences are unmediated by time, place, and social location. Eliason argues that the reification of sexuality is evident in most existing theoretical models of sexual identity formation: these have neglected the ways by which gender, 'race', ethnicity, age, occupation, social class, place of resi-dence, and other important components of living, intersect with sexuality at different times and in different contexts (1996: 52). Such models reflect the liberal humanist assumption that 'lesbian', 'gay' and 'bisexual' designate autonomous, stable persons, rather than subject positions from which to speak. Theorists have failed to consider how the broader socio-historical context shapes the identity categories that are available for subjects to take up. Rather than being fixed, identity categories are constantly evolving and open-ing up new possibilities for being and for subjects to express their sexualities (Eliason, 1996: 55–6).

The deployment of the spatial metaphor of the closet suggests that identity is clear, and that it is simply a question of making it visible, of taking up space (Phelan, 1994: 52). As Namaste (1996) notes, it is a metaphor which presup-poses both the centrality of heterosexuality, and the existence of gays, lesbians, and bisexuals who are *in* the closet. The use of this metaphor makes it impossible to locate oneself outside the dominant discourse. 'In efforts to define a sexual identity *outside* the norm, one needs first to place oneself *inside* dominant definitions of sexuality' (Namaste, 1996: 199). However, 'coming out' is not just an event, it is a process of fashioning a self that did not exist before 'coming out' began. The stability of identity is given not by discovering a deep 'truth' of the self, but rather by participating in historically specific communities and discourses (Phelan, 1994: 52). Among other things, 'coming out' involves participation in the practice of confession. The confes-sion, as Foucault has pointed out, has become 'one of the West's most highly valued techniques for producing truth' (1980: 59). People in the modern West have become so accustomed to confessing that they are unable to see it as an effect of power that constrains them. In fact, the obligation to confess is so ingrained in us that failure to reveal our innermost secrets is seen to be 'at the price of a kind of liberation' (1980: 58). Since the early Christian era, Western peoples have come to believe that the confession provides a privileged path to salvation. It is believed that by telling the 'truth' of what one is and what one does, and what one is thinking, one can be 'free'.

> The confession is a ritual of discourse in which the speaking subject is also the sub-ject of the statement; it is also a ritual that unfolds within a power relationship, for one does not confess without the presence (or virtual presence) of a partner who is not simply the interlocutor but the authority who requires the confession, pre-scribes and appreciates it, and intervenes in order to judge, punish, forgive, console, and reconcile; a ritual in which the truth is corroborated by the obstacles and resis-tances it has had to surmount in order to be formulated; and finally, a ritual in which the expression alone, independently of its external consequences, produces intrinsic modifications in the person who articulates it: it exonerates, redeems, and purifies him; it unburdens him of his wrongs, liberates him, and promises him sal-vation. (Foucault, 1980: 62–3)

As Foucault argued, confessional practices have had an important role in the modern history of sexuality. The deployment of new confessional practices around sexuality reflected a shift in techniques of power, from sovereign power to disciplinary power, whereby subjects were no longer governed chiefly by external imperatives but rather came to govern themselves as subjects requiring detailed work on the self (Foucault, 1980: 115–31). Psychoanalysis has facilitated this work on the self through providing 'a theory of the essential interrelatedness of the law and desire', and by offering a technique for dealing with the effects of the pathologisation resulting from the taboos surrounding sexuality (Foucault, 1980: 129). In its eagerness to embrace new techniques of confession and therapeutics, gay liberation has given inadequate attention to this broader socio-historical context and the particular configurations of power/knowledge that have emerged (Reynolds, 1996).

The practice of 'outing'

Much of the critique of sexual identity politics, described above, can be extended to the practice of 'outing'. In the 1990s, 'outing' began to be promoted by the militant nationalist strands of gay politics as a tactic for challenging the heterosexist idea that one must keep one's 'sexual orientation' quiet. Although the tactic was inaugurated by New York City's now defunct newspaper Outweek, it has been one of the strategies proposed by such groups as ACT UP (Aids Coalition To Unleash Power), FROCS (Faggots Rooting Out Closet Homosexuality), Queer Nation, and Outrage!. With the practice of 'outing', the early Gay Liberationist appeal to lesbians and gay men to 'come out' is transformed from an invitation into a command (Duggan, 1992: 15). As Duggan explains,

> Journalists and activists expose 'closeted' lesbians or gay men in public life, especially those deemed hypocritical in their approach to gay issues. Their goal is to end the secrecy and hypocrisy surrounding homosexuality, to challenge the notion that gay life is somehow shameful, and to show the world that many widely admired and respected men and women are gay. (1992: 15)

Many of the new gay militants reject liberal notions of privacy and the appeal to tolerance that characterise more mainstream gay organizations. Instead, they emphasise publicity, confrontation, self-assertion and direct action. The rhetoric of difference replaces the assimilationist liberal emphasis on similarity with other groups (Duggan, 1992: 15). Gay activism around 'outing' can be seen as a response to the politics of sexual citizenship whereby a large segment of the non-heterosexual population is denied public visibility and participation. Although sexual minorities have become distinct participants within the citizenship of modern capitalist societies, and have become legitimate consumers of sexual and sexualised commodities marketed for their use and enjoyment, they have been accorded only relative and partial rights (Evans, 1993). The partiality of rights and, indeed, the undermining of some established rights, became apparent as a consequence of the official response to HIV/AIDS which, as mentioned earlier, focused on identities rather than acts, and on gays in particular. Sexual minorities have become increasingly frustrated by continuing heterosexism, as reflected in their limited social rights. However, the effectiveness of 'outing' as a political strategy for countering heterosexism is doubtful.

The practice has been highly controversial among both 'gay' and 'straight' communities, on the grounds both of its questionable ethics and its intrusion on established rights. For example, in the United Kingdom in 1995, following the 'outing' of a number of allegedly homosexual bishops by the group OutRage!, there was a great deal of commentary in the British national daily papers about the ethics of the practice. In the case of one prominent 'outed' bishop, fellow bishops and archbishops pledged support for the 'victim', one group deploring the '"reprehensible intrusion" into his private life' (Conaghan, 1995: 9), while another referred to the 'cruel and insensitive' approach of OutRage! (Longley and Fenton, 1995: 1). In this particular instance, the gay organisation Stonewall also issued its own statement condemning 'outing' on the basis that 'it uses homophobia as a weapon to gain revenge on closeted gays said to be harming the community (which community and how, one wonders) or to blackmail them into changing their position' (Massie, 1995: 25). Stonewall, it should be mentioned, is an assimilationist group that has consistently attacked OutRage! for its liberation/activist/community politics (Woods, 1995: 26). (For an overview of the politics and strategies of OutRage!, especially in relation to the British media, and of the rival group Stonewall, see Woods, 1995: 14–19, 24–8.)

Many of the arguments against 'outing' are couched in terms of the right to privacy – the very liberal notion that groups such as OutRage! seek to challenge. The British 'outing' tactic has, without doubt, been effective in revealing the extent of anti-gay prejudice within the press which has long profited from the public exposure of closeted 'homosexuals' and from the maintenance of a wholly private sphere for homosexuality (Watney, 1994: 19). However, like the more established 'voluntary' practice of 'coming out', 'outing' reflects adherence to a conventional identity politics which assumes that there is a simple and uniform 'truth' to 'sexuality', and that individuals are aware of this 'truth' of their nature. As Watney points out, the assumptions underlying 'outing' run counter to contemporary gay political theory which emphasises the imperfect fit between sexual desire and behaviour, on the one hand, and sexual identity, on the other. The tactic is based on a simplistic view of how individuals respond to images and representations, and of how sexual identities are forged (Watney, 1994: 21–2). It does not allow the possibility of individual resistance through the refusal to name oneself and to participate in communities and discourses that serve to 'fix' identity. It is simply assumed that the interests of the individual should be subordinated to the interests of the broader gay and lesbian community. The imperative to 'come out', advocated by avowedly queer groups like Outrage!, sits oddly with the queer emphasis on 'subversion of identity' through deconstruction of identity categories and naming practices. It is based on the dubious assumption that there is a stable truth of the self that can be known and defined with reference to *a* single, identifiable group.

A post-identity politics?

The questions of how one might nurture a politics of difference while avoiding essentialism, and whether or not it is desirable to always avoid involvement in identity politics, are ones that have come to dominate debates in queer theory. Unfortunately, few queer theorists writing in the 1990s have elaborated in detail exactly how, and to what extent, queer politics is different from conventional identity politics, and can make a difference in challenging the power relations of gender, sexuality, class, and 'race'. Queer theory is not without its critics. Dennis Altman (in Berry & Jagose, 1996) is among those who have criticised queer theory on the basis that it is 'written by academics for academics', and has failed to recognise its own roots. The desire for transgression, Altman argues, is 'neither new nor the invention of Michel Foucault, postmodernism or even literary queer theory'. Almost all the ideas were circulating in the early days of Gay Liberation (1969–74). He notes that whereas 'in 1971 dykes and fags risked arrest when they asserted "queer" ideas, . . . today such ideas are more associated with building academic careers' (1996: 9). Gamson, too, has criticised queer theory for its elitism and, more particularly, for its restriction to academic institutions through the use of a highly abstract language (Gamson, 1996: 399). The pressures and demands of academic careerism combined with a strong consumerist ethos, Grant (1995) argues, have contributed to the burgeoning 'queer theorrhea' in the 1990s. Although it is important to raise questions about the politics of queer theory and to examine the context of its production and consumption, many critics seem unduly harsh, and often fail to acknowledge the important insights offered by queer theory.

Clearly, some commentators are hostile towards the politics of queer. Writing from her lesbian feminist position, Sheila Jeffreys (1993) has offered a damning criticism of what she describes as the new liberalism of queer politics on the basis that it denies the different experiences of men and women and the history of gay male misogyny. In her view, queer politics is 'another way in which lesbians are being pulled back into cultural subordination to gay men' (1993: 143). Queer politics is seen as a threat to lesbian feminist politics, and to create yet again a male language which downplays the concerns of feminists about men's objectification of women (for example, pornography) and other forms of male sexual violence (for example, paedophilia). In Jeffreys's view, the postmodern politics of queer, which emphasises the plurality of sexual positionings and 'in which lesbians get homogenised into gay men and "heterosexualities", make a feminist analysis of heterosexuality as a political institution almost impossible' (1993: 146). In their insistent pleas for 'tolerance' for 'diversity' and 'difference', many queer scholars indeed seem to be proposing a kind of liberal pluralist philosophy and politics. As in many discussions of multiculturalism, 'diversity' and 'difference' tend to be reified – treated as monolithic and unchanging things – rather than as constitutive of identities (Scott, 1995: 5–6) In talking about 'queer politics', however, there is a danger of assuming a unanimity of viewpoint and strategy among theorists

that does not in fact exist. While some queer theorists repudiate identity politics and essentialism of any kind, others advocate a mixture of liberal and
radical strategies and the necessity for 'strategic essentialism' as a matter of
survival and for protecting citizen rights. (For some insight into these debates
see Duggan, 1992; Gamson, 1996; Rajchman 1995; Seidman, 1996b.)

A deconstructivist approach to identity

In the effort to avoid the essentialism of identity that has been associated in
particular with the strategies of Gay Liberation, many writers have advocated a semiotic or deconstructivist approach to identity. This approach has
been developed mainly in the humanities, where poststructuralism, particularly of the Derridaean variety, has been highly influential. Diana Fuss, for
example, advocates this approach in her book, *Essentially Speaking* (1989).
Fuss sees a particular need to challenge the reduction of the political to the
personal in reassessing and repoliticising 'identity politics'. Drawing on both
Derrida's deconstruction of 'essence' and Lacan's theory of the constitution
of the subject in language, Fuss argues for a shift in the debate away from a
consideration of the identity of things in themselves and towards an analysis
of *identity statements* (1989: 103). Deconstruction, with its focus on identity
as difference, subverts the possibility of ever finding a secure basis upon
which to construct an identity. 'To the extent that identity always contains the
specter of non-identity within it, the subject is always divided and identity is
always purchased at the price of exclusion of the Other, the repression or
repudiation of non-identity' (1989: 103). A semiotic view of identity, argues
Fuss, dispenses with discussion about 'essence' and instead places language at
the centre of analysis, and allows one to recognise that identity is always
'contingent', 'provisional' and subject to the subversive and destabilising
potential of the unconscious. Fuss takes issue with those poststructuralist
accounts of identity which see difference as a product of the friction between
'easily identifiable and unitary components of identity (sexual, racial, economic, national . . . competing for dominance within the subject' (1989: 103).
Theories of 'multiple identities' which see difference either *between* or *outside*
identity, ignore the radicality of the poststructuralist view which locates differences *within* identity, and leave unchallenged the traditional metaphysical
understanding of identity as unity (1989: 103). The deconstruction of 'identity', Fuss argues, does not necessarily mean the *disavowal* of identity, as
some writers have suggested. Recognition that identity is fictitious makes
those fictions no less powerful. However, one needs to question the assumption that political identities must be secure in order that one can do one's
political work and that 'politics must be steady and localizable, and untrou-
bled by psychic conflict or internal disorder' (1989: 105). Fuss's work is
interesting and provocative, though, in my view, somewhat abstract and inattentive to the practical difficulties associated with mobilising around
'identities' that are not secure.

The activist group Queer Nation exemplifies the complexities and tensions associated with the effort to develop a new poststructuralist or anti-essentialist model of identity politics. Queer Nation, which sprang up in dozens of cities around the United States in the late 1980s and early 1990s, is seen by some commentators as an exemplar of a new or reconceptualised identity politics that employs tactics that can be described as *poststructural*. That is, it is seen to be involved in the task of ' subverting identity' and exposing the assumptions upon which heterosexism is based by celebrating the diversity of the queer community or nation (Slagle, 1995: 93). In his article, 'In defense of Queer Nation: from identity politics to a politics of difference', Slagle argues that while Queer Nation employs many of the strategies that typify identity politics, it takes its collective identity from the fact that members are 'different' (1995: 88). In line with this, it seeks to be inclusive in its membership:

> Queer Nation, in developing a consciousness based on difference, avoids the essentialist nature of the dominant codes and modes of classification (used both by the dominant group and earlier gay and lesbian liberation groups). This group strives to include anyone who feels oppressed by the dominant mainstream. Indeed, Queer Nation *celebrates* difference and diversity in terms of race, class, gender and sexuality among its membership. Queer Nation also strives to include other sexualities that are considered deviant by the dominant system (sado-masochism, for example). (Slagle, 1995: 93)

Given its critique of conventional identity politics and its calls for inclusiveness and celebration of 'difference' and 'diversity', it is difficult to know on what grounds Queer Nation defines its own identity. What exactly is the 'difference' of which queer activists speak and that serves to unite the queer community? And, what are the implications for its politics of the radical deconstruction of 'identity'? Queer Nation's effort to build an organisational structure that is 'non-hierarchical and decentralised' has not been without difficulties. For example, commentators have noted that the group is often disorganised, and that many chapters have disbanded because of unresolvable conflicts (Browning, 1993, cited by Slagle, 1995: 89; Cunningham, 1992: 66). Queer Nation exemplifies the tensions that exist between those who defend boundaries and those who seek to annihilate them. Its adoption of yet another identity category understood in separatist or nationalistic terms, as the name Queer Nation itself implies, demonstrates the difficulty in totally dispensing with an 'essentialist' politics in political activism (Epstein, 1996: 154). The value of Queer Nation's strategy of cultural deconstruction has been questioned by some writers. Gamson, for instance, argues that this strategy does little to touch regulatory institutions, such as law and medicine, that continue to create and enforce gay/straight and male/female divisions (1996: 409). It is his view that Queer Nation and other queer groups adopt a confrontational style of politics that is of unknown or dubious value in terms of challenging the epistemology of sexuality.

Deconstruction plus strategic use of 'identity'

In recognition of the limitations of a strict deconstructivist or semiotic approach to identity and identity politics, a number of more sociologically inclined scholars have recently advocated the deployment of deconstructive strategies in combination with the strategic use of 'identity'. Steven Epstein, for example, notes that the point is not to abandon all forms of identity politics, or to stop studying identity formation, 'but rather to maintain identity and difference in productive tension, and to rely on notions of identity and identity politics for their strategic utility while remaining vigilant against reification' (1996: 156). In a similar vein, Seidman (1996a) comments that one need not completely do away with identity as a category of knowledge and politics, but rather 'render it permanently open and contestable as to its meaning and political role', so that 'decisions about identity categories become pragmatic, related to concerns of situational advantage, political gain, and conceptual utility'. The advantage of conceiving identity as permanently open as to its meaning and use, Seidman argues, is that this allows the public surfacing of differences and the development of a culture which recognises a multiplicity of voices and interests (1996a: 12). Adherence to a strict deconstructivist position, which calls for the complete negation of categories and groups as units of analysis, carries inherent dangers, as Cathy Cohen (1996) observes in her discussion of black gay identities. Such a position ignores both the reality of groups in structuring the distribution of resources, and the importance of group membership in promoting the survival and progress of marginal group members. Thus, she comments, although it is important to recognise the limitations of essentialist theories of 'the black community', there are risks in ignoring the importance of indigenous group structure to the living conditions of marginal groups (Cohen, 1996: 367–8).

Others have warned of the dangers of totally abandoning identity boundaries in the political context of the 1990s. Gamson (1996), for instance, argues that it is politically damaging to undermine identities in a conservative political climate in which social rights are coming under attack, and that it is difficult to make *any* claims without a solid group identity. In the United States at least, he argues, groups that have been most effective in gaining credibility and achieving their political demands are those which have drawn on some notion of a unitary (racial, sexual, gender, or class) identity. Although deconstructionism can be valuable as a tool for countering *cultural* sources of oppression (i.e. popular ideas), it is necessary to appeal to solid identities in order to resist *institutional* sources of oppression. According to Gamson, the particular contribution of queer deconstruction is in raising new questions about collective identities such as 'for whom, when, and how are stable collective identities necessary for social action and social change?' And, 'do some identity movements in fact avoid the tendency to take themselves apart?' (1996: 411–12).

These arguments pertaining to the use of 'identity' and the politics of 'identity politics', which have been brought to the fore in queer discussions about sexuality, are becoming increasingly central to political debates in many societies. There are few areas of theoretical and political discourse where questions about the politics of identity are not now being raised, even if they are not as clearly articulated as they have been in queer writings. Although, as Annamarie Jagose notes, it is improbable that identity politics will entirely disappear with queer, it is likely to 'become more nuanced, less sure of itself, and more attuned to those multiple compromises and pragmatic effects that characterise *any* mobilisation of identity' (1996: 126; her emphasis). Thus, queer's questioning of the assumption of the self-evidence of identity descriptions, including its own, can be seen as its principal achievement (Jagose, 1996: 126).

The queer challenge to thinking about the masculine

Queer theory unsettles contemporary thinking about the masculine, and questions the use of categories in research and writing, and the aims and objects of enquiries. It brings to the fore questions of an epistemological kind that, as I mentioned earlier, have been only rarely addressed in research and writings on 'men', 'manhood', and 'masculine identity'. Although many scholars and activists claim to promote 'pro-feminist' and 'gay-affirmative' policies, few have explicitly and critically examined the theoretical models employed in writings on 'masculine identity'. Theoretical and practical concerns have reflected a strong, if implicit, heterosexist (and 'white', middle-class) bias, and the tendency has been to reduce the political to the personal. An emphasis on the 'burdens of masculinity' or the 'crisis of male identity' within the work of many male writers has effectively cast men as victims of an oppressive social order, while diverting attention from the diverse array of regulations and exclusions that apply to those who do not identify themselves as 'heterosexual', or are not white or European. The essentialism of identity and the underlying identity politics of 'men's studies' and the 'men's movement' have led to the neglect of the analysis of power relations and power/knowledge. In so far as sexuality is dealt with in any detail at all, it tends to be viewed in individual reductionist terms, and in isolation from other aspects of identity and as separate from the social. Most theorists adopt a conventional modernist concept of identity that takes the self as pre-social, unitary, and relatively stable, albeit constrained. The result is that deeply-held cultural assumptions about men, their desires and their identities remain unexamined. The challenges posed by queer theory to thinking about men and 'masculinity' are increasingly difficult to ignore, however, and will need much more serious consideration by scholars and activists who are intent on avoiding essentialism and heterosexism in their own work.

Queer theorists have recently drawn attention to the implicit heterosexist biases of those disciplines that have been central in the production of knowledge about the masculine – namely, psychoanalysis and sociology (Domenici and Lesser, 1995; Seidman, 1996b). As I argued in Chapter 3, psychoanalysis has played a key role, historically, in defining and 'normalising' masculine desire as heterosexual desire that is 'fixed' in the body as an inherent aspect of personhood. These assumptions have been reinforced in recent psychoana-

lytic accounts of masculine identity, especially in object-relations theory (see
Chapter 4). Queer theorists have exposed a heterosexist bias in the underlying
evolutionary theory of psychoanalysis, which assumes procreative heterosexuality as the standard, and confirms the privilege given it by cultural
convention, including psychoanalytic reasoning (Dimen, 1995: 131).
Notwithstanding recent questioning in the social sciences of the kind of
Darwinism on which Freud relied – where every behaviour must have its
reproductive consequences – strict adaptationism has continued to shape
moral ideals, cultural conventions of normality, and political forces. Strict
adaptationism has been a rationale for what Schwartz (1993) calls 'heterophilia': the generally unarticulated idealisation of heterosexuality that
informs our culture and theories of desire (citing Dimen, 1995: 132).
Although heterophilia finds its most concentrated expression in sociobiology,
which holds that all organisms are driven by the imperative to reproduce
successfully, it manifests to varying degrees in many disciplines (Dimen, 1995:
132–3). Sociology, one of the key disciplines in the developing 'men's studies',
has also been shown to reflect an implicit heterosexism through the neglect of
important critical questions relating to the epistemology of sexuality, and
through biases in lines of enquiry and hidden assumptions in theory (see
Seidman, 1996a: 7). Until the late 1960s and early 1970s, sexuality had not
been seen as an important topic for sociological theorisation. And, when it
began to be studied, researchers focused on 'homosexuality' and the 'homosexual role', while paying little attention to the construction of sexual
categories and identities (Epstein, 1996: 146–52). Introductory sociology textbooks have been shown to display an overall heterosexist bias which is
manifest in the choice of topics and examples, in the vocabulary (for example,
the uncritical use of the term 'homosexual'), and in the failure to examine sexuality as a historical and social production (see Phillips, 1991).

The deconstruction of 'gender'

Heterosexist assumptions are imported into research and writing on men
and 'masculinity' most directly through theories of gender. Queer theorists
have pointed to the heterosexual imagery and assumed sexual hierarchy in
theories of gender. According to this hierarchy,

> . . . sexuality that is 'good', 'normal', and 'natural' should ideally be heterosexual,
> marital, monogamous, reproductive, and non-commercial. It should be coupled,
> relational, within the same generation, and occur at home. It should not involve
> pornography, fetish objects, sex toys of any sort, or roles other than male and
> female. Any sex that violates these rules is 'bad', 'abnormal', or 'unnatural'. Bad sex
> may be homosexual, unmarried, promiscuous, non-procreative, or commercial. It
> may be masturbatory or take place at orgies, may be casual, may cross generational
> lines, and may take place in 'public' or at least in the bushes or the baths. It may
> involve the use of pornography, fetish objects, sex toys, or unusual roles. (Rubin,
> 1982: 280–81)

Given the centrality of 'gender' as an analytic concept in late twentieth-
century social thought, it is surprising that scholars have only recently begun

to examine its history and discursive production. Hausman (1995) has recently argued that the idea of gender first arose in the 1950s in the context of efforts to deal with the threat posed to the institution of heterosexuality by intersexuality, or ambiguous sex. Intersexuality has been seen to threaten the binary classification system that has been central to heterosexuality – i.e. the idea of two complementary 'sexes' – and so has been a prime site for the management of normality, particularly through the technologies of bio-medicine. Faced with ambiguities in physical sex, the experts sought to develop a mechanism for deciding how to reassign 'sex'. Articles and case notes of medical experts treating intersexuality in the 1950s reveal that there was a growing concern to bring physical sex into line with how the intersexual person had been reared. John Money and his colleagues, who were then leaders in the study and treatment of intersexuality, developed the idea of gender in order to allow a social and cultural, as opposed to a biological, distinction to be made between the 'sexes'. Their concept of 'gender role' designated one's social status as a boy or man, girl or woman, respectively, which was not established at birth, but was built up cumulatively through experiences.

According to Hausman, this specific usage of gender represented a shift in the twentieth-century meanings of the term which, until then, operated as a synonym for 'sex' (1995: 95). The development of medical technologies of 'sex change' in the 1950s, particularly surgical technologies, was crucial in creating the possibility of enforcing binary gender through the material production of sex (1995: 79). These technologies allowed physicians to materially intervene into the bodies of their subjects in order to bring them into line with the prevailing conception of the 'natural' sexuality – i.e. heterosexuality. In the process, a new subject category, the transsexual, was brought into being, as was a new possibility for claiming personal identity. The story does not end here, however. The psychoanalytic concept of 'gender identity' was then later developed, by Robert Stoller in 1964, in order to further facilitate the case management of intersexuals and transsexuals by allowing subjects to identify an internal sense of authenticity, thus overcoming the sole reliance on external activities and performances – i.e. the 'gender role' (Hausman, 1995: 102–8). The shift from 'gender role' to 'gender identity' offered a rationale for surgical or hormonal sex change in the treatment of intersexual people in the absence of any physiological justification. As Hausman indicates, the development of the gender identity paradigm has had 'far-reaching effects on cultural notions of the relation between the sexed body and its behaviours'. It helped create a new conceptual terrain for 'sex' since those subjects who were unable to represent sex 'authentically' were now presented with the option of 'performing' their 'sex' through 'gender' (1995: 107).

As Chrys Ingraham (1996) argues, theories of gender rely on an implicit heterosexual dualism whereby males and females learn to become men and women through attaining opposite and distinct traits based on sex. It is taken as an unproblematic given that 'opposite sexes' are naturally attracted to each other, much like other aspects of the physical world (for example, magnetic fields). A heterosexual bias can be seen most clearly in theories of 'socialisation', whereby males and females are seen to become men and women attaining opposite and distinct traits based on sex. Many sociological discussions rely on an unstated heterosexual dualism which implies a static and normative understanding of gender. Moreover, few theorists explain the 'necessity' of gender. The theory of gender as an 'achieved' status never addresses the question of 'to what ends gender is acquired' (Ingraham, 1996: 185–6). Ingraham comments that

> Contemporary sex-gender ideology provides limited options for how we organise sexuality, but expanding these options is not simply a matter of attending to marginalized sexualities. Instead, it seems to me that we need to question our assumptions about sex and gender as to how they organize difference, regulate investigation, and preserve particular power relations, especially those linked to institutionalized heterosexuality. (1996: 184)

The sex/gender dualism and its associated nature/culture dualism has been left largely unproblematised by those researching and writing about men and 'masculinity'. 'Sex' has been taken as a pre-given, natural domain, unmediated by culture and history. Thus, the primary concern has been with such questions as: what is definitive of 'manhood' (as a gendered state of being or set of practices)? How does one become a 'man' (as an acquisition of 'gender role' and/or 'gender identity')? And what are the personal implications of the crisis in 'male identity' (loss of 'gender role' and/or 'gender identity')?

A nature/culture dualism is apparent in the work of Bob Connell, for example, who is one of the few recent analysts of 'masculinity' to offer a systematic account of gender, and more specifically gender as a social practice, in his book *Masculinities* (1995). It is reflected in his comments such as: 'gender is a social practice that constantly refers to bodies and what bodies do, it is not social practice reduced to the body' and 'gender exists precisely to the extent that biology does *not* determine the social' (1995: 71; emphasis in original). These comments, part of Connell's argument against 'biological reductionism', reveal acceptance of the idea of an objective and immutable biological realm (i.e. 'sex') that is distinct from and *beyond* the influence of 'culture' (i.e. 'gender'), and, by implication, beyond change. The specific materiality of the body' is taken as a given. Thus, Connell notes at one point that: 'What is more or less constant, through shifts of culture, is the anatomy and physiology of male bodies' (1995: 43). He never enquires into the epistemological foundations of the gender/sex or culture/nature dualism, or asks why it is that particular 'genders' are seen to accrue exclusively to particular 'sexes'. In his chapter on men's bodies, Connell dismisses what he sees as the two major opposing conceptions of the body – biological determinism and social determinism – in favour of a phenomenological approach, or what he calls 'the body-reflexive practice' (1995: 45–66). Again, 'the body' appears as a natural category, unaffected by history and culture. Connell seems not to recognise that the very materialisation of men's bodies as biologically sexed bodies is effected through historically and socially specific discourses, and that this ultimately affects how men experience their bodies, including their sexual desires. For example, genetic theories about natural sex differences in sex drive or about a pre-programmed natural 'sexual orientation' are part of a set of discourses about bodies and their functioning which shape the ways in which subjects 'live' their 'bodies' and experience their relations with others.

Connell's notion of 'the body-reflexive practice' presumes the existence of an autonomous rational self that is located outside time, place, and social location. It is assumed that the body can speak the 'truth' of itself. The subjects whom Connell interviews (1995: 52–64), and who relate their embodied experiences, inform us little about how prevailing discourses of sexuality shape what is known, and can be known, about 'men', 'manhood' and 'masculine identity'. As in many other contemporary writings on 'masculinity/ies', gender appears here as a reified variable to be examined in interaction with other equally reified variables such as 'race' and class (see Chapter 1). Different 'masculinities' are seen to emerge from the interplay between these different variables, with some 'masculinities' becoming dominant ('hegemonic'), and others 'subordinated' or 'marginalised'. Within this scheme, 'homosexual masculinities' appear as fixed identity categories 'at the bottom of a gender hierarchy among men', along with other 'subordinated masculinities', which includes 'some heterosexual men and boys' (1995: 79–9). Connell argues that his use of terms such as 'hegemonic masculinity' and 'marginalized masculinities' 'name not fixed character types but configurations of practice generated in particular situations in a changing structure of relationships' (1995: 81). However, by focusing on gender as a social practice, one is never led to critically interrogate the sex/gender and nature/culture distinctions. Connell's account ignores the widely varying and shifting cultural constructions of 'manliness' and of same-sex behaviour. The limitations of viewing gender and sexuality as fixed, discrete categories becomes immediately apparent when one examines comparative ethnographic research which shows great variability in definitions of manhood, same-sex behaviour, and gender both between *and* within cultures (see, for example, Almaguer, 1991; Cornwall and Lindisfarne, 1994b; Moore, 1994a).

Rethinking the question of sexual identity

The queer critique of sexual epistemology and of identity politics forces us to rethink the question of sexual identity – particularly the idea that people have a 'natural' 'sexual orientation' which is 'normally' 'heterosexual' – and to consider the political and practical implications of the loosening of the connection between sexuality and identity. The critique of the idea of an 'essential' sexual self unsettles assumptions about the meaning of 'gay-affirmative' work as promoted by many 'men's studies' scholars and by sections of the contemporary 'men's movement'. Discussions are often pre-figured by a discourse which takes as given the hetero/homosexual division, and all that that implies: for example, the assumption that subjects have relatively fixed and mutually exclusive identities; the denial of the construction and fluidity of desire; and the marginalisation of those who identify neither as gay nor heterosexual. As queer theorists have pointed out, political projects designed to 'liberate' subjects, whether they be small-scale confessional or therapeutic practices or large-scale social movements, often amount to ways of 'fixing' identities and shaping subjectivities through the knowledges that they generate. It is for this reason that some writers have linked the success of queer politics to the ability to escape definition, and to remain within 'the realm of the mysterious, the shady, the *unknown*' (Angelides, 1994: 75; emphasis in original). Although, as I have noted, queer theory is not without its problems and unresolved dilemmas, it has played an important role in drawing attention to the limitations and implications of a politics which focuses on securing gay rights while leaving unexamined the epistemology of sexuality.

Again, it should be emphasised, the critique of 'identity' does not mean that one should necessarily completely abandon identity as a category of knowledge and politics. Rather, the point is that one needs to remain ever vigilant about the use of 'identity' and alert to the dangers associated with the assumption of shared identity – for example, in gay historiography, noted above. Although the overall impact of queer theory on identity politics is as yet unclear, the emergence of queer theory would seem to signal an important shift in thinking about questions of identity, with more emphasis on the construction and purposes of the putative (sexual) norm, as well as on marginal experience for what this reveals about the broader terrain of power relations. It points to a different approach to sexuality from that developed in sociology and other social science disciplines, which have tended to relegate sexual minorities to the analytic sidelines rather than viewing them as windows into the structuring of power, meaning, and social organisation (Epstein, 1996: 156). As I argued in Chapter 2, recent studies of 'gender bending', 'transsexualism', 'bisexuality' and 'third sexes' or 'third genders' have revealed the complex links between 'gender', 'sexuality', and 'desire', and the fluidity of sexual self-identifications (for example, Elkins and King, 1996; Garber, 1995; Herdt, 1994). More and more, it has come to be recognised that one can have desires that do not correspond with culturally available sexual and gender identities, and physical 'sexes' that do not necessarily correspond with social 'genders'. The recent appearance of a 'transgender movement' has exposed the existence of a vast variety of desiring subjects, and anticipates future evolutions of physical sexes and social genders, the outcome of which is uncertain (Nataf, 1996: 56). This research underlines the arbitrariness of the sexual classificatory system, and the ways in which an appeal to 'nature' may be used to regulate sexual identities by allowing corporeal distinctions to be drawn between the pure and the impure, the hygienic and the unhygienic, the healthy and the unhealthy, the included and the excluded, and the mutable and the immutable. With this work, the notion of a natural 'sexual orientation' is increasingly difficult to sustain. The 'de-naturalising' of the natural that has been integral to queer thinking, as well as to many other areas of contemporary thought, presents us with the opportunity for reflecting upon our normative ideals of masculine identity and, as I will explain in the next and final chapter, opens up the possibility for the emergence of reconceptualised models of identity.

6

Conclusion

Recent developments suggest that academic and popular interest in 'men', 'masculinity' and 'manhood' is undiminished. There is an ever-growing number of academic journals and men's groups exploring definitions of masculinity and male experience, and journalists and authors have found a ready audience for writings about the crises and dilemmas of 'manhood'. Even the Internet has spawned a site on 'manhood' (www.manhood.com.nf) which in 1997 was attracting 80,000 visitors a month (Williams, 1997: 14). In these texts and contexts, questions of whether or not new 'models of masculinity' are emerging and what they might entail are being vigorously debated. Is the macho man dead? Have Sensitive New Age Guys been superseded by the New Lads? Is it possible to celebrate aspects of aggressive masculinity and still demonstrate one's support for feminism? Has feminism destroyed the very idea of manhood? And so on. In Chapter 2, I suggested that such questioning reflects a crisis in definitions of 'masculinity', as they have evolved in the modern West, which is closely linked to a broader 'crisis in modernity'. In that chapter, and in subsequent chapters, I described the background to this crisis, and identified a number of its dimensions, focusing on challenges to the nature/culture dualism, the sex/gender dualism, the mind/body dualism, and the hetero/homosexual dualism. In this concluding chapter, I draw together the major themes of the book, and discuss some implications and questions arising from the analysis as a whole.

I have provided an outline of recent theoretical developments that have unsettled prevailing assumptions about men and 'masculine identity', and hopefully, in the process, have underlined the need for researchers and activists to rethink their categories of analysis and to refocus their enquiries. In Chapter 1, I signalled my concerns about the contemporary field of academic study known as 'men's studies' which, although producing a number of interesting and provocative analyses, has tended to neglect questions of epistemology, the analysis of power relations, and interdisciplinary enquiry. Male writers have overlooked the contributions of those working in such areas as feminist philosophy of science, postmodern feminism, poststructuralist feminism, and queer theory who have offered useful insights into gender, gender relations, sexuality and identity. As I argued, male scholars who claim to be 'pro-feminist' usually engage with only a small fragment of contemporary feminist contributions, and have been over-reliant on a few perspectives, notably sex-role theory, gender theory, learning theory, Jungian theory and object-relations theory – that were originally developed in the social sciences, and then often subsequently reworked by 'second-wave' feminist scholars. They have largely ignored recent historical deconstructionist and poststructuralist work on the body, and remain strongly wedded to outmoded, essentialist notions of identity. Recent theory challenges conventional understandings of 'the body', 'the self', 'sex', 'gender', 'sexuality', and 'identity', and the dualistic and essentialist thinking underlying the construction of these categories, showing them to be historically and socially specific and to operate as regulatory fictions.

One of the major themes of the book has concerned the ways in which natural knowledge has served to 'naturalise' relations of power, seen clearly in the discourse on sexuality and discourse on sex differences. The idea that there exists a pre-discursive natural or biological realm, separate from and unaffected by a cultural realm, or relations of power, is one that is deeply inscribed in modern Western thought, and has offered a powerful constraint on thinking about the masculine and about the possibilities for social change. Almost all contemporary discussions about men and 'masculinity' are pre-figured by a discourse which takes as given the division between nature and culture. Thus, as I argued in Chapter 1, writers have tended to reify and essentialise 'masculinity' (or 'masculinities', as the current parlance would have it) which is seen to designate a fixed property of the natural corporeal body, or an aspect or manifestation of the socialised psyche. However, as I also pointed out, the view that there exist distinct and stable natural and social realms has increasingly come under question. This can be seen in the growing number of critiques of the sex/gender binary. Critics of sex/gender have noted that there has been a tendency to view the biological realm as somehow 'more real' than the cultural realm (see, for example, Hood-Williams, 1997). That is, biology is seen to provide the invariable and unalterable bedrock of, or material base for, social identity and social behaviour.

Conceptions of sex/gender are premised on, and insistently refer to, a tradition of viewing culture as malleable relative to nature: that is, culture, rather than nature, is the thing that can, and indeed should, be changed. This tradition has provided the foundation for the essentialist/constructivist debate that has been especially influential in feminism and in gay and lesbian studies (Sedgwick, 1994: 41). As I argued in Chapter 2, while early second-wave' feminists criticised the nature/culture dualism, as part of their effort to challenge the notion of biology-as-destiny, they did not extend their criticism fully to the derivative sex/gender distinction, and so biological determinism and dualistic thinking have been carried over into feminist theorising in the correspondence of 'sex' with 'nature' and 'gender' with 'culture'. These biases have been replicated in recent thinking and theorising about 'masculinity' and 'male identity'. Although the sex/gender distinction has, arguably, proved useful in the development of a 'second-wave' feminist movement, its practical and theoretical limitations have become increasingly evident. As I have pointed out, recent scholarship has exposed the historical variability of constructions of 'sex', demonstrating the ways in which it has been deployed in the fabrication of the oppositional binaries of male/female and men/women throughout the post-Enlightenment period. The assumption that the biological realm is 'more real' or less mutable than the social realm has led to the view that there are natural limits to social change; that men are 'hard-wired' to be aggressive, competitive, dominating, and so on. It has also led to efforts to alter the bodies of 'homosexuals' (for example, hormonal treatment) in order to make them 'normal', that is 'heterosexual' (see Chapter 3), rather than to question the norms of sexuality.

As many writers have pointed out, there is an implicit sexual dimorphism in the sex/gender division (see, for example, Hood-Williams, 1996: 6). Consistent with long-standing theories about the complementarity of the sexes, described in Chapter 2, there is seen to be a 'natural' attraction between the two 'opposite sexes'. A focus on sex invariably leads to discussions about women's and men's natural, complementary reproductive capacities and destinies, thereby reinforcing heterosexism. If the focus remains on biological sex, the question arises as to how one should classify people who cannot reproduce because they are too young, too old, too malnourished, at the wrong point in the menstrual cycle, etc. (Hood-Williams, 1996: 5; see also Hood-Williams, 1997: 55). Contemporary feminists and queer theorists have underlined the theoretical shortcomings and political implications of continuing adherence to the sex/gender division, particularly its role in reinforcing dominant socio-sexual arrangements (see Chapters 2 and 5). With the emergence of poststructuralist theory, I have argued, the attention has shifted away from viewing categories such as 'sex' and 'sexuality' as natural categories and towards seeing them as discursive constructions, that is products of power/knowledge, that serve to regulate identity. The critique of 'identity' poses significant challenges for entire areas of scholarship and activism. I pointed to the de-stabilising effects of growing 'gender scepticism' on 'second-wave' feminism in Chapter 2, and the impact of the queer critique of 'sexual identity' on gay and lesbian politics in Chapter 5. As I explained in Chapter 2, the critique of 'identity' has also led to a rethinking of the concept of 'race' within anti-racist/post-colonial theory, and to an examination of the interrelations between this category and other regulatory categories.

In Chapter 3, I examined the historical deployment of the categories ' sex', 'sexuality' and 'race' in the historical and social construction of the male body as 'naturally' different from the female body, and how particular male bodies, namely the bodies of white, European, middle-class, heterosexual men have been fabricated as the standard for measuring and evaluating other bodies. To suggest that the body is historically and socially constructed is not to deny its materiality, as some commentators have suggested, but rather to challenge the 'naturalness' of its *specific* materiality. Following Judith Butler (1993), I have argued that the materiality of the body is an effect of power, or a discursive production. Viewing the body in this way, I would contend, is inherently subversive, since it inevitably leads to questions about how this construction is sustained and how the body might be 'reconstructed'. In

Chapter 3, I emphasised that the discursive production of the 'ideal' male body inevitably involves exclusions, whereby some bodies are rendered deviant or pathological: for example, Jews' bodies, the bodies of non-Europeans, and the 'feminised' bodies of 'homosexual' men. This production has been sustained through evolutionary theory, which has provided the source for many of the ideas about the 'ideal' masculine body, particularly its 'natural' adaptability, competitiveness, strength, aggressivity, and sex drive. I pointed out that these ideas are implicit in social organisation (for example, work, the military) and in expert knowledges (for example, psychology, psychoanalysis, and sociology), and that they continue to influence both 'academic' feminist and 'popular' accounts of 'manhood' and 'masculinity' where biological theories are frequently invoked to explain male identity, male behaviour, and social differences between men and women. However, notwithstanding the endurance of these ideas, they are beginning to lose their credibility. The binary divisions between the subject and the object, and the knower and the known, are being questioned, with consequent de-stabilising effects on dominant understandings of the masculine. The idea that it is possible to achieve an unmediated and impartial understanding of human beings – their bodies and subjectivities – although still dominant as an approach to knowledge, is increasingly seen as untenable and as having marginalising effects. The critique of the nature/social binary, it is clear, is intimately connected with the critique of the mind/body dualism, one of the other major themes of the book.

As I pointed out in Chapter 4, the privileging of the 'mind' over the 'body', or the effort to achieve the impartial or 'disembodied' viewpoint, is seen by many feminist and 'pro-feminist' male scholars as characteristic of a distinctly 'masculinist' rationality that is implicated in the domination not only of men over women but also of culture over nature, and Europeans over non-Europeans. These scholars have criticised such rationality for its essentialism and universalism. However, as I explained, critics have not found it easy to avoid these tendencies in their own work. They have been inclined to 'naturalise' differences between men and women, for example in theories about gender and care, theories of moral development, and accounts of the human/nature connection. Sometimes women are portrayed as having intrinsic qualities that are not shared with men, or there is seen to be some universal feminine 'nature' that is opposed to some clearly definable masculine 'nature' – for example, women are seen as 'naturally more caring' than men. A lack of acknowledgement of complexity in social constructions of masculine and feminine identities, and of the existence of competing, sometimes contradictory, discourses of gender and sexuality in different contexts (see my comments below), has led to the replication of dualistic thinking in many avowedly anti-dualistic and anti-essentialist analyses of 'masculinist' rationality. Furthermore, many theorists embrace rather than critique science and its assumptions, as is often the case with psychoanalytic feminists. One of the key points that I emphasised in Chapter 4 was that if one is serious about challenging dualistic, essentialist and hierarchical thinking it is important to remain critical in respect to the use of all categories and concepts. I concluded this chapter by concurring with Iris Marion Young (1990) that impartiality is a regulative ideal that is prone to failure, and that evidence of this can be seen in the emergence of oppositional discourses, such as that represented by the queer movement, which foreground issues of power/knowledge and the politics of representation.

Because rational knowledge is recognised as always being partial and as having exclusionary and oppressive effects, many scholars have recently proposed the concept of 'situated knowledge', or 'embodied knowledge', as the basis for theory and practice. As I observed in Chapter 4, this is seen by many feminists as a prerequisite for avoiding normative, regulative and exclusionary forms of thought. It suggests that the creator of knowledge is made accountable for the knowledge that is produced; that knowledge is always grounded in a *particular* experience. The problem with this concept, however, is that it suggests some permanence to subject position, an assumption which is challenged by poststructuralist thought. If there is no fixed subject position from which to speak, but only a multiplicity of constantly shifting subject positions, is it possible to develop knowledge that can provide a relatively stable and shared basis for identity and political action? The question also arises as to whether or not it is possible to base an identity on something other than 'essence' (for example, skin colour, reproductive capacities, 'sexual orientation', etc.), and indeed whether or not it is politically strategic to always avoid essentialism (Fuss, 1989: 102). The concept of 'strategic essentialism', proposed by some feminist and queer scholars (see Chapters 2 and 5), suggests that identity labels can be strategically employed according to perceived situational advantage, political gain and/or conceptual utility, and indeed must be used in this way if one is to protect and advance social rights in a context of 'backlash' against the gains of feminists and virtually all minority groups. A number of questions remain, however. These include: under what conditions should such strategic mobilisations occur, and who decides what is strategic and which categories of subject are to be involved in any mobilisation around a particular construction of identity? Who can legitimately speak on behalf of others, and on what grounds do they claim such legitimacy? How exactly should identity labels be employed to maximise political advantage? At what point do the disadvantages of strategic alliance of this kind outweigh the advantages, and who decides on this?

Such questions are complex and not easily resolvable, but are crucial for those seeking to develop a new or reconceptualised identity politics that does not assume the existence of fixed, unitary identities or of a strict causal relationship between 'identity' and 'politics'. However, they have barely begun to be examined by 'men's studies' scholars and those people who are exploring the possibilities for developing new, less oppressive social relations. As noted, many scholars remain committed to positivistic science and continue to adhere to reified and essentialist notions of identity, often exhibiting profound ignorance of important developments in social theory. The insights offered by poststructuralist thinkers such as Michel Foucault hardly figure at all in the new 'men's studies' scholarship, even though poststructuralist theorists are centrally concerned with exploring the operations of power relations, the processes by which subjects are constituted, and the possibilities for resistance. One would expect that scholars who are committed to developing anti-racist, anti-sexist, and anti-homophobic theory and practice would be immensely interested in examining the implications of this work for theory and practice. As it happens, the major challenges to thinking about the masculine have originated not with the new cadre of 'men's studies' scholars and 'masculinity' researchers, but with those working in other areas of scholarship.

One of these areas, I have argued (in Chapter 5), is queer studies, which explicitly questions the concept of identity and identity politics. Queer theory emphasises the limits of the politics of minority rights, and focuses attention on the production and effects of the putative norm. I described the particular context in which queer theory emerged: the conservative backlash against 'homosexuality' and the AIDS crisis which brought to the fore the limits of a politics of minority rights and inclusion, and the exclusions and biases that are seen to be associated with gay and lesbian subcultures. The assumption of the authentic self that has underpinned Gay Liberation strategy, I noted, is seen to leave intact the frameworks of knowledge within which sexuality is understood. It never leads one to question the hetero/homosexual division which is seen to 'fix' identities according to this polarity and to deny the diversity and fluidity of sexual self-identifications. Queer emphasises the limitations and implications of gay historiography, which tends to presume 'homosexuality as we know it today', and the gay tactic of 'coming out of the closet', which is premised upon a concept of a unitary, fixed and voluntaristic self. Although the full implications of queer theory for identity politics have yet to be fully realised, and there remain some important unresolved dilemmas and problems in reconciling theory and practice, it raises important questions about the meaning of 'masculine identity', about research priorities, and about the identity politics of the 'men's movement'. With the undermining of the idea of an essential, unitary sexual self, it needs to be asked exactly what it means for an individual to declare a 'sexual orientation', and for scholars and activists to promote 'gay affirmative' policies and practices. What particular strategies might scholars and activists adopt if they wish to advance minority rights and yet avoid fixing and/or imposing an identity on themselves and others? Is it possible for one to represent members of oppressed groups to which one does not belong and, if so, how should one represent these 'others'? (On this question, see particularly Wilkinson and Kitzinger, 1996.)

Queer theory signals the emergence of a new postmodern or postparadigmatic sensibility in relation to the question of sexual identity, focusing on the politics of representation. Postmodernism has highlighted the representational dimension of sexuality, challenging 'the tired habitualization of metaphors', of which the biological metaphor is 'perhaps the tiredest yet most pervasive and powerful' (Plummer, 1996: xi). An increasing amount of academic work in the area of sexuality and gender has focused on language and representation. In line with this, many scholars have turned their attentions to the critical deconstruction of texts, with a view to exposing their implicit biases and supportive representational practices. I referred to queer critiques of psychoanalysis and sociology, disciplines that have strongly shaped our conceptions of 'masculinity' and theories of gender, which were developed originally in the social sciences and then in feminism and, only relatively recently, adopted in studies of men and 'masculinity'. Queer theorists have exposed the role of evolutionary theory in reinforcing heterosexism in Western knowledge. This complements the work of feminists who have also focused on the role of evolutionary biology in the naturalisation of the power relations of gender. There is a need for a more thoroughgoing analysis of the sexual symbolism of the various modern constructions of the masculine, showing how the language of biology and essence converge at different times and in different contexts to reinforce the ideal form of male sexuality as reproductive heterosexuality. It also needs to be recognised how the symbolism of sexuality has operated, and continues to operate, in the service of racism. As I explained in Chapter 3, different sexual connotations have applied to different male bodies: for example, male Jews and young black men have been seen to be characterised by sexualities that are essentially different from that of white, European, heterosexual (i.e. 'normal') men. Queer theory points to the need for a nuanced historical and social constructionist approach to the question of male sexual identity, with greater recognition of the ways in which different categories of identity interact at different times.

The critique of 'identity', exemplified by queer theory, presents a major challenge to those researching and writing about black or ethnic masculine identities. As I mentioned in Chapter 1, there has been a tendency to 'essentialise' the identities of black or ethnic men, and to overlook the extent to which categories and concepts are infused with racist assumptions (see, for example, Julien, 1992; Mercer, 1994: 213–15, 221, 281; Mercer and Julien, 1988). Although 'race' and ethnicity have been, and continue to be, important categories of self-definition for oppressed groups, many people have begun to question the necessity of having to base one's identity on some single, unitary, fixed 'essence', such as skin colour, nationality, or religious belief (see, for example, Rajchman, 1995). Consequently, contemporary black and ethnic scholars are grappling with the question of how to recognise shared experiences of domination resulting from racism and ethnocentrism while avoiding the dangers of simply imposing an identity based on the assumption of a unitary and undifferentiated 'blackness' or 'ethnicity'. Just as queer theorists have turned their critical attentions on the cultural construction of the normal – i.e. heterosexuality – anti-racist and post-colonial scholars have focused their attentions on the construction of 'whiteness' and the processes by which it has been 'naturalised' through ideologies of race and racism (see, for example, Appiah and Gates, 1995; Frankenberg, 1993). This work points to a new approach to the question of 'race' or ethnicity and its interaction with 'masculinity', with a more historical and critical appreciation of how these categories are constituted and how they interact to construct and marginalise particular identities. There is a need for greater recognition of how black and ethnic masculine identities are shaped within dominant relations of power, manifesting in behaviours such as the 'cool pose', found among many Afro-American men (Majors and Billson, 1992), in a specific use of public space (Westwood, 1990), and in endemic violence within black and ethnic communities (see, for example, hooks, 1992). Analyses of this kind are relatively rare, and sociologists and other scholars can be seen to perpetuate stereotypes of black and ethnic men through the approaches that they bring to their work, in their selective use of data, and in their reliance on pre-existing popular images (Duneier, 1992: 137–62).

Although the critique of 'identity' is gaining momentum throughout the humanities and social sciences and is undermining some basic assumptions about 'men', 'masculinity' and 'identity', established 'ideals' of 'manhood' are unlikely to completely disappear. As George Mosse argues in his book, *The Image of Man: The Creation of Modern Masculinity* (1996), the question is not so much about whether the 'manly stereotype' will vanish, but about its erosion and about 'how far it can bend' (1996: 193). As Mosse correctly points out, images of 'masculinity' are not static constructions, but are shaped by social context and prevailing conceptions of society, and so can be expected to undergo constant modification. In the late modern context of a consumer and mass-mediated culture, one can identify a diversity of new images of masculine identity, including androgynous images which are increasingly seen in fashion advertising (see Mosse, 1996: 185–6). Some writers have identified a shift in popular representations of 'masculinity' – condensed in the figure of the 'new man' – which is seen as linked to the development of new consumer institutions and niche markets (see, for example, Mort, 1996; Nixon, 1996). If the history of reactions to past challenges to 'manly' ideals is any guide, however, one can hardly expect that the erosion of entrenched ideals of masculine identity will be abrupt and without some resistance. As noted earlier, within some sections of the 'men's movement' there has been a strong reaction to the changes afoot, with many harking back to an imaginary 'lost identity' – for example, the warrior ideal.

In their discussion of the so-called 'men's movement', Kimmel and Kaufman suggest that economic, political, and social changes, including changes in the nature of work and the rise of the women's movements and the gay and lesbian movements, have affected all men, but perhaps psychologically hardest hit of all were 'middle-class, straight, white men from their late 20s through their 40s' (1994: 261–3).

> For these were not only the men who inherited a prescription for manhood that included economic autonomy, public patriarchy, and the frontier safety valve but also the men who believed themselves entitled to the power that attended on the successful demonstration of masculinity. These men experienced workplace transformation as a threat to their manhood and the entry of the formerly excluded 'others' as a virtual invasion of their privileged space. (Kimmel and Kaufman, 1994: 262)

These are the men, so argue Kimmel and Kaufman, who largely comprise the current 'men's movement', at least in the United States, and who are attracted to the themes trumpeted by Bly, Warren, and their followers: the powerlessness of men, anguish over dominant mothers and absent fathers, the restrictions of the male sex role, the search for the 'lost warrior', and so on. The emergence of a 'men's rights movement' is an understandable, albeit worrying, response in a context of rapid change. However, it also underlines the fragility of the norms of 'manhood' and the constant effort that is required to maintain 'normality'. As Bech (1997) argues, 'manliness' always involves having to prove one's 'manhood'; having to put one's self to the test. However, the avenues for proving one's 'manliness' have narrowed to the point where, for many men, the performance of 'manhood' has become equivalent to proving that they are *not* women, and emphasising their biological sex, sex organs, and/or sexual functioning (Bech, 1997: 131–6). Clearly, some men have much at stake in the dominant conceptions of masculine identity, and can be expected to feel threatened by any challenge to established ideals. However, it is apparent that many people *are* receptive to rethinking some traditional assumptions about 'manhood' and about the relations between men and between men and women. One cause for optimism is the observation that, at least in some societies, the strong links between ideals of masculine identity and heterosexual object choice have been weakened. Those societies where changes to gender stereotypes are occurring most rapidly also happen to be those characterised by a growing tolerance for a wide range of sexual self-identifications.

In Chapters 2 and 3, I emphasised the close historical connections, in the West at least, between the constructions of 'men' and 'women' as polarised identities and the emergence of the 'heterosexual' and the 'homosexual' as distinct identity 'types'. The erosion of the 'homosexual', and hence the 'heterosexual', it has recently been suggested, may well be linked to 'a fragmentation of the totalising notions of man and woman as two binary opposed sets of social, psychological, and sexual qualities' (Löfström, 1997: 36). Henning Bech (1997) notes that in Denmark the development of the notion of 'registered partnerships', or 'homosexual marriages', closely parallels changes in definitions of heterosexual family arrangements and a greater equality between men and women in the public sphere. Arguments prevailing among supporters of 'registered partnerships' have centred on the principle of equality: that 'homosexuals' should gain the right to equal freedom of choice enjoyed by 'heterosexuals' in relation to the privileges and obligations of forming couples (Bech, 1997: 201). It is only possible to argue for such equality, contends Bech, in a context in which there is a diminution of difference between the lifestyles of 'homosexuals' and 'heterosexuals' brought about by the decline in the prestige and importance of the institutions of marriage and the family. In other words, the conditions of life which have formerly characterised 'homosexuality' for much of the modern period – for example, the separation of sex, love, and cohabitation, and a sense of inner self and sexuality – have become common to the extent that there are no longer any valid arguments for denying 'homosexuals' the rights previously accorded the rest of the population. In late modern society, it is no longer convincing to refer to 'the essentially and naturally different personality type of the homo-sexuals, or to their being inherently and particularly respectable *or* alternative – when the non-homosexuals were increasingly exhibiting the same personality traits and becoming equally "respectable" or unrespectable and "alternative"' (Bech, 1997: 201).

Although Denmark has been at the forefront of social reform in the West, Bech contends that the conditions and forms of life in Denmark are not so different from those in the rest of the (North) Western world and so the debate on 'homosexual marriage' is likely to be replicated in other countries as well. However, this change is contingent upon an equalisation of eco-nomic and social opportunities which will allow for a 'relaxed homoge-nization of life-styles' (Bech, 1997: 206). In national socio-cultural contexts characterised by entrenched inequalities in wealth and the lack of a genuine welfare state, such as in the United States, changes do not have the charac-ter of the disappearance of the modern 'homosexual'. In that particular country, the family has remained the bulwark against a modernity which is still considered threatening, and there continues to be a great deal of hos-tility to 'homosexuals' who are seen as situated outside the family (Bech, 1997: 204). In the absence of an equitable shift of wealth and social welfare, argues Bech, it can be expected that many people will revert to traditional values and ways of life, and 'the homosexual may well come to be per-ceived, once again, as the incarnation of the threats of modernity' (1997: 206; see also Bech, 1992: 140–1). For those who are concerned to explore and promote new models of sexual and personal identity, it makes sense to pay heed to such trends, and to consider the conditions thwarting or mak-ing possible changes in the redefinition of identity. As a number of sociol-ogists have recently noted, late modern society would seem to be characterised by individualism in matters of love and sexuality, with an emphasis on 'freedom of choice' and 'personal responsibility' (see particu-larly Beck and Beck-Gernsheim, 1995; Giddens, 1992). Traditional mar-riage and family are losing their regulatory force to be replaced by new norms and forms of self-governance, with diverse consequences for both men and women. New kinds of division of labour between men and women, and the collapse of the public/private division present new possibilities for being that are less strongly linked to the imperatives of reproductive het-erosexuality. (This view is reflected, for instance, in Giddens's notions of the 'pure relationship' and 'plastic sexuality', which imply new personal oblig-ations and contradictions associated with trust, intimacy, and sexual exclu-sivity – see particularly Giddens, 1992: 49–64, 134–57.) Although this sociological work has tended to focus on the implications for the relation-ship between heterosexual men and women (for example, the splitting up of work and home life), one also needs to recognise the potential for develop-ing a plurality of new selves that are less sexually exclusive and more toler-ant of others.

As Foucault's concept of practices of the self suggests, identity is never simply imposed on (pre-social) subjects but involves a process of self-constitution within specific socio-cultural contexts (see, for example, Foucault, 1985, 1986). Through engaging with culturally prescribed or suggested practices of the self, one comes to understand oneself as a subject with a particular way of viewing and acting in the world. Different contexts provide different degrees of 'freedom' for the individual to act, but there is always scope for subverting, resisting, or negotiating the imperatives of personhood (on this point, see particularly McNay, 1992). Subjects may, and indeed routinely do, fail to take up prevailing practices of the self, or subvert or playfully engage with norms. As Henrietta Moore (1994a) has argued, in any context, there exist competing, and potentially contradictory, discourses on gender and sexuality rather than a single discourse, presenting many possibilities for being. This raises a series of questions: what is it that makes people take up particular subject positions as opposed to others? How can one account for differences between people in regard to their self-representations as gendered individuals? Why do men differ from each other in regard to their understandings of 'masculinity' and what it is to be a man, and why do women differ in regard to their understandings of 'femininity' and what it is to be a woman? And, what is the relationship between discourses and personal identities? (Moore, 1994a: 64). Modernity may have created particular 'ideals' of masculine embodiment and subjectivity, but it has also produced oppositional discourses, and created an array of new subject positions and personal 'choices'.

One positive aspect of the postmodernising tendencies in late modern societies is the abandonment of the idea that there is a single truth defining our personal identity that is waiting to be discovered, in favour of the idea that there is a multiplicity of potential subject positions that may be taken up. The 'postmodernisation of sex' involves recognition of the existence of a plurality of possible sexualities and the capacity for the self to revise one's own sexual history and the meaning of any sexual episode (Simon, 1996: 27–34). Judith Butler's performative theory of gender and William Simon's notion of 'sexual scripting' both neatly capture the idea that there is always the potential for improvisation, subversion of normative ideals, and the recasting of scripts (see Butler, 1990a; Simon, 1996: 40–59). Scholars have exposed the limitations and implications of 'identity', and many people now look forward to the emergence of new or reconceptualised models of identity that permit a wider range of sexual and personal possibilities than is implied by the sex/gender system. However, change cannot be expected to occur in the short term, or to be uniform and absolute. 'As it took centuries for the one-sex model of antiquity to give way to the two-sex model of post-Enlightenment, so the vestiges of the nineteenth-century model of sex and gender persist even as competing models emerge on the eve of the twenty-first century' (Nataf, 1996: 57). In this book, I have described some challenges posed by a recent shift in our theoretical understanding of the world to our conceptions of men, masculinity and identity, and pointed to some further and potentially fruitful lines of enquiry and action. As we enter a new millennium, it is timely to reflect upon the normative ideals of masculine identity that have so strongly shaped twentieth-century culture and to consider what might be done to encourage new ways of being.

References

Adam, B.D. (1995) *The Rise of a Gay and Lesbian Movement*. Revised edition. Twayne Publishers: New York.

Almaguer, T. (1991) 'Chicano men: a cartography of homosexual identity and behaviour', *Differences: A Journal of Feminist Cultural Studies*, 3, 2: 75–100.

Angelides, S. (1994) 'The queer intervention: sexuality, identity, and cultural politics', *Melbourne Journal of Politics*, 22: 66–88.

Appiah, K.A. and Gates, H.L. (eds) (1995) *Identities*. The University of Chicago Press: Chicago.

Bacchi, C.L. (1990) *Same Difference: Feminism and Sexual Difference*. Allen & Unwin: Sydney.

Bacchi, C.L. (1996) *The Politics of Affirmative Action: 'Women', Equality and Category Politics*. Sage: London.

Badinter, E. (1995) *XY: On Masculine Identity*. Columbia University Press: New York.

Bech, H. (1992) 'Report from a rotten state: "marriage" and "homosexuality" in "Denmark"', in K. Plummer (ed.), *Modern Homosexualities: Fragments of Lesbian and Gay Experience*. Routledge: London. pp. 134–47.

Bech, H. (1997) *When Men Meet: Homosexuality and Modernity*. Polity Press: Cambridge.

Beck, U. and Beck-Gernsheim, E. (1995) *The Normal Chaos of Love*. Polity Press: Cambridge.

Benjamin, J. and Rabinbach, A. (1989) 'Forward', in K. Theweleit, *Male Fantasies, Volume 2: Male Bodies: Psychoanalyzing the White Terror*. Polity Press; Cambridge. pp. ix–xxv.

Berry, C. and Jagose, A. (1996) 'Australia queer: editors' introduction, *Meanjin*, 55, 1: 5–11.

Besnier, N. (1994) 'Polynesian gender liminality through time and space', in G. Herdt (ed.), *Third Sex, Third Gender: Beyond Sexual Dimorphism in Culture and History*. Zone Books: New York. pp. 285–328.

Best, S. and Kellner, D. (1991) *Postmodern Theory: Critical Interrogations*. The Guilford Press: New York.

Biddulph, S. (1995) *Manhood: An Action Plan for Changing Men's Lives*. Second edition. Finch Publishing: Sydney.

Birke, L.I.A. (1982) 'From sin to sickness: hormonal theories of lesbianism', in R. Hubbard, M.S. Henifin and B. Fried (eds), *Biological Woman – The Convenient Myth: A Collection of Feminist Essays and a Comprehensive Bibliography*. Schenkman Publishing: Cambridge. pp. 71–90.

Blazina, C. (1997) 'Mythos and men: toward new paradigms of masculinity', *The Journal of Men's Studies*, 5, 4: 285–94.

Bleier, R. (1984) *Science and Gender: A Critique of Biology and its Theories on Women*. Pergamon Press: New York.

Bleys, R.C. (1996) *The Geography of Perversion: Male-to-Male Sexual Behaviour Outside the West and the Ethnographic Imagination 1750–1918*. Cassell: London.

Bly, R. (1990) *Iron John: A Book About Men*. Addison-Wesley: Reading, MA.

Bordo, S. (1993) *Unbearable Weight: Feminism, Western Culture, and the Body*. University of California Press: Berkeley and Los Angeles.

Bourke, J. (1996) *Dismembering the Male: Men's Bodies, Britain and the Great War*. Reaktion Books: London.

Bowden, P. (1995) 'The ethics of nursing care and "the ethic of care"', *Nursing Inquiry*, 2: 10–21.

Braidotti, R. (1991) *Patterns of Dissonance: A Study of Women in Contemporary Philosophy*. Polity Press: Cambridge.

Braidotti, R. (1994) *Nomadic Subjects: Embodiment and Sexual Difference in Contemporary Feminist Theory*. Columbia University Press: New York.

Braidotti, R., Charkiewicz, E., Häusler, S. and Wieringa, S. (1994) *Women, the Environment and Sustainable Development: Towards a Theoretical Synthesis.* Zed Books in association with Instraw: London.

Brain, R. (1979) *The Decorated Body.* Harper and Row: New York.

Bravmann, S. (1995) 'Queer historical subjects', *Socialist Review*, 25, 1: 47–68.

Britton, D.M. and Williams, C.L. (1995) '"Don't ask, don't tell, don't pursue": military policy and the construction of heterosexual masculinity', *Journal of Homosexuality*, 30, 1–21.

Browning, F. (1993) *The Culture of Desire: Paradox and Perversity in Gay Lives Today.* Crown: New York.

Buege, D.J. (1994) 'Rethinking again: a defense of ecofeminist philosophy', in K. Warren (ed.), *Ecological Feminism.* Routledge: London. pp. 42–63.

Bullough, V.L. (1994) *Science in the Bedroom: A History of Sex Research.* Basic Books: New York.

Burr, V. (1995) *An Introduction to Social Constructionism.* Routledge: London.

Butler, J. (1990a) *Gender Trouble: Feminism and the Subversion of Identity.* Routledge: New York.

Butler, J. (1990b) 'Gender trouble, feminist theory, and psychoanalytic discourse', in L.J. Nicholson (ed.), *Feminism/Postmodernism.* Routledge: New York. pp. 324–40.

Butler, J. (1993) *Bodies That Matter: On the Discursive Limits of 'Sex'.* Routledge: New York.

Byne, W. (1995) 'Science and belief: psychobiological research on sexual orientation', in J.P. De Cecco and D.A. Parker (eds), *Sex, Cells, and Same-Sex Desire: The Biology of Sexual Preference*, Harrington Park Press: New York. pp. 303–44.

Caputi, J. and MacKenzie, G.O. (1992) 'Pumping Iron John', in K.L. Hagan (ed.), *Women Respond to the Men's Movement: A Feminist Collection.* Pandora: San Francisco. pp. 69–81.

Carrigan, T., Connell, B. and Lee, J. (1987) 'Toward a new sociology of masculinity', in H. Brod (ed.), *The Making of Masculinities: The New Men's Studies.* Allen & Unwin: Boston pp. 63–100.

Carter, S. (1993) 'Risk, masculinity and modernity: understandings of gender and danger in the modern period'. Unpublished PhD thesis, Lancaster University.

Chodorow, N. (1978) *The Reproduction of Mothering.* University of California Press: Berkeley.

Chodorow, N. (1988) *Psychoanalytic Theory and Feminism.* Polity Press: Cambridge.

Christen, Y. (1991) *Sex Differences: Modern Biology and the Unisex Fallacy.* Transaction Publishers: New Brunswick.

Clatterbaugh, K. (1990) *Contemporary Perspectives on Masculinity: Men, Women, and Politics in Modern Society.* Westview Press: Boulder.

Cohen, C. J. (1996) 'Contested membership: black gay identities and the politics of AIDS', in S. Seidman (ed.), *Queer Theory/Sociology.* Blackwell: Cambridge, MA. pp. 362–94.

Cohen, D. (1990) *Being a Man.* Routledge: London.

Cohen, E. (1993) *Talk on the Wilde Side: Toward a Genealogy of a Discourse on Male Sexualities.* Routledge: New York.

Collins, P.H. (1990) *Black Feminist Thought: Knowledge, Consciousness, and the Politics of Empowerment.* Routledge: New York.

Conaghan, D. (1995) 'Bishops angry at "intrusion" by gay group', *Daily Telegraph*, Wednesday, March 15.

Connell, R.W. (1987) *Gender and Power: Society, the Person, and Sexual Politics.* Allen & Unwin: Sydney.

Connell, R.W. (1993) 'The big picture: masculinities in recent world history', *Theory and Society*, 22: 597–623.

Connell, R.W. (1995) *Masculinities.* Allen & Unwin: Sydney.

Cornwall, A. and Lindisfarne, N. (1994a) 'Dislocating masculinity: gender, power and anthropology', in A. Cornwall and N. Lindisfarne (eds), *Dislocating Masculinity: Comparative Ethnographies.* Routledge: London. pp. 11–47.

Cornwall, A. and Lindisfarne, N. (eds) (1994b), *Dislocating Masculinity: Comparative Ethnographies.* Routledge: London.

Crawford, J., Kippax, S., Onyx, J., Gault, U. and Benton, P. (1992) *Emotion and Gender: Constructing Meaning from Memory.* Sage: London.

Cunningham, M. (1992) 'If you're queer and you're not angry in 1992, you're not paying attention; if you're straight it may be hard to figure out what all the shouting's about', *Mother Jones*, May/June: 60–8.

Davis, F. (1992) *Fashion, Culture, and Identity.* The University of Chicago Press: Chicago.

Dawson, G. (1994) *Soldier Heroes: British Adventure, Empire and the Imagining of Masculinities.* Routledge: London.

de Lauretis, T. (1991) 'Queer theory: lesbian and gay sexualities: an introduction', *Differences: A Journal of Feminist Cultural Studies*, 3, 2: iii–xviii.

Deleuze, G and Guattari, F. (1987) *A Thousand Plateaus: Capitalism and Schizophrenia.* University of Minnesota Press: Minneapolis.

Delphy, C. (1993) 'Rethinking sex and gender', *Women's Studies International Forum*, 16, 1: 1–9.

Devor, H. (1987) 'Gender blending females: women and sometimes men', *American Behavioural Scientist*, 31, 1: 12–40.

Diamond, I. and Quinby, L. (eds) (1988) *Feminism and Foucault: Reflections on Resistance.* Northeastern University Press: Boston.

Dimen, M. (1995) 'On "our nature": prolegomenon to a relational theory of sexuality', in T. Domenici and R.C. Lesser (eds), *Disorienting Sexuality: Psychoanalytic Reappraisals of Sexual Identities.* Routledge: New York. pp. 129–52.

Diprose, R. (1994) *The Bodies of Women: Ethics, Embodiment and Sexual Difference.* Routledge: London.

Doell, R.G. (1995) ' Sexuality in the brain', *Journal of Homosexuality*, 28, 3/4: 345–54.

Dollard, J., Miller, N.E., Doob, L.W., Mowrer, O.H., Sears, R.R. (1949; orig. 1939) *Frustration and Aggression,* Seventh edition. Yale University Press: New Haven.

Domenici, T. and Lesser, R.C. (eds) (1995) *Disorienting Sexuality: Psychoanalytic Reappraisals of Sexual Identities.* Routledge: New York.

Donzelot, J. (1980) *The Policing of Families.* Hutchinson: London.

Duggan, L. (1992) 'Making it perfectly queer', *Socialist Review*, 22, 1: 11–31.

Duneier, M. (1992) *Slim's Table: Race, Respectability, and Masculinity.* The University of Chicago Press: Chicago.

Durban, E.F.M. and Bowlby, J. (1939) *Personal Aggressiveness and War.* Columbia University Press: New York.

Dutton, K.R. (1995) *The Perfectible Body: The Western Ideal of Physical Development.* Cassell: London.

Edley, N. and Wetherell, M. (1995) *Men in Perspective: Practice, Power and Identity.* Harvester Wheatsheaf: New York.

Edwards, T. (1990) 'Beyond sex and gender: masculinity, homosexuality and social theory', in J. Hearn and D. Morgan (eds), *Men, Masculinities and Social Theory.* Unwin Hyman: London. pp. 110–23.

Ehrenreich, B. and English, D. (1979) *For Her Own Good: 150 Years of the Experts' Advice to Women.* Anchor Books: New York.

Ekins, R. and King, D. (1996) *Blending Genders: Social Aspects of Cross-Dressing and Sex-Changing.* Routledge: London.

Eliason, M.J. (1996) 'Identity formation for lesbian, bisexual, and gay persons: beyond a "minoritising" view', *Journal of Homosexuality*, 30, 3: 31–58.

Ellis, H. (1900) *Studies in the Psychology of Sex*, Volume 2. The University Press: Leipzig, and F.A. Davis: Philadelphia.

Ellis, H. (1911) *Studies in the Psychology of Sex: Sexual Selection in Man.* F.A. Davis: Philadelphia.

Epstein, J. and Straub, K. (1991) *Body Guards: The Cultural Politics of Gender Ambiguity.* Routledge: New York.

Epstein, S. (1993/94) 'Gay politics, ethnic identity: the limits of social constructionism', *Socialist Review*, 17, 3/4: 9–54.

Epstein, S. (1996) 'A queer encounter: sociology and the study of sexuality', in S. Seidman (ed.), *Queer Theory/Sociology.* Blackwell: Cambridge, MA. pp. 145–67.

Evans, D.T. (1993) *Sexual Citizenship: The Material Construction of Sexualities.* Routledge: London.

Evans, M. (1997) *Introducing Contemporary Feminist Thought.* Polity Press: Cambridge.

Farrell, W. (1994) *The Myth of Male Power: Why Men Are the Disposable Sex.* Fourth Estate: London.

Fausto-Sterling, A. (1992) *Myths of Gender: Biological Theories About Women and Men*, Second edition. Basic Books: New York.

Featherstone, M. (1991) 'The body in consumer culture', in M. Featherstone, M. Hepworth and B.S. Turner (eds), *The Body: Social Process and Cultural Theory.* Sage: London. pp. 170–96.

Flax, J. (1981) 'Why epistemology matters: a reply to Kress', *Journal of Politics*, 43: 1006–24.

Flax, J. (1990) *Thinking Fragments: Psychoanalysis, Feminism, and Postmodernism in the Contemporary West.* University of California Press: Berkeley.

Foucault, M. (1980) *The History of Sexuality. Volume 1: An Introduction.* Vintage Books: New York.

Foucault, M. (1985) *The Use of Pleasure* (translated by R. Hurley). Penguin: Harmondsworth.

Foucault, M. (1986) *The Care of the Self* (translated by R. Hurley). Penguin: Harmondsworth.

Frank, B.W. (1993) 'The "new men's studies" and feminism: promise or danger?', in T. Haddad (ed.), *Men and Masculinities: A Critical Anthology.* Canadian Scholars Press: Toronto. pp. 333–43.

Frankenberg, R. (1993) *White Women, Race Matters: The Social Construction of Whiteness.* University of Minnesota Press: Minneapolis.

Freedman, E.B. (1995) 'The historical construction of homosexuality in the US', *Socialist Review*, 25, 1: 31–46.

Freud, S. (1930) *Civilization and its Discontents. Complete Psychological Works, Standard Edition*, Volume 21. Hogarth: London.

Freud, S. (1962) *Three Essays on the Theory of Sexuality* (translated and edited by James Strachey). Basic Books: New York.

Fuss, D. (1989) *Essentially Speaking: Feminism, Nature and Difference.* Routledge: New York.

Gamson, J. (1996) 'Must identity movements self-destruct?: a queer dilemma', in S. Seidman (ed.) *Queer Theory/Sociology.* Blackwell: Cambridge, MA. pp. 395–420.

Garber, M. (1995) *Vice Versa: Bisexuality and the Eroticism of Everyday Life.* Simon & Schuster: New York.

Gatens, M. (1996) *Imaginary Bodies: Ethics, Power and Corporeality.* Routledge: London.

Genova, J. (1989) 'Women and the mismeasure of thought', in N. Tuana (ed.), *Feminism and Science.* Indiana University Press: Bloomington. pp. 211–27.

Giddens, A. (1991) *Modernity and Self-Identity: Self and Society in the Late Modern Age.* Polity Press: Cambridge.

Giddens, A. (1992) *The Transformation of Intimacy: Sexuality, Love and Eroticism in Modern Societies.* Polity Press: Cambridge.

Gill, R. and Grint, K. (1995) 'Introduction', in K. Grint and R. Gill (eds), *The Gender-Technology Relation: Contemporary Theory and Research.* Taylor & Francis: London. pp. 1–28.

Gilligan, C. (1982) *In a Different Voice: Psychological Theory and Women's Development.* Harvard University Press: Cambridge, MA.

Gilligan, C. (1993) 'Letter to readers, 1993', in C. Gilligan (1982) *In a Different Voice: Psychological Theory and Women's Development.* Harvard University Press: Cambridge, MA. pp. ix–xxvii.

Gilligan, C., Johnston, D.K. and Miller, B. (1988) 'Moral voice, adolescent development, and secondary education: a study at the Green River School'. Cambridge MA project on the psychology of women and the development of girls. Harvard Graduate School of Education, monograph no.3.

Gilman, S.L. (1985) *Difference and Pathology: Stereotypes of Sexuality, Race, and Madness.* Cornell University Press: Ithaca.

Gilman, S.L. (1989) *Sexuality: An Illustrated History.* John Wiley and Sons: New York.

Gilman, S. (1993a) *Freud, Race and Gender.* Princeton University Press: Princeton.

Gilman, S. (1993b) *The Case of Sigmund Freud: Medicine and Identity at the Fin de Siècle.* The Johns Hopkins University Press: Baltimore.

Gilmore, D.D. (1990) *Manhood in the Making: Cultural Concepts of Masculinity.* Yale University Press: New Haven.

Ginsburg, E.K. (1996) 'Introduction: the politics of passing', in E.K. Ginsburg (ed.), *Passing and the Fictions of Identity*, Duke University Press, Durham, NC, and London. pp. 1–18.

Gleason, P. (1983) 'Identifying identity: a semantic history', *Journal of American History,* 69, 4: 910–31.

Goldberg, D.T. (1993) *Racist Culture: Philosophy and the Politics of Meaning.* Blackwell: Cambridge, MA.

Grant, C. (1995) 'Queer theorrhea (and what it all might mean for feminists)', *Trouble and Strife: The Radical Feminist Magazine*, 29/30: 39-45.

Grant, J. (1993) *Fundamental Feminism: Contesting the Core Concepts of Feminist Theory.* Routledge: London.

Grau, G. (1995) *Hidden Holocaust? Gay and Lesbian Persecution in Germany 1933–45.* Cassell: London.

Grosz, E. (1990a), 'Conclusion: A note on essentialism and difference', in S. Gunew (ed.), *Feminist Knowledge: Critique and Construct.* Routledge: London. pp. 332–44.

Grosz, E. (1990b) 'Contemporary theories of power and subjectivity', in S. Gunew (ed.), *Feminist Knowledge: Critique and Construct.* Routledge: London. pp. 59–120.

Grosz, E. (1993) 'Bodies and knowledges: feminism and the crisis of reason', in L. Alcoff and E. Potter (eds), *Feminist Epistemologies.* Routledge: New York. pp. 187–215.

Grosz, E. (1994) *Volatile Bodies: Toward a Corporeal Feminism.* Allen & Unwin: Sydney.

Grosz, E. (1995) *Space, Time and Perversion.* Routledge: New York.

Guillaumin, C. (1995) *Racism, Sexism, Power and Ideology.* Routledge: London.

Halperin, D.M. (1990) *One Hundred Years of Homosexuality: And Other Essays on Greek Love.* Routledge: New York.

Hamer, D. and Copeland, P. (1994) *The Science of Desire: The Search for the Gay Gene and the Biology of Behaviour.* Simon & Schuster: New York.

Hannaford, I. (1996) *Race: The History of an Idea in the West.* The Woodrow Wilson Center Press: Washington.

Haraway, D. (1991) *Simians, Cyborgs, and Women: The Reinvention of Nature.* Routledge: New York.

Harding, S. (1986) *The Science Question in Feminism.* Cornell University Press: Ithaca, NY.

Harper, P. (1993) 'Eloquence and epitaph: black nationalism and the homophobic impulse in responses to the death of Max Robinson', in T. Murphey and S. Poirier (eds), *Writing AIDS: Gay Literature, Language and Analysis.* Columbia University Press: New York. pp. 117–39.

Harstock, N. (1990) 'Foucault on power: a theory for women?', in L.J. Nicholson (ed.), *Feminism/Postmodernism.* Routledge: London. pp. 157–75.

Haumann, G. (1995) 'Homosexuality, biology, and ideology', in J.P. De Cecco and D.A. Parker (eds), *Sex, Cells and Same-Sex Desire: The Biology of Sexual Preference.* Harrington Park Press: New York. pp. 57–77.

Hausman, B.L. (1995) *Changing Sex: Transsexualism, Technology, and the Idea of Gender.* Duke University Press: Durham, NC, and London.

Hearn, J. (1992) *Men in the Public Eye: The Construction and Deconstruction of Public Men and Public Patriarchies.* Routledge: London.

Hekma, G. (1994) '"A female soul in a male body": sexual inversion as gender inversion in nineteenth century sexology', in G. Herdt (ed.), *Third Sex, Third Gender: Beyond Sexual Dimorphism in Culture and History.* Zone Books: New York. pp. 213–239.

Hekman, S.J. (1995) *Moral Voices, Moral Selves: Carol Gilligan and Feminist Moral Theory.* Polity Press: Cambridge.

Henriques, J., Hollway, W., Urwin, C., Venn, C. and Walkerdine, V. (eds) (1984) *Changing the Subject: Psychology, Social Regulation and Subjectivity.* Methuen: London.

Henry, G. and Galbraith, H.M. (1934) 'Constitutional factors in homosexuality', *American Journal of Psychiatry*, 13: 1249–70.

Herdt, G. (ed.) (1994) *Third Sex, Third Gender: Beyond Sexual Dimorphism in Culture and History.* Zone Books: New York.

Herrn, R. (1995) 'On the history of biological theories of homosexuality', in J.P. De Cecco and D.A. Parker (eds), *Sex, Cells, and Same-Sex Desire: The Biology of Sexual Preference*, Harrington Park Press: New York. pp. 31–55.

Hochschild, A.R. (1983) *The Managed Heart: Commercialization of Human Feeling*. University of California Press: Berkeley.

Hoff, J. (1996) 'The pernicious effects of poststructuralism on women's history', in D. Bell and R. Klein (eds), *Radically Speaking: Feminism Reclaimed*. Spinifex: North Melbourne. pp. 393–412.

Hollinger, R. (1994) *Postmodernism and the Social Sciences: A Thematic Approach*. Sage: Thousand Oaks.

Hollway, W. (1984) 'Gender difference and the production of subjectivity', in J. Henriques, W. Hollway, C. Urwin, C. Venn and V. Walkerdine (eds), *Changing the Subject: Psychology, Social Regulation and Subjectivity*. Methuen: London. pp. 227–63.

Hollway, W. (1993) 'Theorizing heterosexuality: a response', *Feminism & Psychology*, 3, 3: 412–17.

Hollway, W. (1995) 'A second bite at the heterosexual cherry' (Observations and Commentaries), *Feminism & Psychology*, 5, 1: 126–30.

Hood-Williams, J. (1996) 'Goodbye to sex and gender', *The Sociological Review*, 44, 1: 1–16.

Hood-Williams, J. (1997) 'Real sex/fake gender', *The Sociological Review*, 45, 1: 42–58.

hooks, b. (1991) *Yearning: Race, Gender, and Cultural Politics*. Turnaround: London.

hooks, b. (1992) *Black Looks: Race and Representation*. South End Press: Boston.

Horrocks, R. (1994) *Masculinity in Crisis: Myths, Fantasies and Realities*. St. Martin's Press: New York.

Ingraham, C. (1996) 'The heterosexual imagery: feminist sociology and theories of gender', in S. Seidman (ed.), *Queer Theory/Sociology*. Blackwell: Cambridge, MA. pp. 168–93.

Irigaray, L. (1993) *Sexes and Genealogies* (translated by Gillian C. Gill). Columbia University Press: New York.

Jackson, D. (1992) *Unmasking Masculinity*. Unwin Hyman: London.

Jackson, S. (1996) 'Heterosexuality and feminist theory', in D. Richardson (ed.), *Theorising Heterosexuality: Telling it Straight*. Open University Press: Buckingham. pp. 21–38.

Jagose, A. (1996) *Queer Theory*. Melbourne University Press: Melbourne.

James, S.M. and Busia, A.P.A. (1993) *Theorizing Black Feminisms: The Visionary Pragmatism of Black Women*. Routledge: London.

James, W. (1901; orig. 1890) *The Principles of Psychology*, Vols 1 and 2. Macmillan: London.

Jeffreys, S. (1993) *The Lesbian Heresy: A Feminist Perspective on the Lesbian Sexual Revolution*. Spinifex: Melbourne.

Johnson, S. (1997) 'Theorising language and masculinity: a feminist perspective', in S. Johnson and U.H. Meinhof (eds.), *Language and Masculinity*. Blackwell: Oxford. pp. 8–26.

Jordanova, L. (1989) *Sexual Visions: Images of Gender in Science and Medicine Between the Eighteenth and Twentieth Centuries*. Harvester Wheatsheaf: Hemel Hempstead.

Julien, I. (ed.) (1992) 'Black is, black ain't: notes of de-essentializing black identities', in G. Dent (ed.), *Black Popular Culture* (A Project by Michelle Wallace). Bay Press: Seattle. pp. 255–75.

Juteau-Lee, D. (1995) 'Introduction: (Re)constructing the categories of "race" and "sex": the work of a precursor', in C. Guillaumin, *Racism, Sexism, Power and Ideology*. Routledge: London. pp. 1–26.

Kaplan, G.T. and Rogers, L.J. (1990) 'The definition of male and female: biological reductionism and the sanctions of normality', in S. Gunew (ed.), *Feminist Knowledge: Critique and Construct*. Routledge: London. pp. 205–28.

Katz, J.N. (1990) 'The invention of heterosexuality', *Socialist Review*, 20(1): 7–34.

Katz, J.N. (1995) *The Invention of Heterosexuality*. Penguin: New York.

Keen, S. (1992) *Fire in the Belly*. Piatkus: London.

Kern, S. (1974) *Anatomy and Destiny: A Cultural History of the Human Body*. The Bobbs-Merrill Company, Inc.: Indianapolis.

Kimmel, M.S. (1987) 'The contemporary "crisis" of masculinity in historical perspective', in H. Brod (ed.), *The Making of Masculinities: The New Men's Studies*. Allen & Unwin: Boston. pp. 121–53.

Kimmel, M.S. and Kaufman, M. (1994) 'Weekend warriors: the new men's movement', in H. Brod and M. Kaufman (eds), *Theorizing Masculinities.* Sage: Thousand Oaks. pp. 259–88.

Kinsman, G. (1993) '"Inverts", "psychopaths" and "normal" men: historical sociological perspectives on gay and heterosexual masculinities', in T. Haddad (ed.), *Men and Masculinities: A Critical Anthology.* Canadian Scholars Press: Toronto. pp. 3–33.

Kitzinger, C. (1996) 'Therapy and how it undermines the practice of radical feminism', in D. Bell and R. Klein (eds), *Radically Speaking: Feminism Reclaimed.* Spinifex: North Melbourne. pp. 92–101.

Kitzinger, C. and Wilkinson, S. (1994) 'Re-viewing heterosexuality', *Feminism & Psychology*, 4, 2: 330–6.

Kohn, M. (1995) *The Race Gallery: The Return of Racial Science.* Jonathan Cape: London.

Krafft-Ebing, R. von (1953; orig. 1886) *Psychopathia Sexualis: A Medico-Forensic Study.* Pioneer Publications: New York.

Laqueur, T. (1990) *Making Sex: Body and Gender from the Greeks to Freud.* Harvard University Press: Cambridge, MA.

LeVay, S. (1994) *The Sexual Brain.* MIT Press: Cambridge, MA.

LeVay, S. (1996) *Queer Science: The Use and Abuse of Research into Homosexuality*. MIT Press: Cambridge, MA.

Lloyd, G. (1984) *The Man of Reason: 'Male' and 'Female' in Western Philosophy.* Methuen: London.

Löfström, J. (1997) 'The birth of the queen/the modern homosexual: historical explanations revisited', *The Sociological Review*, 45, 1: 24–41.

Longley, C. and Fenton, B. (1995) 'Bishop tells of distress at OutRage intimidation', *Daily Telegraph*, Tuesday, March 14.

Lorber, J. (1994) *Paradoxes of Gender.* Yale University Press: New Haven.

Los Angeles County Museum of Art (1983) *Guide to the Exhibit 'An Elegant Art: Fashion and Fantasy in the Eighteenth Century'.* Los Angeles County Museum of Art.

Majors, R. and Billson, J.M. (1992) *Cool Pose: The Dilemmas of Black Manhood in America.* Lexington Books: New York.

Martell, L. (1994) *Ecology and Society: An Introduction.* Polity Press: Cambridge.

Martin, E. (1994) *Flexible Bodies: Tracking Immunity in American Culture – From the Days of Polio to the Age of AIDS.* Beacon Press: Boston.

Martin, K.A. (1993) 'Gender and sexuality: medical opinion on homosexuality, 1900–1950', *Gender & Society*, 7, 2: 246–60.

Massie, A. (1995) 'Terror tactics of the Tatchell gang', *Daily Telegraph*, Wednesday, March 15.

McClintock, A. (1995) *Imperial Leather: Race, Gender and Sexuality in the Colonial Contest.* Routledge: New York.

McGuire, T.R. (1995) 'Is homosexuality genetic? A critical review and some suggestions', in J.P. De Cecco and D.A. Parker (eds), *Sex, Cells and Same-Sex Desire: The Biology of Sexual Preference.* Harrington Park Press: New York. pp. 115–45.

McMahon, A. (1993) 'Male readings of feminist theory: the psychologization of sexual politics in the masculinity literature', *Theory & Society*, 22: 675–97.

McNay, L. (1992) *Foucault and Feminism: Power, Gender and the Self.* Polity Press: Cambridge.

Melosh, B. (1993) 'Manly work: public art and masculinity in Depression America', in B. Melosh (ed.), *Gender and American History Since 1890.* Routledge: London. pp. 155–181.

Mercer, K. (1994) *Welcome to the Jungle: New Positions in Black Cultural Studies.* Routledge: New York.

Mercer, K and Julien, I. (1988) 'Race, sexual politics and black masculinity: a dossier', in R. Chapman and J. Rutherford (eds), *Male Order: Unwrapping Masculinity.* Lawrence & Wishart: London. pp. 97–164.

Metcalfe, A. and Humphries, M. (ed.) (1985) *The Sexuality of Men.* Pluto Press: London.

Middleton, P. (1992) *The Inward Gaze: Masculinity and Subjectivity in Modern Culture.* Routledge: London.

Mies, M. (1993) 'White man's dilemma: his search for what he has destroyed', in M. Mies and V. Shiva, *Ecofeminism.* Fernwood Publications: Halifax, and Zed Books: London. pp. 132–63.

Mies, M. and Shiva, V. (1993) 'Introduction: why we wrote this book together', in M. Mies and

V. Shiva, *Ecofeminism*. Fernwood Publications: Halifax, and Zed Books: London. pp. 1–21.

Miller, J. (1993) *The Passion of Michel Foucault*. HarperCollins: London.

Minton, H.L. (1996) 'Community empowerment and the medicalization of homosexuality: constructing sexual identities in the 1930s', *Journal of the History of Sexuality*, 6, 3: 435–58.

Mohanty, C.T. (1991) 'Under Western eyes: feminist scholarship and colonial discourses', in C.T. Mohanty, A. Russo, and L. Torres (eds) *Third World Women and the Politics of Feminism*. Indiana University Press: Bloomington. pp. 51–80.

Mohanty, C.T., Russo, A. and Torres, L. (eds) (1991) *Third World Women and the Politics of Feminism*. Indiana University Press: Bloomington.

Moir, A. and Jessel, D. (1991) *BrainSex: The Real Difference Between Men and Women*. Mandarin: London.

Money, J. and Tucker, P. (1976) *Sexual Signatures: On Being a Man or a Woman*. Harrap: London.

Moore, H.L. (1994a) *A Passion for Difference: Essays in Anthropology and Gender*. Indiana University Press: Bloomington.

Moore, H. (1994b) 'The problem of explaining violence in the social sciences', in P. Harvey and P. Gow (eds), *Sex and Violence: Issues in Representation and Experience*. Routledge: London. pp. 138–55.

Morgan, D. (1994) 'Theater of war: combat, the military, and masculinities', in H. Brod and M. Kaufman (eds), *Theorizing Masculinities*. Sage: Thousand Oaks, CA. pp. 165–82.

Mort, F. (1996) *Cultures of Consumption: Masculinities and Social Space in Late Twentieth-Century Britain*. Routledge: London.

Mosse, G.L. (1985) *Nationalism and Sexuality: Middle-Class Morality and Sexual Norms in Modern Europe*. The University of Wisconsin Press: Wisconsin.

Mosse, G.L. (1996) *The Image of Man: The Creation of Modern Masculinity*. Oxford University Press: New York.

Mrozek, D.J. (1987) 'The habit of victory: the American military and the cult of manliness', in J.A. Mangan and J. Walvin (eds), *Manliness and Morality: Middle-class Masculinity in Britain and America 1800–1940*. Manchester University Press: Manchester. pp. 220–41.

Murphy, R. (1994) *Rationality and Nature: A Sociological Inquiry into a Changing Relationship*. Westview Press: Boulder.

Namaste, K. (1996) 'The politics of Inside/Out: queer theory, poststructuralism, and a sociological approach to sexuality', in S. Seidman (ed.), *Queer Theory/Sociology*. Blackwell: Cambridge, MA. pp. 194–212.

Nanda, S. (1994) 'Hijras: an alternative sex and gender role in India', in G. Herdt (ed.) *Third Sex, Third Gender: Beyond Sexual Dimorphism in Culture and History*. Zone Books: New York. pp. 373–417.

Nataf, Z.I. (1996) *Lesbians Talk Transgender*. Scarlet Press: London.

Nelkin, D. and Lindee, M.S. (1995) 'The media-ted gene: stories of gender and race', in J. Terry and J. Urla (eds), *Deviant Bodies: Critical Perspectives on Difference in Science and Popular Culture*. Indiana University Press: Bloomington. pp. 387–402.

Nicholson, J. (1993) *Men and Women: How Different Are They?* Oxford University Press: Oxford.

Nixon, S. (1996) *Hard Looks: Masculinities, Spectatorship and Contemporary Consumption*. UCL Press: London.

Oudshoorn, N. (1994) *Beyond the Natural Body: An Archeology of Sex Hormones*. Routledge: London.

Oudshoorn, N. and Wijngaard, M. van den (1991) 'Dualism in biology: the case of sex hormones', *Women's Studies International Forum*, 14, 5: 459–71.

Oyěwùmí, O. (1997) *The Invention of Women: Making an African Sense of Western Gender Discourses*. University of Minnesota Press: Minneapolis.

Pahl, R. (1995) *After Success: Fin-de Siècle Anxiety and Identity*. Polity Press: Cambridge.

Park, R.J. (1987) 'Biological thought, athletics and the formation of a "man of character": 1830–1900', in J.A. Mangan and J. Walvin (eds), *Manliness and Morality: Middle-Class Masculinity in Britain and America 1800–1940*. Manchester University Press: Manchester. pp. 7–34.

Parker, A., Russo, M., Sommer, D. and Yaeger, P. (eds) (1992) 'Introduction', in A. Parker, M. Russo, D. Sommer and P. Yaeger (eds), *Nationalisms and Sexualities*. Routledge: New York pp. 1–18.

Penn, D. (1995) 'Queer theorising: politics and history', *Radical History Review*, 62 (Spring): 24–42.

Petersen, A.R. and Davies, D. (1997) 'Psychology and the social construction of sex differences in theories of aggression', *Journal of Gender Studies*, 6, 3: 309–20.

Petersen, A.R. and Lupton, D. (1996) *The New Public Health: Health and Self in the Age of Risk*. Sage: London.

Phelan, S. (1994) *Getting Specific: Postmodern Lesbian Politics*. University of Minnesota Press: Minneapolis.

Phillips, S.R. (1991) 'The hegemony of heterosexuality: a study of introductory texts', *Teaching Sociology*, 9, 4: 454–63.

Pleck, J. (1981) *The Myth of Masculinity*. MIT Press: Cambridge, MA.

Plummer, K. (ed.) (1981) *The Making of the Modern Homosexual*. Barnes & Noble Books: Totowa.

Plummer, K. (1996) 'Foreword: symbols of change', in W. Simon, *Postmodern Sexualities*. Routledge: London. pp. ix–xvi.

Plumwood, V. (1992) 'Feminism and ecofeminism: beyond the dualistic assumptions of women, men and nature', *The Ecologist*, 22: 8–13.

Rajchman, J. (ed.) (1995) *The Identity in Question*. Routledge: New York.

Ramazanoğlu, C. (ed.) (1993) *Up Against Foucault: Explorations of Some Tensions Between Foucault and Feminism*. Routledge: New York.

Rapp, R. (1995) 'Heredity, or: revising the facts of life', in S. Yanagisako and C. Delaney (eds), *Naturalizing Power: Essays in Feminist Cultural Analysis*. Routledge: New York. pp. 69–86.

Reynolds, R. (1996) 'Confessing to change: Gay Liberation and the deployment of therapeutic and confessional practices', *Meanjin*, 55, 1: 138–52.

Rich, A. (1980) 'Compulsory heterosexuality and lesbian existence', *Signs: Journal of Woman in Culture and Society*, 5, 4: 631–60.

Richardson, D. (ed.) (1996a) *Theorising Heterosexuality: Telling It Straight*. Open University Press: Buckingham.

Richardson, D. (1996b) 'Heterosexuality and social theory', in D. Richardson (ed.), *Theorising Heterosexuality: Telling It Straight*. Open University Press: Buckingham. pp. 1–20.

Riley, D. (1988) *'Am I That Name?' Feminism and the Category of 'Women' in History*. University of Minnesota: Minneapolis.

Robinson, V. (1996) 'Heterosexuality and masculinity: theorising male power or the male wounded psyche?', in D. Richardson (ed.), *Theorising Heterosexuality: Telling It Straight*. Open University Press: Buckingham. pp. 109–24.

Roper, M. (1994) *Masculinity and the British Organization Man Since 1945*. Oxford University Press: Oxford.

Roscoe, W. (1994) 'How to become a berache: toward a unified analysis of gender diversity', in G. Herdt (ed.) *Third Sex, Third Gender: Beyond Sexual Dimorphism in Culture and History*. Zone Books: New York. pp. 329–72.

Rose, N. (1989) *Governing the Soul: The Shaping of the Private Self*. Routledge: London.

Rotundo, A. (1993) *American Manhood: Transformations in Masculinity from the Revolution to the Modern Era*. Basic Books: New York.

Rowley, H. and Grosz, E. (1990) 'Psychoanalysis and feminism', in S. Gunew (ed.), *Feminist Knowledge: Critique and Construct*. Routledge: London. pp. 175–204.

Rubin, G. (1975) 'The traffic in women: notes on the "political economy" of sex', in R. Reiter Rayna (ed.), *Toward an Anthropology of Women*. Monthly Review Press: New York. pp. 157–210.

Rubin, G. (1982) 'Thinking sex: notes for a radical theory of the politics of sexuality', in C. Vance (ed.), *Pleasure and Danger: The Politics of Sexuality*. Routledge & Kegan Paul: Boston. pp. 267–319.

Russett, C.E. (1989) *Sexual Science: The Victorian Construction of Womanhood*. Harvard University Press: Cambridge, MA.

Rutherford, J. (1992) *Men's Silences: Predicaments in Masculinity*. Routledge: London.

Saltonstall, R. (1993) 'Healthy bodies, social bodies: men's and women's concepts and practices of health in everyday life', *Social Science & Medicine*, 36, 1: 7–14.

Sarup, M. (1993) *An Introductory Guide to Poststructuralism and Postmodernism*. Second edition. Harvester Wheatsheaf: Hemel Hempstead.

Sawicki, J. (1991) *Disciplining Foucault: Feminism, Power and the Body*. Routledge: New York.

Sayer, A. (1997) 'Essentialism, social constructionism, and beyond', *The Sociological Review*, 45(3): 453–87.

Schiebinger, L. (1986) 'Skeletons in the closet: the first illustrations of the female skeleton in eighteenth-century anatomy', *Representations*, 14 (Spring): 42–83.

Schiebinger, L. (1989) *The Mind Has No Sex? Women in the Origins of Modern Science*. Harvard University Press: Cambridge, MA.

Schiebinger, L. (1993) *Nature's Body: Gender in the Making of Modern Science*. Beacon Press: Boston.

Schwartz, D. (1993) 'Heterophilia: the love that dare not speak its aim', *Psychoanalytic Dialogues*, 3: 643–52.

Scott, J. (1995) 'Multiculturalism and the politics of identity', in J. Rajchman (ed.), *The Identity in Question*. Routledge: New York. pp. 3–12.

Scully, D. and Bart, P. (1973) 'A funny thing happened on the way to the orifice: women in gynecology textbooks', *American Journal of Sociology*, 78: 283–88.

Sedgwick, E.K. (1994) *Epistemology of the Closet*. Penguin: London.

Seidler, V.J. (1987) 'Reason, desire, and male sexuality', in P. Carlan (ed.), *The Cultural Construction of Sexuality*. Tavistock: London. pp. 82–112.

Seidler, V.J. (1988) 'Fathering, authority and masculinity', in R. Chapman and J. Rutherford (eds), *Male Order: Unwrapping Masculinity*. Lawrence & Wishart: London. pp. 272–302.

Seidler, V.J. (1989) *Rediscovering Masculinity: Reason, Language and Sexuality*. Routledge: London.

Seidler, V. (1994) *Unreasonable Men: Masculinity and Social Theory*. Routledge: London.

Seidler, V.J. (1995) 'Men, heterosexualities and emotional life', in S. Pile and N. Shrift (eds), *Mapping the Subject: Geographies of Cultural Transformation*. Routledge: London. pp. 170–91.

Seidman, S. (1996a) 'Introduction', in S. Seidman (ed.), *Queer Theory/Sociology*. Blackwell: Cambridge, MA. pp. 1–29.

Seidman, S. (ed.) (1996b) *Queer Theory/Sociology*. Blackwell: Cambridge, MA.

Sennett, R. (1994) *Flesh and Stone: The Body and the City in Western Civilization*. Faber and Faber: London.

Shaw, M. (1991) *Post-military Society*. Polity: Cambridge.

Shilling, C. (1993) *The Body and Social Theory*. Sage: London.

Silberstein, L.R., Mishkind, M.E., Striegel-Moore, R.H., Timko, C. and Rodin, J. (1989) 'Men and their bodies: a comparison of homosexual and heterosexual men', *Psychosomatic Medicine*, 51, 3: 337–46.

Simmons, C. (1993) 'Modern sexuality and the myth of Victorian repression', in B. Melosh (ed.), *Gender and American History Since 1890*. Routledge: London. pp. 17–42.

Simon, W. (1996) *Postmodern Sexualities*. Routledge: London.

Simpson, J.A. and Weiner, E.S.C. (1989) *The Oxford Dictionary*. Volume Nine. Second edition. Clarendon Press: Oxford.

Skelton, T. (1995) '"Boom, bye, bye": Jamaican ragga and gay resistance', in D. Bell and G. Valentine (eds), *Mapping Desire: Geographies of Sexualities*. Routledge: London. pp. 264–83.

Slagle, R.A. (1995) 'In defense of Queer Nation: from identity politics to a politics of difference', *Western Journal of Communication*, 59 (Spring): 85–102.

Soper, K. (1995) *What is Nature? Culture, Politics and the Non-Human*. Blackwell: Oxford.

Spivak, G.C. (1993) *Outside the Teaching Machine*. Routledge: New York.

Springhall, J. (1987) 'Building character in the British boy: the attempt to extend Christian manliness to working-class adolescents, 1880–1914' in J.A. Mangan and J. Walvin (eds), *Manliness and Morality: Middle-Class Masculinity in Britain and America 1800–1940*. Manchester University Press: Manchester. pp. 52–74.

Stanley, L. and Wise, S. (1993) *Breaking Out Again: Feminist Ontology and Epistemology.* New edition. Routledge: London.

Stein, A. and Plummer, K. (1996) '"I can't even think straight": "queer" theory and the missing sexual revolution in sociology', in S. Seidman (ed.), *Queer Theory/Sociology.* Blackwell: Cambridge, MA. pp. 129–44.

Stein, E. (ed.) (1992) *Forms of Desire: Sexual Orientation and the Social Constructionist Controversy.* Routledge: New York.

Stember, C.H. (1976) *Sexual Racism: The Emotional Barrier to an Integrated Society.* Elsevier: New York.

Stoltenberg, R. (1989) *Refusing to be a Man: Essays on Sex and Justice.* Breitenbush Books, Inc.: Portland.

Terman, L.M. and Miles, C.C. (1936) *Sex and Personality: Studies in Masculinity and Femininity.* McGraw-Hill: New York.

Terry, J. (1995) 'Anxious slippages between "Us" and "Them": A brief history of the sexual search for homosexual bodies', in J. Terry and J. Urla (eds), *Deviant Bodies: Critical Perspectives on Difference in Science and Popular Culture.* Indiana University Press: Bloomington. pp. 129–69.

Theweleit, K. (1987) *Male Fantasies, Volume 1: Women, Floods, Bodies, History.* Polity Press: Cambridge.

Theweleit, K. (1989) *Male Fantasies, Volume 2: Male Bodies: Psychoanalyzing the White Terror.* Polity Press: Cambridge.

Thorndike, E.L. (1921; orig. 1913) *Educational Psychology Vol. 1: The Original Nature of Man.* Teachers College, Columbia University: New York.

Tuana, N. (1989) 'The weaker seed: the sexist bias of reproductive theory', in N. Tuana (ed.), *Feminism and Science.* Indiana University Press: Bloomington. pp. 147–71.

Vance, C.S. (1989) 'Social construction theory: problems in the history of sexuality', in D. Altman, C. Vance, M. Vicinus and J. Weeks (eds), *Homosexuality, Which Homosexuality?* International Conference on Gay and Lesbian Studies. GMP Publishers: London. pp. 13–34.

Waldby, C., Kippax, S. and Crawford, J. (1995) 'Epidemiological knowledge and discriminatory practice: AIDS and the social relations of biomedicine', *The Australian and New Zealand Journal of Sociology*, 31, 1: 1–14.

Wallace, M. (1990) *Black Macho and the Myth of Superwoman.* Verso: London.

Warner, M. (1993) 'Introduction', in M. Warner (ed.), *Fear of a Queer Planet: Queer Politics and Social Theory.* University of Minnesota Press: Minneapolis.

Warren, A. (1987) 'Popular manliness: Baden Powell, scouting, and the development of manly character', in J.A. Mangan and J. Walvin (eds), *Manliness and Morality: Middle-class Masculinity in Britain and America, 1800–1940.* Manchester University Press: Manchester, pp. 199–219.

Warren, K. (1994) 'Toward an ecofeminist peace politics', in K. Warren (ed.), *Ecological Feminism.* Routledge: London. pp. 179–199.

Watney, S. (1994) 'Queer epistemology: activism, "outing", and the politics of sexual identities', *Critical Quarterly*, 36,1: 13–27.

Watney, S. (1997) *Policing Desire: Pornography, Aids and the Media.* Third edition. Cassell: London.

Weedon, C. (1987) *Feminist Practice and Poststructuralist Theory.* Blackwell: Oxford.

Weeks, J. (1977) *Coming Out: Homosexual Politics in Britain from the Nineteenth Century to the Present.* Quartet Books: London.

Weeks, J. (1985) *Sexuality and Its Discontents: Meanings, Myths and Modern Sexualities.* Routledge & Kegan Paul: London.

Weeks, J. (1995) *Invented Moralities: Sexual Values in an Age of Uncertainty.* Cambridge: Polity Press.

Westwood, S. (1990) 'Racism, black masculinity and the politics of space', in J. Hearn and D. Morgan (eds), *Men, Masculinities and Social Theory.* Unwin Hyman: London. pp. 55–71.

Wieviorka, M. (1995) *The Arena of Racism.* Sage: London.

Wilkinson, S. and Kitzinger, C. (eds) (1993) *Heterosexuality: A Feminism and Psychology Reader.* Sage: London.

Wilkinson, S. and Kitzinger, C. (1994a) 'The social construction of heterosexuality', *Journal of Gender Studies*, 3, 3: 307–16.

Wikinson, S. and Kitzinger, C. (1994b) 'Dire straights?: Contemporary rehabilitations of heterosexuality', in G. Griffen, M. Hester, S. Rai and S. Roseneil (eds), *Stirring It: Challenges for Feminism.* Taylor & Francis: London. pp. 75–91.

Wilkinson, S. and Kitzinger, C. (1996) *Representing the Other: A Feminism and Psychology Reader.* Sage: London.

Williams, S. (1997) 'Here come the new lads: men behaving not too badly', *The Australian Magazine*, March 1–2: 10–17.

Witleson, S. (1978) 'Les différences sexuelles dans la neurologie de la cognition: implications psychologiques, sociales éducatives et cliniques', in E. Sullerot (ed.), *Le fait féminin.* Fayard: Paris. pp. 287–303.

Woods, C. (1995) *State of the Queer Nation: A Critique of Gay and Lesbian Politics in 1990s Britain.* Cassell: London.

Young, B. (1993) 'Feminism and masculinism: a backlash response', in T. Haddad (ed.), *Men and Masculinities: A Critical Anthology.* Canadian Scholars Press: Toronto. pp. 313–32.

Young, E. (1996) 'Confederate counterfeit: the case of the cross-dressed civil war soldier', in E.K. Ginsburg (ed.), *Passing and the Fictions of Identity,* Duke University. Press: Durham. pp. 181–217.

Young, I.M. (1990) *Justice and the Politics of Difference.* Princeton University Press: Princeton.

Young, I.M. (1995) 'The ideal of community and the politics of difference', in P.A. Weiss and M. Friedman (eds), *Feminism and Community.* Temple University Press: Philadelphia. pp. 233–57.

Young, R.J.C. (1995) *Colonial Desire: Hybridity in Theory, Culture and Race.* Routledge: London.

Index